Liberal Democracy and its Critics

*Perspectives in Contemporary
Political Thought*

EDITED BY

April Carter and Geoffrey Stokes

Polity Press

Copyright © this collection Polity Press 1998

First published in 1998 by Polity Press in association with Blackwell Publishers Ltd.

Editorial office:
Polity Press
65 Bridge Street
Cambridge CB2 1UR, UK

Marketing and production:
Blackwell Publishers Ltd
108 Cowley Road
Oxford OX4 1JF, UK

Published in the USA by
Blackwell Publishers Inc.
Commerce Place
350 Main Street
Malden, MA 02148, USA

ISBN 0-7456-1919-3
ISBN 0-7456-1920-7 (pbk)

A catalogue record for this book is available from the British Library and has been applied for from the Library of Congress.

Typeset in 11 on 13 pt Garamond
by Best-set Typesetter Ltd., Hong Kong
Printed in Great Britain by TJ International, Padstow, Cornwall

This book is printed on acid-free paper.

Liberal Democracy and its Critics

Contents

Preface and Acknowledgements

This collection of essays explores how some of the most significant contemporary social and political theorists understand democracy, and what they contribute to democratic theory. The idea for the book arose out of the Political Theory Group for staff and postgraduate students within the Department of Government at the University of Queensland, and members of the group have written chapters in their areas of special interest. The main aim, however, is to represent the most important strands in debates on contemporary philosophy and political theory. We therefore asked six other contributors, who have special expertise on those we wanted to include, to write chapters.

We are very grateful to the Department of Government for making us a grant towards final preparation of the book. Special thanks are due to Jason de Rooy, who coordinated the Political Theory Group. We also thank all those members of the group who contributed helpful comments in the discussion of the original papers. We are grateful to Kylie Stephen and Katherine Welton who shared responsibility for technical editing, and to Karen Gillen for compiling on the index. We are also greatly indebted to Karen La Rocca for her expertise and patience in compiling the book and incorporating all the revisions, Ros Nicol for her help with typing and Tony Bunney for his technical assistance.

April Carter
Geoffrey Stokes

Contributors

Margaret Canovan is Professor of Political Thought at Keele University. Her publications on Hannah Arendt include two books; the second is *Hannah Arendt: A Reinterpretation of Her Political Thought* (Cambridge University Press, 1992). She has also published books on populism, and on G. K. Chesterton as a radical populist, as well as articles on many aspects of political thought. Her most recent book, *Nationhood and Political Theory*, was published by Edward Elgar in 1996. She is now working on a study of populism and democracy.

April Carter is Senior Lecturer in the Department of Government, University of Queensland. Her books include *Authority and Democracy* (Routledge, 1979), *Democratic Reform in Yugoslavia* (Frances Pinter, 1982), *The Politics of Women's Rights* (Longman, 1988) and *Peace Movements, International Protest and World Politics* (Longman, 1992). She has written a number of recent articles on citizenship and is now working on a book on global citizenship.

Don Fletcher is Reader in Politics at the University of Queensland. He is the editor of *Reading Rushdie* (Rodopi, 1994) and author of a number of recent papers including 'Political identity in contemporary Australian literature: Malouf and Carey', in G. Stokes (ed.), *The Politics of Identity in Australia* (Cambridge University Press, 1997), and 'Imagining gender: Politics, postmodernism and feminist science fiction', in B. Sullivan and G. Whitehouse (eds), *Gender, Politics and Citizenship in the 1990s* (University of New South Wales Press, 1996).

John Horton is Reader in Political Theory at Keele University. He is author of *Political Obligation* (Macmillan, 1992). He has recently edited

Liberalism, Multiculturalism and Toleration (Macmillan, 1993) and co-edited *After MacIntyre* (Polity, 1994) and *Literature and the Political Imagination* (Routledge, 1996).

Mark Kingwell is Associate Professor of Philosophy at the University of Toronto. He is the author of *A Civil Tongue: Justice, Dialogue, and the Politics of Pluralism* (Pennsylvania State University Press, 1995), which won the 1997 Spitz Prize in political theory; and *Dreams of Millennium: Report from a Culture on the Brink* (Viking, 1996), which was a finalist for the 1997 Gordon Montador Prize in social commentary. His latest book is: *Better Living: In Pursuit of Happiness from Plato to Prozac* (Viking, 1998).

Chandran Kukathas is Associate Professor in the School of Politics, University College, University of New South Wales, at the Australian Defence Force Academy, and is an editor of *The Journal of Political Philosophy*. He is the author of *Hayek and Modern Liberalism* (Clarendon, 1990) and co-author of *Rawls: A Theory of Justice and its Critics* (Polity, 1990). He has published various papers on contemporary political thought, and is currently completing a book on the politics of cultural diversity.

Martin Leet is completing a doctoral dissertation on Habermas and critique in the Department of Government, University of Queensland. He has published articles in the *Political Theory Newsletter*, *The Australian and New Zealand Journal of Sociology* and the *Journal of Public Policy*.

Lois McNay is Lecturer in Politics and Fellow of Somerville College, Oxford University. She is the author of *Foucault and Feminism: Power, Gender and the Self* (Polity, 1992) and *Foucault: A Critical Introduction* (Polity, 1994). She is currently working on a book, *Gender Reconfigured*, which explores the crossover between French social theory and feminist thought.

Geoffrey Stokes is Reader in the Department of Government, University of Queensland, Foundation Director of the Centre for Democracy and co-editor of the *Australian Journal of Politics and History*. He has edited *The Politics of Identity in Australia* (Cambridge University Press, 1997) and *Australian Political Ideas* (University of New South Wales Press, 1994) and co-authored *Accounting for the Humanities* (Institute for Cultural Policy Studies, 1991). His book *Karl Popper: Philosophy, Politics and Scientific Method* is to be published by Polity in 1998.

Barbara Sullivan teaches political theory and gender politics at the University of Queensland. She has recently authored *The Politics of Sex: Prostitution and Pornography in Australia since 1945* (Cambridge University Press, 1997), and co-edited (with Gillian Whitehouse) *Gender, Politics and Citizenship in the 1990s* (University of New South Wales Press, 1996) and (with Glyn Davis and Anna Yeatman) *The New Contractualism?* (Macmillan, 1997).

Katherine Welton is a postgraduate student and tutor in the Department of Government at the University of Queensland. She is currently completing a doctorate on the concept of objectivity in feminist theories of knowledge and has published articles on feminist thought in the *Political Theory Newsletter* and in *Women and Politics*.

Jonathan Wolff is Reader in Philosophy, University College London and editor of *The Proceedings of the Aristotelian Society*. He is the author of *Robert Nozick* (Polity Press and Stanford University Press, 1991) and *An Introduction to Political Philosophy* (Oxford University Press, 1996) and has published a series of papers on the problem of political obligation. He is currently working on the concepts of equality, competition and exploitation, and is co-authoring (with Veronique Munoz Dardé) a students' guide to Rawls in the Routledge Philosophical Guide Book series.

Introduction: Liberal Democracy and its Critics

April Carter and Geoffrey Stokes

Parliamentary multi-party democracy is now widely accepted as the dominant expression of the democratic ideal in most parts of the world. This historical transformation has occurred alongside the ostensible ascendancy of capitalism over state socialism and the declining influence of Marxist ideas. The 'triumph' of democracy in the 1990s has brought to prominence *liberal* democratic ideas and institutions as well as renewing support for free-market capitalism. For all its virtues, however, liberal democracy continues to generate dispute among both its defenders and its critics. Commentators upon established Western democracies, for example, have increasingly expressed doubts about the strength of their own political institutions.[1] One reason for this is that the apparent victory of liberal democracy has occurred at the same time that tendencies towards social disintegration and widespread voter alienation have become more obvious within many Western countries. These concerns have continued to prompt questions about the philosophical foundations for, and defence of, liberal democracy. The critics of liberal democracy have come from within the liberal democratic tradition and from outside it.

The vigour and scope of these critiques suggest that arguments about democracy remain crucial to both politics and political theory. Such debates over the meaning and substance of democracy provide part of the rationale for this book and our purpose is to explore the contributions made by major figures in contemporary social and political thought. The theorists have been chosen both for their relevance to intellectual controversy in the 1990s and for their wider impact on philosophy and political theory. None of them is primarily a theorist of democracy, although they have all played a role in defining key themes and problems in that field. Where some theorists discuss democracy more directly and in more detail than others, they all throw light on long-standing controversies within democratic theory.

The eleven theorists selected represent a range of philosophical positions and reflect varying political, cultural and generational contexts. Some of the theorists aim to justify liberal democracy; others are critical of the basic tenets of liberalism, even if they endorse certain liberal values. A number of the theorists are influenced by Marxism, but they would generally no longer call themselves Marxists. Many of the theorists contribute to significant disputes between liberalism and republicanism as well as between elitism and participation. They engage with the problem of whether liberal individualist or communitarian conceptions of democracy should prevail. A few theorists are centrally concerned with clarifying issues within the terms of older disputes between liberalism and socialism, whilst others are more committed to articulating claims to justice by groups previously excluded from exercising power or influence in liberal democracies. A number of the writers either assume or argue in support of universal principles, whereas others challenge universalism on various epistemological and political grounds. The perspectives of feminism and the politics of difference combine to provide a point of departure in dealing with identity politics. Attention is given also to proposals for a deliberative democracy which attempts to transcend liberalism and republicanism. Further questions about the meaning and efficacy of democracy are raised by poststructuralist critiques of power and knowledge.

All the theorists set important items on the intellectual agenda for contemporary democratic theory. This range of theoretical and political concerns results in very different priorities when discussing liberal democracy. While almost all accept that representative institutions provide the necessary framework for democratic politics, most also seek to extend the scope of democratic activity within and beyond those institutions. Yet, multi-party representative democracy does not mark the limits of democratic theory or its political practice. The subject of democracy requires more extensive analysis under a number of different conceptual subcategories.

Democratic Elitism and Participatory Critiques

One central theme is the connection between liberalism and democracy, which is not as close as use of the term 'liberal democracy' might imply. There is a historic tension between the ideals of liberalism and those of democracy. Classical liberalism stresses the importance of individual and minority rights, the rule of law and constitutional limits on government power. Democracy, on the other hand, places more emphasis upon popular participation and popular sovereignty. Historically, the growth of authoritarian mass movements of the 1930s and the rise of totalitarian regimes were often attributed in part to the excesses of democracy. Liberal distrust of majorities, or of passionate minorities claiming to represent the popular will, has often provided the rationale for elitist interpretations of representative democracy.[2]

The different priorities of liberalism and democracy may be seen in the work of Friedrich Hayek, one of the most sophisticated theorists of individualism and constitutional liberalism. Hayek articulates the main themes of elitist democratic theory such as distrust of majority opinion, rejection of the ideal of collective self-rule and the belief that democracy is not of intrinsic value. Nonetheless, he also maintains that liberal democratic procedures are the best way to secure other goods. Chandran Kukathas discusses in his chapter the nature of Hayek's elitism and its implications for his approach to democracy. Yet, Hayek's attitudes to democracy are somewhat ambivalent and have been partly influenced by changing historical circumstances. As Kukathas notes, Hayek was less critical of democracy during and immediately after the Second World War than in his later writings.

The tensions between liberalism and democracy recur in major debates between theorists of elitist democracy and advocates of greater participation during the 1960s and 1970s.[3] At this time radical student, worker and civil rights movements in North America and Western Europe challenged the prevailing assumptions of liberal representative democracy and advocated participatory democracy. New left concerns were evident in many theoretical critiques of democratic elitism and in a defence of the democratic values of participation. Carole Pateman (included in this book primarily for her role as a pioneer of feminist political theory) first became known for her book *Participation and Democratic Theory*, which defended the ideal and the possibility of participatory practices.[4]

Critics of elitist democracy often established their case upon a revived defence of the significance of values in political theory in opposition to the influential claims of positivist political science. Leading political scientists, such as David Easton, tended to adopt certain positivist assumptions about knowledge, one of which was the requirement to distinguish clearly between empirical claims and value judgements and to avoid contaminating the former with the latter.[5] Values were also thought to be largely emotional preferences and not subject to rational discussion or selection. The critics pointed out that value judgements could not be easily separated from factual ones and that commitments to values were not necessarily irrational. More important, they claimed that the pursuit of neutrality deprived democratic theory of one of its most enduring and important responsibilities which was to articulate political ideals. By confining political theory to the formulation of generalizations derived from empirical studies of the operation of Western parliamentary systems, the elitists were giving moral approval to what existed. The norms of 'democratic realism' foreclosed significant criticism of liberal democracy and severely curtailed discussion of options for radical transformation. For these reasons, the defence of the classical tradition of political thought in the English-speaking world articulated in the 1960s came primarily from those inclined both to refute the claims of behavioural political science and to criticize existing forms of liberal democracy.[6] The writings of Charles Taylor, one of the theorists discussed in this book, fall into this category. His landmark article 'Neutrality in political science' shows both the impossibility and the undesirability of maintaining value freedom or value neutrality in making empirical judgements.[7]

Republican Critiques of Liberal Democracy

A major strand within Western political thought which has challenged liberalism and advocated a strong, participatory concept of citizenship is republicanism. Republican thought draws on the political heritage of classical Greece and Rome, and is often associated with Rousseau's concept of the general will. Republican writers generally suggest a radical alternative to liberal understandings of individualism and stress the over-riding importance of community and the public good. Where the liberals (classical and neo-classical) see the priority of protecting individual freedom from incursions by the state (negative liberty), republicans argue for the priority of 'positive freedom' which may subordinate individuals and their private interests to the greater good of the whole community. The republicans also suggest institutional alternatives to parliamentary democracy. Although defenders of the republican ideal were rare in the English-speaking world in the 1950s and early 1960s, Hannah Arendt stands out as an exception. Arendt was the most distinguished exponent of republicanism in this period and her contribution to democratic theory is discussed in Margaret Canovan's chapter.

Arendt sought to re-establish an understanding of what is entailed in authentic political activity. She pursued this project through critiques of Western political thought and reflections on political events, past and present. Arendt found examples of political action and participatory democracy in 'council democracy', the spontaneous creation of soviets or councils in diverse revolutionary contexts, in revolutionary France and

Russia, and most recently in Hungary in 1956. Her interpretation of the significance of council democracy diverged from radical Marxism or anarcho-syndicalism which tended to focus on worker control of industry. Arendt's goal was to indicate a possible political alternative to a parliamentary and multi-party system.[8] Arendt did not expect to see council democracy implemented in the West but, like several other theorists discussed in this book, she saw some hope for the future in the political movements of the 1960s and 1970s, which she believed offered significant examples of participatory politics and responsible citizenship. As Canovan points out, however, despite Arendt's insights into modern politics, there are serious practical limits to her proposals for council democracy. Furthermore, Canovan concludes that Arendt's injunctions against political discussion of social and economic matters cannot be sustained.

Civil Society: Different Interpretations

Republicanism has not provided the only ideal of a participatory alternative to the Western parliamentary and multi-party system. During the 1980s, many opposition groups in Eastern Europe ceased to believe in the possibility of significant democratic reforms within communist party states. Such groups still hoped to find a third way between Western capitalism with its parliamentary institutions and Soviet socialism based on a one-party state. Workers' self-management in industry and democratically controlled autonomous social organizations independent of the state were two of the major strategies proposed. Dissidents in Poland, Hungary, Czechoslovakia and East Germany developed a cooperative style of politics with an emphasis on debate and democratic decision-making, which some of them tried to carry over into government after 1989. Nevertheless, the initial hopes that opposition-style politics might provide a satisfactory alternative to Western multi-party democracy soon dissipated.[9]

Anti-communist dissidents revived the concept of 'civil society' to be found in Marx's critique of capitalism and competitive individualism, but reinterpreted it to denote the potential for individual moral choice, independent organization, autonomous action and social solidarity.[10] Civil society stood for all that communist party regimes tried to suppress through their comprehensive system of party control, and the opposition envisaged its gradual growth within, but independent of, the communist state. Václav Havel, who had always rejected reform communism, became one of the leading theorists of 'anti-political politics', or civil society.

Havel shares with Arendt a commitment to a polity based on citizen responsibility, which would be the opposite of both the mass conformity imposed under totalitarianism, and the perceived irresponsible individualism and political apathy of Western consumer society. He also shared with Arendt in his dissident writings a deep distrust of a politics dominated by political parties. After Havel became President of the new Czechoslovak state, however, he accepted the necessity of both parliamentary institutions and party politics, which he had previously criticized, and therefore embraced a revised theory of democracy. He now sees civil society as safeguarding individual choice, but also providing opportunities for a sense of community and the exercise of social responsibility, which may counteract the lack of civic spirit among most of the population as well as the selfish partisanship manifest in the official sphere of democratic party politics. In her chapter, April Carter argues that although Havel has contributed to the revival of the notion of civil society and underlines the political importance of moral responsibility, his views on institutional reform and economic matters remain undeveloped.

Liberal Individualism versus Communitarian Critiques

Questions about the relative priority to be given to individual and community in democratic theory also arise in the context of debates between liberal individualism and communitarianism. John Rawls formulates a distinctive individualist, contractarian model of the foundation of a just democratic politics. Indeed, the major revival of political philosophy in North America and the UK is often attributed to Rawls's influential *A Theory of Justice*, published in 1971. Rawls, whose contribution to democratic theory is discussed by Jonathan Wolff, provides an ambitious justification of the universal principles underlying liberal societies. Rawls begins from a hypothetical social contract that enshrines the principles of individual liberty, genuine equality of opportunity and a justifiable distribution of economic goods. With its emphasis upon these principles, Rawls's work is a variant of 'social liberalism' that differs considerably from the market-oriented views of Hayek. Although Rawls has often been interpreted as providing universalist foundations for justice, in his later writings he stresses that he is drawing on his inherited cultural context, and in so doing he explicitly provides a philosophical justification of the values and institutions of the USA. These qualifications may limit the application of Rawls to other political domains but, as Wolff suggests, they do not rule out criticism of US institutions. In addition, Rawls reminds us of an important truth which familiarity may obscure: that liberal democracy still represents a remarkable political and intellectual achievement.

Rawls's ideal contractarian model and the individualist basis of actual liberal societies have come under attack from a number of theorists often identified as 'communitarians'. Despite significant differences among them, the communitarians are united in their claim that individuals do not exist independently of the society and culture within which they acquire their values, beliefs and perceptions of the social world. Communitarians, like Taylor and Walzer, criticize the excessive individualism they see as implicit in classical liberal ideology.[11] They also repudiate theories which conceptualize politics as a type of market place in which voters and leaders are represented simply as buyers and sellers. Although communitarianism can also have conservative connotations because of its respect for existing communities and their traditions, both Taylor and Walzer are on the left. Taylor was associated with the new left and, in particular, with the Canadian New Democratic Party. Walzer identifies himself, in the context of US politics, as a social democrat. Both Taylor and Walzer claim that the liberal emphasis on individual rights and corresponding contractual obligations provides neither an adequate understanding of citizenship, nor a full sense of the potential of democracy.

As John Horton points out in his chapter, Taylor argues that an effective democratic government requires a sense of shared beliefs and goals. Yet, despite his sympathy for values embodied in republicanism and an aversion to those versions of liberal democracy which stress instrumental pursuit of interests, Taylor rejects Rousseau's vision of the general will. This is not only because he is aware of Jacobin and Leninist perversions of this ideal, but also because he is drawn more to a Hegelian concept of politics that combines pluralism with a unifying moral and political consciousness. Horton concludes that Taylor's achievement is to indicate why a democratic polity requires a sense of the common good that also recognizes basic individual rights and cultural diversity. The difficulty remains of how such goals may be achieved in political practice.

Michael Walzer's *Spheres of Justice* is a response to Rawls that also stresses social complexity. For Walzer, there is not one set of principles relevant to justice, but different, culturally defined, understandings of justice in different spheres of life. If principles from one sphere are imposed upon another, Walzer contends, the result is domination. Mark Kingwell's essay explores the implications of *Spheres of Justice* for Walzer's general theory of democracy. Kingwell also examines the role Walzer assigns to social and political criticism in his ideal of democratic citizenship. In the sphere of politics, all citizens are expected to be potential critics. A number of commentators dispute Walzer's method of argument to claim that he cannot derive his substantive theoretical recommendations from an analysis of the existing culture. Kingwell concludes, however, that Walzer's defence of democracy is based not upon a narrow interpretation of the contingent facts of contemporary political culture, but upon a deeper, critical understanding of what is central to the longer heritage and practices of our social and political life.

Feminist Critiques: Participation, Universalism and the Politics of Difference

Although both Carole Pateman and Iris Marion Young, the feminist theorists examined in this collection, are drawn to participatory democracy, they also repudiate republicanism. In her feminist mode, Pateman is highly critical of liberalism for maintaining the subordination of women. Despite liberalism's formal commitment to political equality, it fails to take account of the significance of the private sphere for the operation of the public sphere and overlooks the fact that women still tend to be dominated by men in both spheres. Pateman is even more critical of participatory democrats who recognize the significance of economic inequalities, but who fail to address issues of gender. Her goal, as Barbara Sullivan shows in the chapter on Pateman, is to extend democratic participation to the realm of private or family life. One of Pateman's achievements is that she has helped to make feminist critique a significant part of contemporary debates about democracy.[12] By examining the masculine bias of dominant conceptions of citizenship, she has also contributed a feminist perspective to discussions about citizenship and republicanism.[13] In her appraisal, however, Sullivan contends that Pateman's critiques are limited by an unwarranted essentialism about the nature of women and sexual relations. This feature of her work may be attributed to the fact that, unlike many recent feminists, Pateman has not turned to postmodernism which challenges both essentialism and universalism. Although Pateman recognizes that universal claims have been used to exclude women and other groups from the political process, she also observes that universal ideas have been used as a basis to claim inclusion. She argues that, in the world of the 1990s, a creative rethinking of universalism is needed, rather than its rejection.

Young, by contrast, formulates a very specific critique of the 'universal' principles underlying republican ideals of participatory democracy. In particular, she submits that universalist claims tend to mask the dominant and oppressive beliefs of those who are most powerful. Young notes that democratic discourse in the USA has, in the past, excluded indigenous people, black and Mexican Americans as well as women. To a large extent, for Young, this discourse still screens out the interests and experiences of these and other less politically powerful groups.[14] Young's central theoretical concern, as Don Fletcher indicates in his chapter, is to reconceptualize social justice, which she claims has focused too exclusively on distribution and ignored the importance of both economic and cultural forms of oppression. She points out how the increasing claims of aboriginal and different ethnic groups to a greater degree of political power and autonomy have contributed to demands for a politics of difference. Young argues that democratic theory needs to be reformulated to take account of these concerns.

As an advocate of the 'politics of difference', Young also provides detailed proposals for group representation to enable different 'voices' to influence policy-making. To explain the origins of domination and the need for this type of politics, Young looks to Michel Foucault's analysis of cultural oppression. She takes up Foucault's idea of the 'normalizing gaze' which demonstrates how all those who do not fit the dominant, white, heterosexual, male norms are placed at the political margins. Her normative prescriptions, however, draw upon the work of a very different writer, Jürgen Habermas. To formulate her own ideal concept of 'communicative democracy', Young takes up a Habermasian conception of deliberative democracy while rejecting his universalism.

Deliberative Democracy and Problems of Justification

Habermas provides a philosophical justification of democracy and articulates a theory of deliberative democracy. As Martin Leet indicates in his chapter, both are closely linked to his concepts of rationality and communicative action. In the modern world, Habermas explains, societies are no longer integrated by strong traditions and religious beliefs and have become increasingly pluralistic. What holds them together are the ideals embodied in the process of reaching consensus through rational communication and a widespread acceptance of these procedures of argument. A concept of democracy is therefore inherent in the communicative practices of modern Western society. This general conception of rational communication has then to be translated into political institutions to create a workable model of democracy.

On Habermas's account, deliberative democracy combines elements of both liberalism and republicanism. Like liberal democracy, deliberative democracy requires an institutional framework to protect free discussion among equal citizens. Like republicanism, it sees democratic deliberation as a good in itself. Given its foundations in Habermas's discourse ethic,[15] however, it does not assume, as republican theory does, that such discussion necessarily has the aim of persuading others to a different point of view.[16] 'Discourse theory,' Habermas contends, 'has the success of deliberative politics depend not on a collectively acting citizenry but on the institutionalization of the corresponding procedures and conditions of communication.'[17] Leet raises the practical criticism that Habermas's requirement for impartiality in democratic deliberation may be too demanding. An inability to agree on what impartiality means may lead to a failure to overcome preliminary disagreements, for example, which may produce disaffection with democracy. In taking the deliberative path, Habermas may be abandoning one of the strengths of liberal democracy which is its capacity to reach non-violent accommodations over problems that do not allow for consensus.

The question of justifying democracy is one of Richard Rorty's main concerns. Rorty is best known as a postmodern philosopher who argues for the contingency of all knowledge claims. He is therefore sceptical about the possibility or the need to provide philosophical justifications for democratic institutions and practices, let alone any universal justification. This starting point brings him into direct conflict with Habermas and Rawls in particular, who both focus on problems of justification. Rorty claims that if democracy promotes a peaceful and tolerant society it provides its own justification. Given his belief that philosophy is a private, not a public enterprise, Rorty thinks that philosophical debate not only is unable to provide a foundation for democracy, but also distracts attention from practical political goals. Instead, Rorty focuses on the need for procedures which make conversation possible. As Katherine Welton notes in her chapter, he acknowledges a debt to Habermas and adopts his argument that decisions should be accepted if they are the outcome of undistorted communication. Rorty also deploys Rawls's concept of 'reflective equilibrium' – a process of mutual adjustment of principles and judgements – to indicate the kind of procedure necessary for reaching decisions. He shares with Rawls a commitment to liberal principles such as tolerance and a tendency to accept American institutions. Moreover, in his essay 'The priority of democracy to philosophy', he claims a kinship with the later Rawls in his explicit reliance on his inherited culture and values. Politically therefore, he tends to reject the postmodern label. He also exemplifies the claim that it is possible to combine philosophical radicalism with conventional political liberalism. Welton concludes that, for all the sophistication of Rorty's radical, anti-foundationalist epistemology, his democratic theory is underdeveloped. It is based upon a number of unsustainable assumptions about the difference between the public and private spheres and neglects important issues of political power.

Radical Critiques of Power and Domination in Liberal Democracy

Philosophical radicalism is allied to uncompromising political radicalism in the work of Michel Foucault, the last theorist considered in this book. Foucault questions not only universalist thinking but also general social theories like Marxism which attempt to explain society as a whole. His work on madness, punishment and sexuality provided a vivid and influential critique of Enlightenment rationalism, liberal values and beliefs about progress. The thrust of his writings suggests that in liberal societies individuals, far from being free, are subjected to subtle forms of discipline imposed by dominant concepts of the normal. Although Foucault provides a fundamental critique of liberal democracy, he is precluded from offering a positive elaboration of democratic theory. This conclusion, however, should be modified in two directions. Lois McNay demonstrates in her chapter that, despite the apparently pessimistic implications of his analysis, Foucault has inspired those committed to radical change. Moreover, his later work on an 'ethics of the self' suggests greater scope for individual autonomy and also for social change. Indeed, in some of his own political protests Foucault suggests the potential for resistance to abuse of power. McNay examines how radical democratic theorists, namely Chantal Mouffe and Ernesto Laclau, begin from Foucault's understanding of power, and demonstrates how his later work on the self has influenced William Connolly's concept of 'agonistic' democracy. Despite these efforts, McNay argues that there are significant conceptual difficulties in using Foucault to develop democratic theory. Whereas all the other theorists in this book envisage constructive forms of power challenging domination, Foucault's stress on the disciplinary nature of power prevents him from recognizing the potential for political change within democratic systems.

Contemporary Issues for Liberal Democracy

The discussion above points to a number of interrelated problems that will continue to confront liberal democracy in the late 1990s and beyond. Liberal democracy and its critics cannot avoid dealing with: (a) the tensions between claims to recognition of difference and the maintenance of unity within a larger community, also expressed in debates over universalism and particularity; (b) disagreements about the relationship between the state and civil society, expressed in debates over civic virtue, social capital and associational democracy; (c) questions about the practical requirements of deliberative democracy and more fundamental disputes over its theoretical foundations; and (d) the different demands of national and international principles and institutions, expressed in debates over global democracy and global citizenship.

The Politics of Identity and Difference

Issues of domination and power are central for a politics of identity or difference and are evident in political movements for feminism, gay liberation, and ethnic and indigenous rights. In a number of liberal democracies, for example, indigenous peoples have made distinctive claims to group or cultural rights. In the countries of the former Soviet bloc, ethnic claims have dominated politics in ways highly destructive to the principles of liberalism, including those of tolerance and the requirement for reform by peaceful means. The main impetus is often the quest for recognition and expression of a cherished or neglected identity which also entails a struggle for institutional or symbolic power. This politics may take one of two forms in which activists either seek cultural recognition, economic resources and limited forms of political autonomy within a nation state, or pursue more radical strategies for self-determination or secession and the creation of separate states.[18]

Those seeking recognition within liberal democracy often make claims to diverse cultural rights and state provision for different languages and religions.[19] This form of politics may also include claims for support for and acceptance of groups defined by significant difference, such as those of gender, sexual preference and physical disability. The trend towards an increasingly diversified society that acknowledges special group rights has, as Fletcher notes in his discussion of Young, alarmed some political theorists.[20] One of their fears is that group identification will undermine any sense of belonging to a common polity and therefore undermine the conditions for effective democracy. A related concern is that the claims to group rights can foster ideological intolerance between different sectors of the population. Far from promoting an egalitarian basis for reasoned deliberation, identity politics can promote disharmony and political violence.[21]

It must be said that where the politics of identity and difference does not involve political independence or secession, it generally represents a radical kind of pluralism. The earlier concept of liberal pluralism depicted and even celebrated the competition for influence upon governmental policy that occurred among strong pressure groups, such as business and trade unions. The pluralism of identity and difference politics, however, signifies claims to attention by oppressed groups previously without much power. Partly for this reason, their demands for recognition are often more unsettling to previously dominant liberal principles of equal treatment of individuals and those of a single national loyalty. Although critics like Sheldon Wolin are not unsympathetic to 'the new pluralism of cultural difference', they point to its tendency to undercut the assumptions of 'commonality' to which the politics of difference must inevitably appeal.[22] To put it another way, the advocates of a politics of difference do not explain satisfactorily how their theories can dispense with the universalism they have criticized in others. Furthermore, without recourse to general principles, it is difficult to determine which claims to identity and difference ought to be recognized and which rejected. The recognition of differences raises other concerns that extend beyond protecting rights and the proper functioning of democratic institutions. They pertain to the problems of maintaining political integration and find expression in another kind of pluralism founded upon cooperative voluntary activities in the sphere of civil society.

Civil Society and Associational Democracy

The deep conflicts arising from violent ethnic nationalism in many democratizing societies, and the widespread disenchantment with established liberal democracies elsewhere, have provoked theorists to look beyond the formal political institutions. One important issue here is how to foster or retain some minimal unity and commitment to democracy among diverse groups. In different ways, the solution is thought to lie in promoting citizenship.[23] Central to the recent work of a number of liberal and socialist theorists is an emphasis upon democratic citizenship and a unifying civic identity. What unites a number of these disparate citizenship theorists, however, is their emphasis upon civil society and associational democracy. Those who regard civil society as the foundation of democratic citizenship seek to establish or strengthen democratic political culture through voluntary institutions.[24]

Nonetheless, there are significant differences of emphasis among the civil society theorists. Those liberals, for example, who have expressed doubts about the capacity of market transactions to encourage democratic virtues of civility, self-restraint and mutual trust have looked to the formative role of voluntary associations. Writers like Robert Putnam claim further that the strength of good, democratic, government may be measured by the levels of participation in organizations such as choral societies, soccer clubs and cooperatives.[25] Where the stocks of 'social capital' are low, he argues, so also the commitment to democratic participation and good government is weak.

Although democratic socialists, particularly Cohen and Rogers and Paul Hirst, also acknowledge the educative role of voluntary or 'secondary' associations, they tend to see them more as an essential vehicle for democratic empowerment which gives greater political force to the idea of pluralism.[26] For Hirst, the role of associational democracy is to 'supplement and extend' representative democracy.[27] Walzer considers participation in voluntary associations to be essential, but because he also recognizes that they can be narrow minded, self-interested and parochial, he proposes a 'critical associationalism' that allows the members to reform their views and organizations.[28]

Both the liberal and the socialist versions of 'civil society politics' propose a means of extending democratic participation beyond formal political institutions, but in a way that emphasizes individual choice. These theorists see such participation giving greater life to the body politic.[29] The problem remains of determining the optimum relationship between voluntary associations and the state. Among the socialists, associational democracy appears to require a strong state that can bring about economic intervention in markets and implement those redistributive policies that would give effect to the legitimate demands of associations. For liberals too, strong government would be needed to protect the rights of both those in associations and those who may be threatened by them.[30] Furthermore, where one advantage of civil society politics was thought to be its capacity to foster citizenship and a minimal civic unity, the practical outcomes may be the opposite. The inherent possibilities of entrenching divisions encountered above with the 'politics of difference' also confront associational democracy. Without some restraining influence, the pursuit of narrow, sectional interests can lead to a disabling political conflict. One proposed response is to incorporate the values and procedures of deliberative democracy not only into associational activity but also into more formal political institutions.

Deliberative Democracy

Given the possibility of political fragmentation and conflict inherent in identity politics and the strong pluralism of civil society politics, we must ask whether there are any common grounds for non-violent, democratic discussion and decision between groups. This is where Habermas's discourse theory of deliberative democracy offers an innovative alternative. Deliberative democracy aims to provide both a justification of democracy and a set of procedures that encourage 'rational and moral capacities for agreement'.[31] Its distinguishing feature is the requirement that democratic rules and procedures are intended to protect and enhance democratic deliberation as a good in itself and are not just a means for ordering, defending and criticizing individual preferences.

Deliberative democracy therefore differs from liberal democracy, in which the procedures of voting, representation and protection of rights largely have an instrumental value based upon their capacity to produce and change governments, limit their powers, or facilitate political participation. The deliberative conception also rejects the classical liberal theory which interprets society purely in terms of market relations and understands politics as an aggregation of individual interests to be realized through state action. Yet, deliberative democratic theory not only accepts liberal assumptions of pluralism within societies and the emphasis upon the importance of procedures, but also acknowledges that instrumental politics is part of democracy.

Deliberative democracy is also close to the republican ideal, in that both presuppose autonomous citizenship and public use of reason. It takes from republicanism the assumption that the democratic process itself has intrinsic value, but in a weaker sense than republicans imply. Habermas departs from republicanism in rejecting Rousseau's emphasis on civic virtue and the goal of unanimity based on a consensual community, and, therefore the contemporary republican tendency to see public discourse in terms of 'collective ethical self-understanding'.[32]

There are two major kinds of criticism that can be levelled against Habermas. One is that he largely accepts the existing institutions of liberal democracy and does not give any practical guidance on how to give institutional substance to the values implicit in his work. Nonetheless, some supporters of deliberative democracy, James Fishkin, for example, do make specific proposals to institutionalize permanent citizen deliberation.[33] The second debate centres on Habermas's claim that deliberative democracy is based upon universal principles specifying the conditions for rational discussion. Critics, like Young and Walzer, query both the possibility and desirability of universalism and the exclusive emphasis upon rationality. Lynn Sanders has argued forcefully that deliberative democratic theory's demand for discussion that is 'rational, moderate, and not selfish' excludes those ordinary citizens from participating who do not have these skills or capacities for self-restraint.[34] A more fundamental question is whether the deliberative ideal in some modified form is compatible (as Young claims) with the politics of identity and difference.

Transnational Democracy and Global Citizenship

These theoretical and practical issues have become conspicuous in discussions of international and global problems. Just as the relevance of democratic principles is no longer confined to national or subnational representative political institutions, so too it is arguable that democratic procedures must extend beyond national borders. In response to perceptions of increasing globalization, a number of democratic theorists have reaffirmed moral and political responsibilities that transcend the nation state. Although the concept of 'globalization' is contentious, and is applied to many different things, it is commonly used to describe world-wide processes of economic, technological and cultural integration.[35] One of its main characteristics is the growth of global markets and the weakening of the power of nation states over their economies.[36] Indeed, the ideals of Hayekian economics and liberalism, exemplified in the free movement of capital and labour, can be seen as defining the logic of a global market economy.[37] Economic logic of that kind, however, has serious implications for the capacities of democratic states to exercise control over key public policies and institutions. The extent to which globalization seems to undermine democratic power within the state has prompted David Held and others to advocate measures to institutionalize new global democratic controls over market and environmental forces.[38]

These globalizing tendencies have encouraged two related programmes of inquiry. The first returns us to the problem of the possible grounds for universalist thought, while the second takes universalism as given and explores the notion of global citizenship. Rawls's *A Theory of Justice*, for example, has sometimes been criticized for failing to pursue far enough the logic of its arguments and for not extending his concept of justice to the world as a whole.[39] Despite the contemporary tendency to reject universalism, several theorists in this book do lean towards a cosmopolitan sense of moral and political responsibility.

A common context for such leanings is given by the problems of increasing racism and xenophobia and the need to tackle global injustice. This is the case for Pateman, for example, who takes up the issue of globalization and the problems of defining citizenship in purely national terms.[40] Habermas also touches on the ultimate ideal of 'global citizenship' in discussing both the non-nationalist conception of citizenship embodied in late-eighteenth-century republicanism and the prospects for European citizenship within the European Union.[41] Havel expresses a poignant and specifically moral formulation of cosmopolitanism:

> We are all familiar with the threats that hang over the world today. . . . We all know what conflicts lie dormant within humanity, now that a single global civilization is pushing people from different spheres of culture ever closer together, thus inevitably arousing their determination to defend their

identity against this pressure toward uniformity. But what are we doing to avert these dangers or confront them? . . . we have entirely ignored one of the pillars of the European tradition – universalism, the commandment to think of everyone, to act as everyone should act, and to look for universally acceptable solutions.[42]

For Havel, the universal outlook is a moral and practical necessity for resolving difficult problems; it is not a topic offered for philosophical contention. Indeed, this assumption is embedded in the commitments to international human rights. International movements for peace, human rights and the environment also embody the universal principles inherent in global citizenship. The implications of these cosmopolitan tendencies, their philosophical foundations, and the possible institutional models for future development will all be issues in the emerging debate on global democracy.

Conclusion

The extent and speed of the democratic transition in Europe in early 1989 led Francis Fukuyama to proclaim the 'end of history'. This he represented as the 'endpoint of mankind's ideological evolution and the universalization of liberal democracy as the final form of human government'.[43] From the essays in this book, it can now be seen even more clearly how Fukuyama overstated the case. Debate continues over the very nature of liberal democracy, its distinctive principles, its diverse institutional forms and the proper grounds for its defence. To varying degrees, the theorists in this book, and *their* critics, have contributed to the renewal of democratic theory. Accordingly, it is as important now as in 1989 to recognize that ideological struggles over democratic theory and practice have not ended. Just as a democratic politics thrives on robust criticism, discussion and debate, so also does democratic theory. In liberal democracies, where democratic realism still provides the underpinning assumptions of elite political practices that are oriented primarily to elections and managing political conflict, the search for democratic alternatives is vital. Where people do not have basic human rights and the security of the rule of law, however, or the capacity to vote and change governments by peaceful means, the political requirements of the situation are somewhat different. For those who live under dictatorship, even the mundane 'realism' of elitist versions of democracy may appear utopian.

Notes

1 See the discussion by Barry Hindess, 'Democracy and disenchantment', *Australian Journal of Political Science*, 32:1 (1997), 79–92.

2 The best known expression of democratic elitism is Joseph Schumpeter's 1943 book *Capitalism, Socialism and Democracy*, in which he argues that the primary role of citizens is to choose between competing elites in elections. Schumpeter based his interpretation of democracy on what he saw as the stubborn realities of the American and British democratic practices. Whereas some advocates of greater participation drew upon liberal theorists such as J. S. Mill to refute Joseph Schumpeter's claim, others looked beyond liberalism to republican or socialist ideas.

3 Political scientists, such as Robert Dahl, writing in the United States in the 1950s, modified Schumpeter's account to allow a central role for 'pressure groups', but still reproduced his elitist emphasis. See e.g. the theory of polyarchy in *A Preface to Democratic Theory* (Chicago, University of Chicago Press, 1956). Dahl later significantly shifted ground to espouse economic democracy, as evident in his *A Preface to Economic Democracy* (Cambridge, Polity, 1985).

4 This book is one of the most frequently cited contributions to the literature.

5 David Easton, *The Political System: An Inquiry into the State of Political Science* (New York, Knopf, 1953).

6 See the essays in H. S. Kariel (ed.), *Frontiers of Democratic Theory* (New York, Random House, 1970) and in C. A. McCoy and J. Playford (eds), *Apolitical Politics: A Critique of Behavioralism* (New York, Thomas Y. Crowell, 1967). See especially, G. Duncan and S. Lukes, 'The new democracy', *Political Studies*, 11 (1963), 156–77.

7 C. Taylor, 'Neutrality in political science', in P. Laslett and W. G. Runciman (eds), *Philosophy, Politics and Society*, third series (Oxford, Basil Blackwell, 1967), pp. 25–57.

8 Arendt's arguments influenced Benjamin Barber's book *Strong Democracy* (Berkeley, CA, University of California Press, 1984) which outlines a republican vision of a democratic alternative to liberal ideology and institutions.

9 See Neal Ascherson, '1989 in Eastern Europe: Constitutional representative government as a "return to normality"?', in J. Dunn (ed.), *Democracy: The Unfinished Journey 508 BC to AD 1993* (Oxford, Oxford University Press, 1992), pp. 221–37.

10 The theoretical evolution of the concept of civil society from Locke through Adam Ferguson to Hegel and Marx is complex, and has invested the term with different connotations. See J. A. Hall (ed.), *Civil Society: Theory, History, Comparison* (Cambridge, Polity, 1995).

11 Although Taylor and Walzer are often classed as communitarians, both are unhappy with the label. Taylor argues that such a distinction is based on an oversimplified contrast between individualism and collectivism.

12 On feminism and democracy, see Anne Phillips, 'Must feminists give up on liberal democracy?', in D. Held (ed.), *Prospects for Democracy* (Cambridge, Polity, 1993), pp. 93–111, and Susan Mendus, 'Losing the faith: Feminism and democracy', in Dunn, *Democracy*, pp. 207–19.

13 See C. Pateman, 'Citizen male', *Australian Left Review*, 137 (1992), 30–3.

14 I. M. Young, 'Polity and group difference: A critique of the ideal of universal citizenship', *Ethics*, 99 (1989), 250–74.

15 See Seyla Benhabib, 'Towards a deliberative model of democratic legitimacy', in S. Benhabib (ed.), *Democracy and Difference* (Princeton, NJ, Princeton University Press, 1996), p. 70.

16 Joshua Cohen, 'Procedure and substance in democratic theory', in Benhabib, *Democracy and Difference*, p. 100.

17 Jürgen Habermas, 'Three normative models of democracy', in Benhabib, *Democracy and Difference*, p. 27.

18 See Geoffrey Stokes, 'Introduction', in Geoffrey Stokes (ed.), *The Politics of Identity in Australia* (Melbourne, Cambridge University Press, 1997), p. 8.

19 Young and Taylor, amongst others, have explored the arguments for, and implications of, recognizing the claims by groups to maintain their different cultural identity and the problems it poses for liberal theory. Taylor has also been politically involved for a long period with the claims of his own province of Quebec to linguistic and political autonomy or independence. See also the essays in I. Shapiro and W. Kymlicka (eds), *Ethnicity and Group Rights*, *NOMOS XXXIX* (New York, New York University Press, 1997).

20 See, for example, the critique by C. Kukathas, 'Are there any cultural rights?', *Political Theory*, 20:1 (1992), 105–39 and W. Kymlicka, 'The rights of minority cultures: Reply to Kukathas', *Political Theory*, 20:1 (1992), 140–6.

21 J. B. Elshtain, *Democracy on Trial* (New York, Basic Books, 1995), see ch. 3 'The politics of difference'.

22 S. S. Wolin, 'Democracy, difference and re-cognition', *Political Theory*, 21:3 (1993), 464–83.

23 For a general overview of the revived interest in citizenship see W. Kymlicka and W. Norman, 'Return of the citizen: A survey of recent work on citizenship theory', *Ethics*, 104 (1994), 352–81.

24 See L. Diamond, 'Rethinking civil society: Towards democratic consolidation', *Journal of Democracy*, 5:3 (1994), 4–17. Diamond excludes profit-making activity but includes economic organizations like business associations and trade unions. He also excludes political parties seeking state power and movements seeking to extinguish pluralism.

25 Robert D. Putnam, 'What makes democracy work?', *IPA Review*, 47:1 (1994), 31–4.

26 See Joshua Cohen and Joel Rogers, *Associations and Democracy* (London, Verso, 1995) where they argue for 'associative democracy'.

27 See Paul Hirst, 'Associational democracy', in Held, *Prospects for Democracy*,

pp. 112–35, and his *Associative Democracy* (Amherst, MA, University of Massachusetts Press, 1994).

28 See Michael Walzer, 'The civil society argument', in C. Mouffe (ed.), *Dimensions of Radical Democracy: Pluralism, Citizenship, Community* (London, Verso, 1992), pp. 89–107, and M. Walzer, 'The concept of civil society', in M. Walzer (ed.), *Toward a Global Civil Society* (Providence, RI, Berghahn, 1995), pp. 1–27.

29 Australian writings include M. Krygier, 'The sources of civil society', *Quadrant* (October 1996), 12–22 and (November 1996), 26–32, and E. Cox, *A Truly Civil Society*, 1995 Boyer Lectures (Sydney, ABC Books, 1995).

30 See Kymlicka and Norman, 'Return of the citizen', p. 364.

31 Nancy Rosenblum, 'Democratic character and community: The logic of congruence', *The Journal of Political Philosophy*, 2:1 (1994), 67–97, esp. p. 93.

32 Habermas, 'Three normative models of democracy', p. 24.

33 J. S. Fishkin, *Democracy and Deliberation: New Directions for Democratic Reform* (New Haven, CT, Yale University Press, 1991).

34 Lynn Sanders, 'Against deliberation', *Political Theory*, 25:3 (1997), 347–76.

35 See R. Robertson, *Globalization* (London, Sage, 1992).

36 One of the disputes occurs over whether economic globalization is the result of irreversible, structural trends or whether it is largely due to national governments deliberately weakening economic controls and reducing the size of the public sector. For a sceptical view of the inevitability of globalization see P. Hirst and G. Thompson, *Globalization in Question: The International Economy and the Possibilities of Governance* (Cambridge, Polity, 1996).

37 O. O'Neill, 'Transnational justice', in D. Held (ed.), *Political Theory Today* (Cambridge, Polity, 1991), pp. 276–304.

38 Kukathas takes up Held's argument and criticizes it from a Hayekian perspective.

39 Charles Beitz, *Political Theory and International Relations* (Princeton, NJ, Princeton University Press, 1979), pp. 128–76.

40 C. Pateman, 'Democracy and democratization', *International Political Science Review*, 17:1 (1996), 5–12.

41 J. Habermas, 'Citizenship and national identity: Some reflections on the future of Europe', *Praxis International*, 12:1 (1992), 1–19.

42 V. Havel, 'The hope for Europe', *New York Review of Books*, 63:8 (20 June 1996), 38–41. See also V. Havel, 'Transcendence and the search for common principles', *Quadrant* (May 1995), 9–12.

43 Francis Fukuyama, 'The end of history?', *The National Interest* (summer 1989), 4, and his 'Reply to my critics', *The National Interest* (winter 1989–90), 21–8. See also Fukuyama's book *The End of History and the Last Man* (London, Hamish Hamilton, 1992).

1

Friedrich Hayek: Elitism and Democracy

Chandran Kukathas

We have no intention, however, of making a fetish of democracy. It may well be true that our generation talks and thinks
too much of democracy and too little of the values which it
serves.

Friedrich Hayek, *The Road to Serfdom*[1]

Contemporary political theory is awash in competing conceptions and
analyses of democracy. Democratic models range from 'technocratic
visions of government to conceptions of social life marked by extensive
political participation';[2] and theorists of democracy are scarcely less
numerous. Not least among the reasons for democracy's prominence
in contemporary political writing is the significance of the global political
phenomenon of 'democratization'. We live in an age of democracy
fetishism.

In these circumstances, what, if anything, does Friedrich Hayek have to
offer our understanding of democracy? Hayek is best known as a critic of
socialism and, later, of the welfare state, and as a defender of a classical
liberal doctrine of limited government. While he has addressed some issues
in democratic theory, he has scarcely done so at length; and to the extent
that he has, he has been, at best, ambivalent about his commitment to
democracy. Moreover, it could be argued that Hayek's critique of democratic rule not only rests on a particularly narrow conception of democracy, but also invokes an alternative – the free market – which is beset by
similar (and arguably greater) problems of power and domination. Why,
then, trouble to examine Hayek's contribution to democratic theory?

It is the contention of this essay that Hayek, despite his ambivalence, does indeed have something to offer the student of democratic theory and of democratization. He has something to offer less because of his analysis of the processes of modern democracy than because of the light thrown on the democratic state by his thought more generally. This chapter begins by outlining Hayek's view of democracy and then turns to the problem of explaining Hayek's ambivalent attitude towards it. Once this is done it will be possible to draw out more clearly the contribution Hayek has to make to democratic theory.

Background: Intellectual Context and Wider Philosophy

To understand Hayek's view of democracy it is important to recognize that it springs from his social and political philosophy more generally, which is in turn shaped by the circumstances of Hayek's intellectual and political development. Although born in Austria (in 1899), where he completed his education with doctorates in law and political science, Hayek spent most of his academic life in Britain and the United States. Leaving the Austrian Institute of Economic Research (of which he was Director), Hayek became Tooke Professor of Economics and Statistics at the London School of Economics in 1931, and remained there until his move to the Committee on Social Thought at the University of Chicago in 1950. It was this period in Britain that was critical to the development of his political thinking. This was partly because it was in this period that Hayek made his reputation as an economist: indeed, the 1930s and 1940s had a profound effect on Hayek's thought, as well as on his career.

The critical development was the emergence of Nazism in Germany. Under the influence of Ludwig Mises, Hayek had already embarked on research into economic problems of socialism and by 1936 had produced a number of influential papers on the question of economic calculation under central planning. After the Nazi rise to power, and eventually the outbreak of war, however, Hayek's concerns broadened into an interest in the political challenge posed by totalitarianism – a challenge presented to the West both by German Nazism and by Soviet communism. That challenge, for Hayek, was nothing less than a threat to civilization. Holding this view led him not only down a path of public activism, but also into political philosophy; for it convinced him that the articulation of the intellectual alternative to totalitarianism was a matter of urgency. Not least important among his reasons for this conviction was his view that totalitarian ideas were at the core of the socialist thinking which was gaining popularity even in Britain, which was facing the wrong direction on the road to serfdom.

It is in these assumptions that the central ideas of Hayek's thought have their beginnings. Human society, for Hayek, is a spontaneous order which, while the product of human intention, is not the result of human design, and is too complex to plan or control. To think that it can be consciously ordered is an illusion because no individual or agency is capable of acquiring the knowledge that would be needed to do so. Socialism was the most recent, and also the noblest, form of this illusion. But it was an illusion nonetheless.

A good society, then, could not be one informed by the principles of socialism but would have to be a liberal social order. The great bulk of Hayek's social thought is devoted to the task of describing and defending the principles of a liberal social order. Such a society, he argued, was a free society in which individuals were at liberty to make use of their knowledge to pursue their own ends, under the protection of the rule of law. A free society, for Hayek, was a society under law.

In stressing the importance of the rule of law, Hayek is not simply calling for the impartial enforcement of law – important though that may be. The rule of law, he argues, is 'not a rule of law, but a rule concerning what the law ought to be, a meta-legal doctrine or a political ideal'.[3] It requires that the law possess three important attributes: (1) that its rules be general and abstract; (2) that they be known and certain; and (3) that they respect individual equality before the law.[4] Underlying these imperatives is Hayek's concern that law should not be arbitrary; for in his understanding, a free society is one in which individuals are not subject to the arbitrary will of another. It is this belief which also lies at the core of Hayek's conviction that the common law is a better guarantee of freedom than legislation, and that freedom and the rule of law are possible, ultimately, only in a society which is a 'spontaneous order' rather than in any kind of planned society. For only in such a society can the role of judge be restricted to that of an upholder of an abstract order or system of rules which has itself no goals or purposes other than facilitating the peaceful pursuit of individual ends by diverse individuals.[5] A good society, in this understanding, is not a society marked by collective self-rule but one marked by obedience to rules. This was the key to upholding freedom.

Hayek's View of Democracy

For Hayek, 'Democracy is essentially a means, a utilitarian device for safeguarding internal peace and individual freedom.'[6] This attitude, already evident in *The Road to Serfdom* (1944), was one Hayek still held when he came to write *The Constitution of Liberty* (1960): 'However strong the general case for democracy, it is not an ultimate or absolute value . . . It is probably the best method of achieving certain ends, but not an end in itself.'[7] In this understanding, democracy amounts to a decision procedure. When collective action needs to be taken to lay down coercive rules of conduct, the decision should be in accordance with the view of the majority. This principle is commended, however, largely because it is most likely to command general assent. Democracy is thus a decision procedure which allows for peaceful change.

In adopting this lukewarm attitude towards democracy Hayek's concern is to distance himself from those he describes as 'doctrinaire democrats', for whom democracy means popular sovereignty and, so, the unlimited and unlimitable rule of the majority.[8] For Hayek, democracy is not the fundamental or master value in politics, since it is not the value which holds the political community together: 'A group of men normally become a society not by giving themselves laws but by obeying the same rules of conduct.'[9] A free society exists when people accept common principles of conduct, and when majorities agree to submit to these principles even when it may be in their immediate interest to violate them. Democracy is no more than a decision procedure. In a free society it is constrained by a higher order requirement that that procedure should not have unlimited application: some matters simply should not be the subject of democratic decision. Democracy does not guarantee the right decisions will be reached. Power in the hands of the people is still power; and power, or might, does not make right.

In spite of these reservations, however, Hayek thinks that democracy can be justified by three arguments, each of which is conclusive.[10] The first is that, when opinions conflict, it is less wasteful to determine which should prevail by counting numbers than by fighting. The second is that democracy is an important safeguard (though not a guarantee) of individual liberty. The third is that democracy has the power to educate the majority, which learns by participation in the process of rule and thereby also makes available a wider range of able people to be selected for office.

Yet having said that democracy is justifiable, most of Hayek's writing on the topic is devoted to an analysis of the excesses and dangers of democracy. In *The Road to Serfdom* he warns of the dangers of treating democracy as the main value threatened by the rise of totalitarianism. This mistake he thinks responsible for the 'misleading and unfounded belief that so long as the ultimate source of power is the will of the majority, the power cannot be arbitrary'.[11] This belief is mistaken because democratic control does not, by its mere existence, prevent power from becoming arbitrary: 'If democracy resolves on a task which necessarily involves the use of power which cannot be guided by fixed rules, it must become arbitrary power.'[12] In *The Constitution of Liberty* he cautions against the idea of government guided by majority opinion. First, he argues, it is important that that opinion be independent of government, emerging from a spontaneous process rather than as the product of government direction. And this condition, he insists, also requires 'the existence of a large sphere independent of majority control in which the opinions of the individual are formed' (making the case for democracy and the case for freedom of speech 'inseparable').[13] Secondly, he suggests that majority decisions should not be trusted too readily since they tell us only what people want at a given moment, and not what it is in their interest to want if they were better informed. Majorities can be persuaded and minority opinion can become a majority one.[14] Indeed, more often than not, it is the minority who are enlightened, and it is its capacity to lead the majority that brings progress.[15] Finally, majority decisions are 'peculiarly liable, if not guided by accepted common principles, to produce overall results that nobody wanted'.[16] A government seeking to control affairs by judging every case on its merits 'usually finds itself having to observe principles not of its own choosing and being led into action that it never contemplated'.[17]

This last point is one Hayek elaborates at great length in volume 3 of *Law, Legislation and Liberty*, the work in which Hayek's disdain for the democratic process is most strongly evident. Here, again, Hayek begins by emphasizing the importance of democracy, claiming to be 'profoundly disturbed by the rapid decline of faith in it'.[18] But what follows is a vigorous attack on democratic politics as interest group politics: 'Under the existing system . . . every small interest group can enforce its demands, not by persuading a majority that the demands are just or equitable, but by threatening to withhold that support which the nucleus of agreed individuals will need to become a majority.'[19] Modern democratic government, in Hayek's view, is a system in which bargaining or deal-making, rather than deliberation in order to reach substantive agreement, is the order of the day. Political parties, in this situation, are 'little more than coalitions of organized interests whose actions are determined by the inherent logic of their mechanics rather than by any general principles or ideals on which they are agreed'.[20]

In Hayek's analysis, the reason for our being in this predicament lies partly in the expansion of the purposes of government and, so, of the scope of democracy. The domination of government by coalitions of organized interests is 'the inescapable result of a system in which government has unlimited powers to take whatever measures are required to satisfy the wishes of those on whose support it relies'.[21] To limit the powers of organized interests it is necessary to limit the powers of government. But Hayek also offers another important thesis about the root of democracy's malaise. This is the argument that, in modern representative assemblies, two very different functions have become confused: *legislation* and *government*. Indeed, the function of government – the administration of common means for public purposes – has come to dominate. The problem is that responsibility for governing and rule-making is placed in the hands of a single body, giving rise to a condition which is inconsistent with the separation of powers and the rule of law. Hayek explains: 'The ideal of a democratic control of government and that of the limitation of government by law are thus different ideals that certainly cannot be both achieved by placing into the hands of the same representative body both rule-making and governmental powers.'[22]

It is this last concern in particular that leads Hayek to consider the question of what alternative political arrangements might be more defensible. The result of his reflections is the 'model constitution' described in volume 3 of *Law, Legislation and Liberty*. Under this constitution there would be two representative bodies, one charged with the task of stating the general rules of just conduct, and another entrusted with the task of government. Hayek thinks that the deleterious effects of parties and party politics would be reduced (if not eliminated altogether) by a system of non-renewable fifteen-year terms for elected representatives to the legislative assembly (eligible for office only at age forty-five), and by making members of the governmental assembly ineligible for election to the legislative assembly. The interest of Hayek's proposals themselves aside, what is important about his discussion of a model constitution is that it reveals his concern to contain power and dethrone politics.

Yet, at the same time, Hayek continually reiterates his commitment to democracy, and expresses his fear that people are losing faith in democracy. What seems strange about this is the tension between Hayek's unremitting hostility to democratic politics and his avowed concern for the fate of democracy. 'I am anxious,' he writes, 'to rescue the true ideal from the miscredit into which it is falling.'[23] Nevertheless, if Hayek's description of the democratic process is correct, he seems to be doing more to discredit it than to rescue it. The question, then, is: how is Hayek's ambivalence towards democracy to be explained?

Explaining Hayek's Ambivalence towards Democracy

Hayek, undoubtedly, would deny that he is in any way ambivalent about democracy: his concern is to show how democracy has been corrupted, and to explain how it might be recovered. And this explanation of his apparent ambivalence clearly must be considered. But there is another explanation which is also worth examining. Put most bluntly, this explanation is that Hayek is an elitist or even a kind of a Leninist, who distrusts the masses and doubts their wisdom. Like the tradition of Austrian economists from which he draws, and like the Marxists, he is scornful of majority opinion as a form of false consciousness.[24] Does either explanation account for Hayek's ambivalence?

Hayek's own explanation must be counted as unsatisfactory. Even though he asserts that he is not against democracy but only against corrupted versions of it, or that he is really concerned to rescue the democratic ideal which has miscarried in modern times, Hayek never explains convincingly what 'true democracy' amounts to. If democracy is little more than a procedure for changing rulers peacefully, and if it is quite possible to talk coherently of totalitarian democracy, it is hard to see how democracy could be regarded as anything more than a formal feature of a political system. And this makes it hard to see why one would feel particularly upset, let alone 'profoundly disturbed', about the 'decline in faith' in democracy. If the recovery of true democracy is important, true democracy must be something more substantial. Yet here there are two problems. First, Hayek himself has insisted that democracy is not a substantive value. Second, if true democracy is given substance by building other considerations or values into 'democracy', there is a risk that what ends up being argued for is not so much democracy as the other values that it serves.

Hayek, in fact, runs into both these problems. The first is a straightforward problem of inconsistency: he asserts that democracy is not a substantive value but, when he defends it, he defends it in terms which assume that it is. In the second case, however, he commits the sin of giving democracy substance by implying that real democracy exists only when particular types of democratic regimes – liberal democratic regimes – exist, but at the same time without managing actually to explain what are the elements of true democracy. Indeed, Hayek really only tells us what real democracy is not. It is not, among other things, the operation of interest group politics, or unrestricted majority rule. But this leaves us little wiser about the nature of the democracy he wishes to rescue.

One intriguing suggestion Hayek offers to clarify his argument is the proposal that we adopt the word 'demarchy' to describe the ideal he wishes to uphold. The Greek word 'democracy' was formed by combining *demos*, meaning people, with *kratein*, meaning 'to exercise power'. But *kratein*, unlike the alternative verb *archein*, stresses brute force rather than government by rule. 'Demarchy' might be a word which better captures what it is that Hayek has in mind, since it indicates one important feature of the polity he wants to defend: it embodies the ideal of an equal law for all.[25] But this solution is also unsatisfactory. In part, the trouble is that coining new words does not really help when the problem calls for the explication of concepts. As C. S. Lewis explained, language, although not an infallible guide, 'contains, with all its defects, a good deal of stored insight and experience. If you begin by flouting it, it has a way of avenging itself later on. We had better not follow Humpty Dumpty in making words mean whatever we please.'[26] On top of that, the use of the term 'demarchy' only gives us a vague sense of what Hayek's version of what he (sometimes) and others (generally) call 'democracy' *connotes*. What the term denotes remains unacceptably opaque.

All in all, Hayek's explanation does little to help us understand the ambivalence which is so evident in his discussion of democracy. This offers strong grounds for the suspicion that he is really not in favour of mass democracy but rather favours some form of elitism. And there is good reason to think this. Most obviously, even while asserting his concern for the fate of democracy, he employs the term 'democracy' to describe the practices of which he is so critical. His criticisms of interest group politics and of majoritarianism are offered as criticisms of democracy. Here it is worth noting also that the phenomenon of interest group politics he describes is one which some democratic theorists also recognize, though are much less critical of. Democratic pluralists, for example, have argued that democracy does involve a bargaining among competing interests in a process in which power is dispersed (imperfectly, to be sure) among a multitude of competing interests. Whatever the weaknesses of this process, it brings us (or so they argue) as close as is possible to a regime of political equality.[27] In attacking what he sees as interest group politics he is, in fact, attacking theories of democratic pluralism. If Hayek's view of democracy could find any sympathizers among his contemporaries it would most likely be Joseph Schumpeter.[28]

There are other reasons for thinking of Hayek as an elitist. As Andrew Gamble points out, Hayek thought 'most things of value in the development of civilization were the work of minorities', who were often persecuted by majorities.[29] Even socialism he thought owed its great political success in the twentieth century to the efforts of intellectuals who proselytized on its behalf. If civilization was to survive the socialist onslaught, he believed, what was needed was not a turning to the masses or to self-government but better leadership from the classical liberal intellectual elite. Its task, Hayek argued, was to make the defence of freedom and the rule of law a crusade which would attract the best minds in society.[30]

Yet tempting though it may be to accept this as an explanation of

Hayek's ambivalence about democracy, in the end it will not do. The crucial point here is that, while Hayek is, in many respects, an elitist, he is not a Leninist. While he sees elites as the driving forces of progress, or as the engines of civilization, he also retains a powerful distrust of elites which is consistent with the central commitments of his thought. Those commitments see him repudiate with relentless hostility all doctrines of centralization. While Lenin's overriding concern was to have the intellectual vanguard seize the commanding heights so as to transform the state, Hayek's goal is to persuade intellectuals to resist, and persuade others to resist, the temptation to take power. More than this, he argued for moves to put obstacles, mostly in the form of legal rules, in the way of elites to reduce the scope of their activity. Most of Hayek's practical proposals are less for specific measures to be taken to achieve particular outcomes than for steps to reduce the capacity of elites to exercise power – and any form of monopoly power in particular. In the economic sphere his arguments for the denationalization of money provide an important example. In politics, his arguments for free speech and for the rule of law are important precisely because (in his thought) they are arguments put against the idea of any sovereign power having the right to direct the legal order or society more generally.

Yet, if neither elitism nor Hayek's own self-description can explain his ambivalent attitude towards democracy, what can? In the end, two complementary explanations are necessary. The first is a historical explanation, while the second one is conceptual.

The historical explanation is to suggest that Hayek's ambivalence about democracy reflects, to some degree, the development of his thought, which becomes increasingly hostile towards democracy. In his first major political work, *The Road to Serfdom*, while he is wary enough of democracy to warn against mistaking it for all that is valuable in political life, he is less critical of democracy than in most of his major writings. In part this may have been the result of his motives in writing of the dangers of totalitarianism at a time when Britain was still at war with Germany, and the USSR was on the side of the Allies. Whatever his reservations about democracy, he was careful not to let his warnings about the totalitarian dangers inherent in central planning be undermined by giving the impression that he was against democracy. In the period immediately after the war, when the threat to Western civilization came no longer from Nazi Germany but from Soviet communism, Hayek felt that the most important contribution he could make would be to help build a broadly based coalition of intellectuals united by their opposition to totalitarianism. This conviction saw the creation in 1947 of the Mont Pélèrin Society as an international society of anti-totalitarian scholars. But the price that had to be paid for the building of this coalition was the admission into the fold of a diversity of intellectual and political viewpoints, ranging from conservatism to democratic socialism.[31] At this time, to criticize democracy would not have been prudent, particularly when the differences between the free West and the Eastern bloc were drawn in terms of a conflict between democracy and communism. Nonetheless, as the perceived dangers of communism and totalitarianism in the West receded, Hayek became freer to criticize more forcefully those political developments about which he first expressed concern in 1944.

Accordingly, by the time he came to write *Law, Legislation and Liberty*, when the central planning variant of socialism was no longer a serious political issue, Hayek could offer a more direct challenge to the institutions of the welfare state, of which he had become increasingly critical. Indeed, it is in *Law, Legislation and Liberty* that the criticism of democracy is most vigorous, and the tone of the criticism most hostile. Hayek's ambivalence about democracy is therefore partly explained by his increasing reservations about democratic politics and his greater willingness to express them.

But that is still not quite the whole story. After all, even in *Law, Legislation and Liberty*, Hayek continues to pay a kind of homage (some may say lip-service!) to democracy. Why should he continue to do so? The reason may be that, when dealing with the issues of democratic government, Hayek is thinking about the concept of democracy in two different ways.

When he is attacking democracy what he has in mind is democracy as collective self-rule, which he generally equates with majority rule. It is the idea of democracy as a principle of self-government for which Hayek has very little time. In part this is because he does not particularly value self-government, since self-government is not inconsistent with tyrannical government. In part, it is also because he thinks this deludes people into thinking that they are governing themselves when they are really being directed by others. Morover, he is critical of democracy understood in this way because he sees it as leading to the politics of interest group conflict.

When Hayek is praising democracy, however, he does not seem to be thinking of democracy as a principle of collective self-rule. Rather, he appears to think of democracy as a kind of *regime*, with its own particular, and highly desirable, characteristics, the most notable of which is liberty. When discussing democracy in this vein, he writes less of self-government or majority rule than of the freedom for which such a society stands. 'The belief in democracy,' Hayek quotes, 'presupposes belief in things higher than democracy.'[32] A democratic society is one which enjoys certain protections against tyranny, and safeguards of its freedoms.[33] No less important, a democracy is a society in which equality before the law prevails. For Hayek, the great aim of the struggle for liberty has been equality before the law, and this equality is found typically in democratic regimes. Thus he writes, in *The Constitution of Liberty*:

> This extension of the principle of equality to the rules of moral and social conduct is the chief expression of what is commonly called the democratic spirit – and probably that aspect of it that does most to make inoffensive the inequalities that liberty necessarily produces.[34]

When writing favourably of democracy, Hayek ties it closely to the notion of a regime operating under the rule of law. Indeed, in writing of the importance of democracy for the preservation of the *Rechtsstaat*, he observes that 'democracy will not exist long unless it preserves the rule of law.'[35]

In all these cases Hayek's praise of democracy turns into criticism when he ceases to focus on the values he thinks it serves. He remains attached to democracy in so far as he remains wedded to the assumption that those regimes which uphold liberty, equality and the rule of law tend to be democratic regimes. But, in the end, it is these other concerns which dominate his thought. His attachment to democracy is less an attachment to self-rule than an attachment to the liberalism which defines his political ideas more generally.

Lessons from Hayek?

Given the ambiguities in Hayek's analysis of democracy, and the guarded nature of his endorsement of democratic government, it looks doubtful that much could be gained for democratic theory by any serious examination of his thought. Certainly, it appears unlikely that modern theorists of discursive and deliberative democracy would find much in Hayekian democratic theory that would move them in any way. At best, Hayek might seem a little out of date; at worst, irrelevant.

Nonetheless, Hayek does have something to offer the student of democracy. This is less because of Hayek's own theory of democracy than because of the challenge posed by his analysis of modern democracies, and by his thought more generally, to democratic theory. This challenge has not gone unnoticed. In his own work on democracy, David Held has devoted considerable attention to the problem of responding to the Hayekian challenge. Held's analysis and response are worth considering in some detail, not only because they illustrate the significance of Hayek for democratic theory, but also because the objections which might be raised against Held reveal why Hayek's thought carries within it more radical implications than have so far been recognized.

In Held's account, Hayek is the principal author of a model of democracy called 'legal democracy'. Its principle of justification is this:

> The majority principle is an effective and desirable way of protecting individuals from arbitrary government and of maintaining liberty. However, for political life, like economic life, to be a matter of individual freedom and initiative, majority rule must be circumscribed by the rule of law. Only under these conditions can the majority principle function wisely and justly.[36]

The key features of this model of democracy, according to Held, are the constitutional state, the rule of law, and a free market (and civil society more generally) subject to minimal state intervention. The general conditions necessary for the operation of this model of democracy include political leadership guided by liberal principles, modest levels of bureaucratic regulation, restrictions on the operation of interest groups, and international free trade.[37]

In Held's view, this model of democracy is a model of the minimal state. Furthermore, this model, he argues, is marked by a number of flaws which he identifies in a critique of Hayek's social thought. While there is much to agree with in Hayek's arguments attacking the planned economy, Held concedes, he has failed to appreciate the complexity of contemporary capitalism. The Soviet conception of a command economy was indeed a failed economic and political project, and largely for the reasons Hayek specified. These included:

> an arrogant and misplaced presumption of knowledge about people's needs and wants, a crisis of 'excessive information' which could not be properly evaluated in the absence of market prices and costs, and the pursuit of coercive political programmes in diverse domains, from economic management to cultural life.[38]

But while Hayek had been right about all this, he had failed to see that his model of a liberal free-market order was becoming 'ever more at odds with the modern corporate capitalist system'.[39] He did not appreciate the importance of the massive asymmetries of power and resources which were 'systematically reproduced by the market economy but also buttressed by liberal democratic governments themselves'.[40] For Held, the reality of the modern free market is that it is 'marked by complex patterns of market formation, oligopolistic and monopolistic structures, the imperatives of the system of corporate power and multinational corporations, the short-term logic of commercial banking houses and the economic rivalry of regional power blocs'.[41] In these circumstances, Held maintains, it is simply not possible to claim, as Hayek and others on the new right do, that markets are 'simply free, responsive mechanisms of collective choice'.[42]

This critique is pressed further in Held's work when he argues that leaving the market to solve fundamental problems of resource generation and allocation misses the roots of many economic and political difficulties. These include inequalities within and between states which are the source of conflict, the erosion of manufacturing industry in some countries while it remains protected in others, the emergence of huge world-wide financial flows which may destabilize national economies, and the development of transnational problems of the earth's commons, ranging from global warming to the spread of toxic pollutants. Moreover, pushing back the boundaries of the state and cutting back on government activity exacerbate the difficulties suffered by the most vulnerable members of society.[43] On top of this, Held argues, to try to remove certain issues from politics (as Hayek suggests) would reduce the sphere of democratic debate and control, and also end up denying the least well-off the capacity to pursue the courses of action Hayek thinks they should have the liberty to take.[44]

Perhaps the most interesting aspect of Held's work is his own response to the condition he describes (and which he thinks Hayek has failed to appreciate). Having recognized the extent of globalization, Held offers a 'cosmopolitan model' of democracy as one more suitable for a global age. Modern society, he argues, has transformed the nature of sovereignty. Held argues:

> If the agent at the heart of modern political discourse, be it a person, a group or a collectivity, is locked into a variety of overlapping forces, developments and communities – domestic, international and transnational – then the proper 'home' of politics, and the model of democratic autonomy especially, becomes a puzzling matter.[45]

In the modern world sovereignty has to be reconceived and the cosmopolitan model is his attempt to do so. What cosmopolitan democracy would attempt to do is to 'entrench and develop democratic institutions at regional and global levels as a necessary complement to those at the level of the nation-state'.[46] This is on the assumption that the nation state will continue to be of significance, but that a layer of governance will be

necessary to constitute a limitation of national sovereignty. The hope is
that we will see the construction not only of new democratic institutions
but also of 'broad avenues of civic participation in decision-making at
regional and global levels'.[47] Indeed, Held envisages a global movement
bringing about regional parliaments, international referenda and the
democratization of international governmental organizations, including
(possibly) a reformed UN assuming the role of an authoritative assembly
of all democratic states.[48]

The question, however, is what are we to make of this critique of
Hayek, and the philosophical direction then taken by the critic? This
question has a particular significance given that Hayek advanced a view of
liberalism which emphasized its nature as an internationalist creed, and
indeed the nature of capitalism as an economic system which did not
recognize national, or any other political, boundaries. But is Held
right?

While some of the points Held makes are sound, his critique of Hayek
is not as decisive as it might appear. More important, the theoretical
conclusions Held wishes to pursue themselves run up against challenges he
does not really consider – challenges posed substantially by Hayek's political ideas.

The first, and most obvious, point with which Hayek might take issue
is Held's charge that he had failed to appreciate the complexity of capitalism. If anything, Hayek made a career of emphasizing the complexity of
the economic order, and stressing that it was not something which could
be confined within national boundaries and controlled by political
authorities trying to act as economic managers. For him, globalization was
not a phenomenon of the late twentieth century but already an important
feature of economic activity a century before. Where Hayek differs from
Held, however, is in a claim that also differentiated him from those of his
critics who thought him mistaken about the folly of central planning. This
is the claim that the increase in complexity necessitates less rather than
more central control. The greater the size and complexity of the economic
order, Hayek had argued against central planners, the greater the need to
decentralize decision-making, since the informational difficulties confronting the central planner were insuperable. In his later political writings
Hayek extended this analysis to the welfare state and the international
order, arguing against central direction because the growth of complexity
brought with it a growth in ignorance. Knowledge was so dispersed, and
so much a matter of tacit understandings and local scope, that attempts at
central direction threatened to result in discoordination. In this regard,
then, Held's criticism that Hayek has failed to appreciate capitalism's
complexity is unpersuasive. It simply repeats an old charge made against

Hayek as the critic of central planning – one which, even Held concedes, saw Hayek thoroughly vindicated.

Equally, it is a mistake to suggest that Hayek, or others in his camp, did not recognize the reality of modern corporate power, and the economic rivalry of regional power blocs. One of the most important strands of Hayek's social thought is the persistent critique of monopoly power, which arises in most damaging form when buttressed by legal sanctions supplied by the state. Hayek's targets here included not only trade unions but also corporations. His recommendations ranged from the removal of legal privileges to changes in corporate laws which he thought gave companies powers (such as the power to determine whether or not to pay dividends) which distanced them from the control of shareholders.

As for the argument that removing some issues from politics would harm the vulnerable by reducing the sphere of democratic debate, it does not tell against Hayek's position. For Hayek has argued that what passes for democratic debate is, in the end, only a matter of elite appeal to selected interests, with the most powerful winning. Hayek would undoubtedly agree with Held that there are massive asymmetries of power, and that these are buttressed by governments. To take Hayek to task in any convincing fashion it would be necessary to show that this is not so, and that democratic debate and control can be something other than a process manipulated by political elites.

This brings us, then, to a consideration of Held's own model of cosmopolitan democracy as a model for the politics of globalized society, and one which might provide an alternative to the Hayekian view disdaining democracy. The interesting point of contrast between Held and Hayek here is in their attitudes towards sovereignty. Held's view is that the global condition demands a reconceiving of sovereignty and that reconceiving sovereignty means extending the reach of democratic practice beyond the nation state. Hayek's view, by contrast, anticipates the very reverse as a necessary development. What has to be challenged, he argues, is the 'constructivistic superstition of sovereignty'.[49]

Hayek's argument here emerges most usefully in his construction of a 'model constitution' in *Law, Legislation and Liberty*. He offers two important reasons for presenting this construction (after emphasizing that his interest is *not* in proposing a scheme for present application). The first is that such a construction may be illuminating in as much as it forces us to reflect upon how the tacit presuppositions which are the foundations of successful democracies might be embodied in constitutions designed for new, emerging democracies. Secondly, the principles embodied in the scheme outlined might illuminate matters in our endeavours to create 'new supra-national institutions'.[50] These reasons reveal the prescience of

Hayek's theoretical efforts, not least because they anticipate the preoccu-
pations which have dominated the politics of democratization in the post
Cold War era.

What is most striking about the model constitution Hayek offers,
however, is in the structure of authority it elaborates. 'If it be asked where
under such an arrangement "sovereignty" rests,' Hayek observes, 'the
answer is nowhere – unless it [temporarily][51] resides in the hands of the
constitution-making or constitution-amending body.'[52] Hayek is not
asserting here that authority is irrelevant or unnecessary. Far from it. What
he is saying is, first, that authority is not hierarchical in structure, or
located unambiguously within boundaries within which it is unlimited in
scope; and second, that in the imagined society of his model constitution
there are no clear boundaries, and there are many sources of authority,
none of which is sovereign.

Hayek's concern, therefore, is to combat what he sees as the modern
preoccupation with creating sovereign powers to shape and control social
life. His own prescriptions are for a move in the opposite direction. The
solutions to the problems of social life are to be found not in the development of institutions of governance but in the preservation of a structure of
competition among authorities in which none can acquire enough power
to prevail. Hayek's hostility to democracy is the product of this outlook.
For his target, in the end, is sovereignty, which is an idea he identifies with
absolutism: 'In the Western world unlimited sovereignty was scarcely ever
claimed by anyone since antiquity until the arrival of absolutism in the
sixteenth century. It was certainly not conceded to medieval princes and
hardly ever claimed by them.'[53] Yet even then, he insists, it was not really
accepted as legitimate until after the advent of modern democracy.
Democracy, for him, 'has inherited the tradition of absolutism'.[54]

The challenge this thought poses for modern democracy is an important one. For if Hayek is right, democratic theorists like David Held are
responding to the growing complexity of modern society in precisely the
wrong way, seeking, in the name of democracy, to develop structures of
authority which run the risk of creating sovereigns with powers too great
and, so, too dangerous. The answer, however, is to worry less about the
construction of democratic authority but to limit its scope, and to try to
ensure that there remains space for a diversity of competing authorities,
none of which can become pre-eminent.

In the eyes of his critics, Hayek's democratic theory, like his classical
liberalism, presents a somewhat old-fashioned face. Yet in many ways, the
challenge he presents suggests an outlook which is strikingly modern, if
not postmodern. Michel Foucault has suggested, in his own analysis of
power, that 'We need to cut off the King's head', adding that 'in political

theory that has still to be done.'[55] Hayek's contribution to democratic theory has been made not by any effort of reconstruction but by an attempt at decapitation.

Notes

1 F. A. Hayek, *The Road to Serfdom* (London, Routledge and Kegan Paul, 1976), p. 52.
2 D. Held, *Models of Democracy*, 2nd edn (Cambridge, Polity, 1996), p. 295.
3 F. A. Hayek, *The Constitution of Liberty* (London, Routledge and Kegan Paul, 1976), p. 206.
4 Hayek, *Constitution of Liberty*, pp. 207–9.
5 I have discussed Hayek's theory of the rule of law in greater depth in my *Hayek and Modern Liberalism* (Oxford, Clarendon Press, 1989), pp. 148–64. See also J. Shearmur, *Hayek and After: Hayekian Liberalism as a Research Programme* (London, Routledge, 1996), esp. pp. 88–91. Shearmur argues (convincingly) that Hayek's ideas on the nature of law were profoundly changed by his reading of Bruno Leoni's *Freedom and the Law*.
6 Hayek, *Road to Serfdom*, p. 52.
7 Hayek, *Constitution of Liberty*, p. 106.
8 Hayek, *Constitution of Liberty*, p. 106.
9 Hayek, *Constitution of Liberty*, pp. 106–7.
10 Hayek, *Constitution of Liberty*, pp. 107–8.
11 Hayek, *Road to Serfdom*, p. 52.
12 Hayek, *Road to Serfdom*, p. 53.
13 Hayek, *Constitution of Liberty*, p. 109.
14 Hayek, *Constitution of Liberty*, p. 109.
15 Hayek, *Constitution of Liberty*, p. 110.
16 Hayek, *Constitution of Liberty*, p. 111.
17 Hayek, *Constitution of Liberty*, p. 111.
18 F. A. Hayek, *Law, Legislation and Liberty*, vol. 3, *The Political Order of a Free People* (London, Routledge and Kegan Paul, 1982), p. 5.
19 Hayek, *Law, Legislation and Liberty*, vol. 3, p. 10.
20 Hayek, *Law, Legislation and Liberty*, vol. 3, p. 13.
21 Hayek, *Law, Legislation and Liberty*, vol. 3, p. 15.
22 Hayek, *Law, Legislation and Liberty*, vol. 3, p. 26.
23 Hayek, *Law, Legislation and Liberty*, vol. 3, p. 98.
24 This explanation is offered in a passing remark in A. Gamble, *Hayek: The Iron Cage of Liberty* (Boulder, CO, Westview, 1996), p. 97.
25 Gamble, *Hayek: The Iron Cage*, pp. 39–40.
26 C. S. Lewis, *The Four Loves* (London, Harper Collins, 1977), p. 8.
27 The classic statement of this view is still Robert Dahl's *A Preface to Democratic Theory* (Chicago, University of Chicago Press, 1956). For Dahl's

reservations about these earlier views see, in particular, his *Dilemmas of Pluralist Democracy: Autonomy versus Control* (New Haven, CT, and London, Yale University Press, 1982); and *Democracy and its Critics* (New Haven, CT, and London, Yale University Press, 1989).

28 See J. Schumpeter, *Capitalism, Socialism and Democracy* (London, Allen and Unwin, 1943).

29 Gamble, *Hayek: The Iron Cage*, p. 96.

30 See in particular F. A. Hayek, 'The intellectuals and socialism', in his *Studies in Philosophy, Politics and Economics* (London, Routledge and Kegan Paul, 1967), pp. 178–94.

31 I have expounded Hayek's rationale for the establishment of the society at greater length in 'Hayek and modern liberalism' (unpublished MS), drawing from letters and other papers from the Hayek Archive at the Hoover Institution, Stanford University.

32 Wilhelm Hennis, quoted in Hayek, *Law, Legislation and Liberty*, vol. 3, p. 4.

33 Hayek, *Law, Legislation and Liberty*, vol. 3, p. 5.

34 Hayek, *Constitution of Liberty*, p. 85.

35 Hayek, *Constitution of Liberty*, p. 248.

36 Held, *Models of Democracy*, p. 261.

37 Held, *Models of Democracy*, p. 261.

38 D. Held, *Democracy and the Global Order: From the Modern State to Cosmopolitan Governance* (Cambridge, Polity, 1995), pp. 248–9.

39 Held, *Models of Democracy*, p. 260.

40 Held, *Models of Democracy*, pp. 260–1.

41 Held, *Models of Democracy*, p. 261.

42 Held, *Models of Democracy*, p. 262.

43 Held, *Models of Democracy*, p. 262.

44 Held, *Models of Democracy*, p. 263.

45 Held, *Models of Democracy*, p. 353.

46 Held, *Models of Democracy*, p. 354.

47 Held, *Models of Democracy*, p. 354.

48 Held, *Models of Democracy*, p. 355.

49 Hayek, *Law, Legislation and Liberty*, vol. 3, p. 33.

50 Hayek, *Law, Legislation and Liberty*, vol. 3, p. 108.

51 The printed text reads 'temporally resides'; but I am assuming here that this is an error, and that the passage only makes sense if the world 'temporarily' is substituted.

52 Hayek, *Law, Legislation and Liberty*, vol. 3, p. 123.

53 Hayek, *Law, Legislation and Liberty*, vol. 3, p. 34.

54 Hayek, *Law, Legislation and Liberty*, vol. 3, pp. 34–5.

55 'Truth and power', in M. Foucault, *Power/Knowledge: Selected Interviews and Other Writings, 1972–77*, ed. Colin Gordon (New York, Pantheon, 1980), p. 121.

2

Hannah Arendt: Republicanism and Democracy

Margaret Canovan

Although Hannah Arendt never wrote a book about democracy, her work has important implications for democratic theory. At the time of her death in 1975 she was known as a champion of participatory politics and regarded in some quarters as a utopian idealist. Since that time, momentous cases of 'Arendtian' politics in the real world have led many political theorists (including some concerned specifically with democracy) to pay more attention to her understanding of politics itself as a peculiarly open-ended and unpredictable activity. There are, then, two different contributions to democratic theory to be found in her work: firstly an alternative republican vision of what democracy might be, and secondly an original but persuasive account of what political action is.

Arendt was highly critical of existing liberal democratic systems[1] and favoured what (following the classical republican tradition) she usually spoke of as 'public freedom': direct participation in politics by ordinary citizens. This alternative vision of a decentralized system based on what she called 'councils' is a minor but recurrent theme throughout her writings.[2] As we shall see, her views on this subject are unusual, and have been criticized for elitism. They do, however, have the virtue of confronting a problem often evaded by radical democrats, namely the tension between the ideal of grassroots political action on the one hand and twentieth-century experiences of mass politics on the other.

Apart from this concern for participation, her political theory has more fundamental implications for democracy because she rethinks politics itself, focusing attention on the plural and spontaneous nature of action. Her rethinking is in many ways encouraging for democrats. For example, she stresses the openness of the future, the capacity of political actors to make new beginnings and do the unexpected. She points out how apparently helpless individuals can act in concert to generate power among themselves (as the members of Solidarity did in Poland). The anti-communist revolutions of 1989 can in some respects be seen as vindicating her faith in the permanent possibility of action by those who choose to accept the responsibility of citizens.[3] Within established liberal democracies, grassroots initiatives ranging from the American civil rights movement[4] to protests against motorways bear witness to the potency of this sort of informal politics.

On the other hand, she also draws attention to some more disturbing implications of human plurality and spontaneity. Because political action goes on among plural persons, not among robots, its outcomes are unavoidably unpredictable and uncontrollable. The traditional democratic aspiration for the people to 'take power' in order to 'determine their own future' is therefore illusory. Furthermore, even when the outcomes of political action are desirable, they are also contingent and fragile, dependent on the continuing action of those who care about the political realm. Above all, no political philosophy can tell political actors what to do or provide a blueprint for action. Within the public space that opens up amongst active citizens, participants can learn from one another and develop their capacity for judgement, but in the end they have to judge and act 'without bannisters', as Arendt put it, and with no way of ensuring that their initiatives and decisions will turn out well.[5]

In her work, original trains of thought are interwoven in a way that makes it difficult to summarize her ideas or to disengage her views on democracy from other facets of her thought. In what follows, however, I shall attempt to do so as far as is feasible, beginning with the work on totalitarianism that led her to rethink the nature of political action, looking at the general implications of this for democracy, and then turning to her interest in direct popular action and her advocacy of participatory citizenship. In conclusion I shall attempt a critical assessment of this aspect of her thinking.

Background: Arendt's Life

Inhabitants of Western liberal democracies in the late twentieth century, accustomed to a humdrum round of electoral campaigns based on 'the feel-good factor', may think that Arendt's vision of the heroism and tragedy of politics is highly coloured. To understand her we need to take a less parochial view, remembering the catastrophic experiences that made her a political thinker, above all the destruction of the European Jewish community into which she was born in Germany in 1906. Her family was secularized, assimilated and well-to-do. As a brilliant young student of theology and classical philosophy she was quite uninterested in 'the Jewish question' or in politics generally. It was the rise of Nazism amid the political, economic and social instability of Weimar Germany that forced her to pay attention to such matters. She began to move in Zionist circles, acting on the principle that (as she later expressed it) '"When one is attacked as a Jew, one must defend oneself *as a Jew.*" Not as a German, not as a world-citizen, not as an upholder of the Rights of Man.'[6] Any other response (she believed) failed to confront the reality of the situation. She came to terms intellectually with this new salience of Jewishness by way of a critical study of an earlier Jewish German intellectual, Rahel Varnhagen, a prominent figure in the German Romantic movement of the early nineteenth century.[7]

Hitler's rise to power in 1933 was a shattering blow, not least because it was welcomed by many German intellectuals. In particular, the enthusiastic Nazism of the philosopher Martin Heidegger, who had been not only Arendt's teacher but her lover, left her with a lasting suspicion of philosophical approaches to politics. Heidegger, whom she believed to be the greatest contemporary philosopher, had (she reflected) followed in the footsteps of Plato in betraying democracy and supporting tyranny. Was there perhaps an inherent antagonism between the solitary ivory tower of the thinker and the bustling pluralism of the political arena? Arendt wrestled with this conundrum for the rest of her life.

Fleeing to exile in France, she plunged into practical work within the Zionist movement. Her engagement with Zionist politics, however, was always vociferously critical, and by her own account she learned to think politically from a non-Jewish fellow refugee, Heinrich Blücher, a revolutionary socialist who had in extreme youth joined in Rosa Luxemburg's Spartacist uprising in Germany. In 1941, Arendt and Blücher, now married, managed to escape from occupied France to the USA. There she embarked upon a study of anti-semitism that eventually turned into *The Origins of Totalitarianism*, published in 1951. This book made her famous, and from then until her death in 1975 she continued to work as an independent thinker and writer, holding a succession of guest professorships in American universities, but belonging to and establishing no school. Her publications include *The Human Condition, Between Past and Future, On Revolution, Eichmann in Jerusalem* (which caused a great deal of controversy among her fellow Jews), *Men in Dark Times, Crises of the Republic* and (posthumously published and incomplete) *The Life of the Mind.* Large numbers of articles, papers and lectures (some of them now being published for the first time) make up a vast and intensely idiosyncratic corpus of writings.

Totalitarianism and Political Action

In her first major political work, *The Origins of Totalitarianism*, Arendt characterized 'totalitarianism' (Stalinist as well as Nazi) as a new kind of political phenomenon with antecedents in imperialism. Like all her work, the book is complex, but from the point of view of her thinking about democracy two connected aspects are particularly significant. In the first place, she emphasized that totalitarian movements had attracted mass support. Besides referring to large numbers, 'mass' in this connection has a special meaning for her, evoking the legacy of war, revolution, hyper-inflation and unemployment and the formation of 'masses' out of disinte-grated 'classes'. Following such traumatic events, large numbers of people in Europe had become 'superfluous', as she puts it, with no place in the world, no membership even of an exploited class in which they could find solidarity. These uprooted masses were attracted by the propaganda of totalitarian movements, which offered certainty – insight into the sup-posed forces of history, a guide to an inevitable future, protection against 'the never-ending shocks which real life and real experiences deal to human beings and their expectations'.[8]

Although the establishment of totalitarian regimes was in no sense inevitable, and was made possible by specific circumstances, Arendt be-lieved that many general features of modernity tend to generate 'masses': people, that is, who are only too ready to swallow totalitarian propaganda and to devote themselves to a movement which promises them certainty. If this is true, it is evidently bad news for democracy. The experience of McCarthyism in the United States further weakened her trust in the common sense of the electorate. As we shall see, her views on participatory politics show traces of these experiences. Her reflections on totalitarianism also had more fundamental implications for her thinking about politics in general and popular participation in particular.

Totalitarianism as analysed by Arendt found its apogee in the concen-tration camp. What made this institution crucial was not only the terror practised there, but above all what seemed to her to be the systematic destruction of human plurality and spontaneity. In the course of what she described as an attempt to change human nature,[9] human beings were reduced to creatures like Pavlov's dogs, bundles of reactions with no capacity for taking an individual action or thinking an independent thought. She came to believe that this assault on individuality lay at the heart of the system: being a quest for total power, totalitarianism could not tolerate the existence of real human beings. Individual initiative and plural viewpoints are essential characteristics of humanity. In the interests of total power, therefore, an attempt had been made (supported by the mass psychology of 'superfluous' people) to crush out all such individuality and initiative. Systematic terror pressed human beings together into a single gigantic robot that would follow the supposedly inexorable laws of nature or history in the way described by totalitarian ideology.[10]

Reflecting on the incompatibility between total power and human plurality, Arendt came to the conclusion that it is plurality – the fact that we are all the same precisely in being *different*, and that each of us is capable of acting spontaneously and of thinking our own thoughts – that is at the heart of being human, and that finds its clearest expression in politics. Startlingly, however, she realized that although it had taken totalitarian regimes to make a systematic attempt to eradicate this plurality in practice, political philosophers had in some ways prepared the ground by ignoring plurality in their theories. It was perhaps not by accident that philosophers of the stature of Heidegger and Plato had sympathized with one-man rule, for philosophers had looked at politics from the standpoint of the solitary thinker engaged in his single-minded pursuit of truth. Ever since Plato, each major philosopher had wanted to impose his truth upon the multifarious opinions of the public arena, failing to see that plural viewpoints and plural initiatives are at the heart of politics.

These wider implications of totalitarianism, and the need for funda-mental reflections on the human condition, became clearer to Arendt as her focus shifted from Nazism to an aspect of totalitarianism omitted from her book, namely the debt Stalinism owed to Marxism.[11] Marx had himself rebelled against the Western tradition of political philosophy by exalting practice above abstract theory and material life above ideas. Arendt believed, however, that despite these apparent reversals he had in fact perpetuated age-old philosophical misunderstandings of human activ-ity, and therefore of politics. What he and others had missed (as Arendt sought to explain in *The Human Condition*) was the significance of human plurality, the fact that 'men, not Man, live on the earth and inhabit the world.'[12] In so far as human beings are just another species of animal, engaged in the routine business of keeping themselves alive – what Arendt calls 'labour' – the differences between us may not have great significance. But the practical activities that mark us out as human beings are distinct from labour. One of them – 'work' in Arendt's terminology – creates the human 'world' of civilization that provides a setting for our lives as distinct individuals; but the other, 'action', most clearly reveals human distinctive-ness, and is the form of activity that is most relevant to politics.

If human beings merely *behaved* in routine and predictable ways, there might be a place for domination and administration, but not for politics. Politics is possible and necessary because we can also *act*. That is, we can interrupt our ordinary behaviour by taking the initiative and doing the unexpected. When we act, we reveal that we are free beings, as Rosa Parks and Martin Luther King did in the American South, and as Lech Walesa and his comrades in Solidarity did in Poland. So utterly unpredictable are such actions that Arendt describes the capacity to act as 'the one miracle-working faculty of man'.[13] As the place of action, politics is also the arena in which freedom in this characteristically Arendtian sense of beginning of something new can be most fully displayed and enjoyed.

Arendt maintained that almost all political thinkers have interpreted politics predominantly in terms of *work*, seeing it as a matter of making something out of material that has to be dominated and transformed, as wood is turned into a table or chair. The ideal republic is to be constructed according to the philosopher's blueprint. But this understanding of politics implies that someone – perhaps Plato's philosopher king or Rousseau's lawgiver – acts as a master craftsman and treats everyone else as raw material for the work of art. The crucial feature of the human condition left out of this picture, but that lies at the root of politics, is that human beings are plural actors. Action is a matter of initiative and creativity, but it is always *interaction*: we never start with a clean sheet on which we can scribble what we please. Instead we take initiatives that need the cooperation of others, and launch proposals into the tangle of contending opinions and actions. Politically, action is almost inseparable from speech. To suppose, however, that such speech could or should converge on a single rational viewpoint or issue in a single general will is (once again) to underestimate the significance of human plurality, which means that new actors, new initiatives and new points of view are continually entering the public arena.[14]

Reinterpreting politics in terms of action of this kind has profound implications. For one thing, it means that the time-honoured notion of politics as *rule* by a sovereign power is fundamentally misleading, particularly where democracy is concerned. That model implies a degree of control over the outcomes of one's actions that is possible only if others' capacity for action is drastically curtailed. In particular, the idea of 'rule by the people' supposes that plural individuals with separate viewpoints and capacities for initiative have disappeared into a single subject. Free politics (of the kind practised by the citizens of ancient Athens, of which she wrote in tones of admiration) implies rule by no one; aspirations to rule and exercise sovereignty have been left behind (in the household, in which, as she recognized, women and slaves were indeed subject to domination). Arendt maintained that political philosophers ever since Plato have misrepresented the experience of free politics,[15] with the result that although the possibilities of action amongst citizens were periodically rediscovered (notably in revolutionary situations) those involved found it hard to describe and to defend their experience.

Although the interaction involved in free politics cannot be a matter of exercising sovereignty, it can, as Arendt stressed, generate power. She maintained, indeed, that political power always rests upon 'action in concert', and that even tyranny cannot function without some degree of active support. But power is fluid and unstable. Instead of being a solid resource that is possessed by a government and that needs to be 'seized' by revolutionaries, it is an energy that is generated when people act together and dissipated when they cease to do so.[16] They can preserve that power only through mutual commitment, consolidating it by agreements that bridge over the spaces between them. Power can leak away quite suddenly from regimes that appeared impregnable, and be generated by individuals who seemed to be helpless until they came together in public and began to act. Arendt's message is therefore that ordinary citizens can be free and powerful; not by waiting for someone in authority to give them power, but by having the courage to act in concert and create their own public space. Such spaces do not need pre-existing institutions, but come into existence among those who act together. Above all, action is unpredictable. Human beings really do have the capacity to work miracles in the sense of doing the totally unexpected.[17]

Revolution and Participation

While Arendt was articulating her understanding of action in *The Human Condition*, political events, in the form of the abortive Hungarian Revolution of 1956, seemed to provide striking confirmation of it. An apparently entrenched system of domination abruptly lost power: insignificant people, emerging suddenly out of obscurity, turned into citizens and came together at the grassroots to create their own public spaces and to generate new power through action in concert. This promising beginning was speedily crushed by the military force of the Warsaw Pact governments (which could at that time still count on the compliance of their troops) but it helped to turn Arendt's attention to the phenomenon of revolution, its failures and its possibilities.

The result, *On Revolution*, is a complex and many-stranded set of reflections on the contrasted cases of the American and French Revolutions of the late eighteenth century. Both began (like the Hungarian uprising) with the exhilarating experience of liberation, as subjects threw off the shackles of rule and discovered the unexpected possibility of acting together in public. In the French case, exhilaration rapidly turned to tragedy as freedom disappeared in the Terror. Controversially, Arendt attributed this outcome to the irruption into politics of 'the social question'. Mass poverty, which had always existed, suddenly rose to the top of the political agenda as starving crowds were mobilized by the revolution. In conditions of premodern economic scarcity, political action could not in fact do anything to remedy the misery of the poor. Once their suffering was brought into the spotlight of the political arena, however, its sheer urgency made concern with establishing a lasting republic seem merely heartless.[18]

The American experience was much more successful in that the revolutionaries did manage to make the difficult transition from experiencing revolutionary liberation to establishing 'a new house where freedom can dwell',[19] a republic with 'lasting institutions'. This was easier for them than for the French revolutionaries, partly because the unprecedented prosperity of the (white) poor in America kept 'the social question' lower down the political agenda, and partly because the founders of the new republic could build upon a tradition of political action going back to the Pilgrim Fathers. For those early British settlers had, Arendt maintained, almost inadvertently discovered for themselves 'the elementary grammar of political action'.[20] Arriving in a wilderness where the authority of the British monarchy was too distant to be effective, they had constructed their own body politics from the ground up, using as their building blocks binding agreements with one another at a face-to-face level. When 'the people' subsequently rose in rebellion against King George, and later adopted the Constitution, they were a people articulated in local bodies where individuals were used to acting together and able to authorize representatives whom they could trust. In defiance of the Hobbesian and Rousseauian tradition of thinking about political power as a legal sovereignty that would be undermined by being divided, Arendt argued that the Americans knew by experience that a state with many different arenas in which power is generated is more powerful than one with a single centre.

Arendt contrasted this kind of articulated, federated people, generating power in their local assemblies, with 'the people' invoked by the French revolutionaries, which never got beyond being either a legal fiction (a mere substitute for the sovereign monarch) or else the starving mob in the streets. She also contrasted it, however, with modern mass electorates, including that in the USA, which had failed to live up to its revolutionary promise of political freedom enjoyed by active citizens. Although at the time of its founding the American Republic had been spared the stress of mass poverty, she believed that it was now under threat from a different kind of social problem, mass consumerism, the 'pursuit of happiness' in the sense of private affluence. Echoing many of her predecessors in the classical republican tradition, Arendt observed that 'freedom and luxury have always been thought to be incompatible.'[21] She added, linking the two kinds of 'social question': 'while it is true that freedom can come only to those whose needs have been fulfilled, it is equally true that it will escape those who are bent upon living for their desires.'[22] The public interest and the welfare of the republic may mean as little to those who are born to shop as to those who are born to starve.

The trouble with modern democracy, in her view, is 'the invasion of the public realm by society',[23] by which she means that instead of sharing concern for the public interest, people use politics as a collective device for serving private interests and concerns. The public arena is occupied by career politicians, while voters in general have become consumers. Neither is in a position to debate public affairs and form genuine opinions about them. Professional politicians, versed in the arts of selling consumer goods, try to get themselves elected by appealing more or less blatantly to the private interests of voters. Voters, meanwhile, make their choice not by considering any public interest (for which they have no responsibility) but simply by deciding which party has most to offer them as private individuals. The process of election seemed to Arendt a gigantic exercise in bribery. Experience earlier in the century of the many 'unpolitical' Germans who supported Hitler out of equally blinkered concern with their own private interests made her fear that this kind of relation to politics was not only corrupt, but dangerous.

It would be a mistake to suppose that she had no appreciation of modern liberal democracy. Although experience of the unstable and ideologically divided party systems of the Weimar Republic in Germany and the Third and Fourth Republics in France gave her a sceptical view of party politics, she was well aware of the value of political systems that protected civil liberties and were to some degree responsible to their subjects. In particular, the two-party system of government in Britain and the USA, in which opposition is both legitimate and responsible, seemed to her vastly superior to the centralizing and autocratic tendencies harboured (she believed) by most versions of representative government existing at the time.[24] She sometimes conceded, moreover, that the USA had not entirely succumbed to professional politics, but retained some features of the federated grassroots citizen power from which it had begun.[25]

What it had *not* done, however, was to institutionalize the 'public freedom' experienced during the Revolution. The Founding Fathers' federal structure had not made enough room for direct local participation in politics (for example through revitalized town meetings) in which subsequent generations would have been able to take the responsibility and experience the 'public happiness' of acting as citizens. Arendt maintained that Thomas Jefferson had (too late) seen 'the danger . . . that all power had been given to the people in their private capacity, and that there was no space established for them in their capacity of being citizens'.[26] In spite of being in many ways remarkably successful in making the transition from revolution to a lasting republic, the Founders had failed to preserve the revolutionary spirit.

The final chapter of *On Revolution* is concerned with this 'lost treasure' of revolution. Arendt's claim was that the experience of public freedom in action among citizens, though rediscovered over and over again in revolutionary situations, was effectively preserved neither in the institutions of the American Republic nor in the European revolutionary tradition, which was dominated by the memory of the failed French Revolution. In accordance with her view of the proper relationship between political thought and political action, Arendt's purpose was not so much to set out a programme for the reconstruction of democracy as to recover the memory of forgotten experiences.

> Experiences and even the stories which grow out of what men do and endure, of happenings and events, sink back into the futility inherent in the living word and the living deed unless they are talked about over and over again.[27]

The experiences she particularly wished to recover and preserve concerned what she often refers to as 'the council system'. This was an embryonic form of participatory republic based on a federation of face-to-face groupings that had, she believed, appeared again and again in the course of revolutions, only to be crushed in the interests of a centralized state. For example, grassroots activity during the French Revolution had taken the form not only of popular agitation over 'the social question' but also of the spontaneous formation of self-governing bodies. Some of these had federated themselves into the Paris Commune, and had (at least in part) been organs that enabled citizens to concern themselves with the public interest.[28] Though similar bodies quickly sprang up across the country, these 'first organs of a republic which never came into being'[29] were rapidly taken over and destroyed by the Jacobin party, a fate emblematic of that later encountered by the soviets during the Bolshevik Revolution.

What seems remarkable to Arendt is that despite the neglect of such popular organs of self-government within the revolutionary tradition, much the same thing, 'councils, *soviets* and *Räte*', appeared spontaneously and quite unexpectedly in revolution after revolution in the nineteenth and twentieth centuries – in the Paris Commune of 1871, in the Russian Revolutions of 1905 and 1917, in 1918–19 in Germany and in 1956 in Hungary. All of them were destroyed, often by parties which claimed to be revolutionary. In Arendt's view, it was the repeated invention or discovery of something so unexpected, 'the absence of continuity, tradition, and organized influence that makes the sameness of the phenomenon so very striking'.[30] It might be objected that recognition of such a phenomenon could be found in the writings of anarchists like Proudhon or Bakunin. Arendt stresses, however, that the councils in question were not anarchist, but aimed at the establishment of a new polity which would be federated from below, and a new form of government based on the direct participation of citizens. These were 'spaces of freedom',[31] and in their combination of grassroots participation with federation into a wider republic she believed she could see the possibility of a genuine alternative to the centralized representative democracies of today, one in which public freedom might be genuinely enjoyed.

This 'new form of government' had of course in each case failed to flourish, and was to that extent a lost cause. In an interview given in 1970, five years before her death, Arendt addressed the question of whether speculation along these lines was utopian. Discussing the problems of international relations in a nuclear age, she suggested that a new kind of state no longer built on the concept of sovereignty was needed, and that the only alternative (though one which had never so far got beyond the embryonic stage) was the kind of republic built up out of federated councils which had regularly been adumbrated in the course of revolutions. Her enthusiasm for this was evident.

> In this direction, I think, there must be something to be found, a completely different principle of organization, which begins from below, continues upward, and finally leads to a parliament.[32]

Nevertheless, she made it clear that what she was doing was commenting on events and possibilities (bearing in mind the openness of the future and the inventiveness of human beings) rather than presenting a model: 'Whether this system is a pure utopia – in any case it would be a people's utopia, not the utopia of theoreticians and ideologies – I cannot say.' And she added: 'if you ask me now what prospect it has of being realized, then I must say to you: very slight, if at all. And yet perhaps, after all – in the wake of the next revolution.'[33]

Participation and Elitism

Arendt's views on 'the council system' have attracted a great deal of criticism. The critics have focused not on her attempted recovery of these

revolutionary experiments in participation (or even on her speculations
about what future revolutions might bring) but on a few pages at the end
of *On Revolution*. There she considers some of the implications that such
a 'council system' would have if it ever came into being. Most of her
readers have been startled to find that the price of citizen participation
seems to be the loss of what most of us think of as democracy, resulting in
rule by a self-chosen elite. The context of this discussion is her observation,
a few pages earlier, that

> what we today call democracy is a form of government where the few rule,
> at least supposedly, in the interest of the many. This government is demo-
> cratic in that popular welfare and private happiness are its chief goals; but
> it can be called oligarchic in the sense that public happiness and public
> freedom have again become the privilege of the few.[34]

Under the 'council system', by contrast, public freedom – the opportunity
to take action – would be available not just to those few professional
politicians, but to citizens in general, provided that they were prepared to
take up the opportunity to participate.

Crucially, Arendt differs from most theorists of participatory democracy in accepting that most people will not want to involve themselves in
public affairs, and that, by implication, they will thereby exclude themselves from a share in power. Although all human beings are in principle
capable of taking the initiative, and therefore of engaging in the dynamic
interaction that she calls 'public freedom', she knows that most prefer
private life. Her discussion is unusually frank and unvarnished, and she is
not afraid to use the term 'elite' for those who choose to involve themselves
in public affairs, and even to refer to the resulting form of government as
'aristocratic'. Looking back at historical experience, she observes that
'freedom, wherever it existed as a tangible reality, has always been spatially
limited', a matter of 'islands in a sea' or 'oases in a desert'.[35] Those moved
by the 'political passions' of courage, ambition, public happiness and
public freedom have always been a minority. She speaks not only of 'the
responsibility that falls automatically upon those who care for the fate of
those who do not', but, less engagingly, of 'the bitter need of the few to
protect themselves against the many' in order to enjoy their island of
freedom.[36]

Like other forms of government, then, the 'council system' would mean
rule by an elite. The difference would be that instead of being an elite of
professional politicians answerable to the mass of voters, this would be an
elite of those who care about public affairs, and any citizen could in

principle be part of it. All who wished to do so could participate at the base level, and might also be among the deputies who would go to the next level in the federation, not as representatives of a party line but as individuals trusted by their peers. But those who did not make the effort to attend would simply have no influence on the discussions or the choices; the 'council system' 'would spell the end of general suffrage as we understand it today'. The joys and responsibilities of public life would belong to 'those few from all walks of life who have a taste for public freedom . . . Politically, they are the best, and it is the task of good government and the sign of a well-ordered republic to assure them of their rightful place in the public realm.'[37]

This forthright defence of a democratic version of 'aristocratic' politics is accompanied by an equally controversial attempt to distinguish politics from 'administration' and to keep 'social' matters out of politics. Arendt observes that when 'councils' emerged in the course of revolutions, they regularly made things difficult for themselves by failing to do this. 'The fatal mistake of the councils has always been that they themselves did not distinguish clearly between participation in public affairs and administration or management of things in the public interest.'[38] As a result workers' councils tried to run the factories, usually with disastrous results. This could not work, according to Arendt, because politics and management demand quite different qualities. It would not in her view be the task of the participating citizens of a federated republic to 'run the economy' – a way of thinking about politics which in any case merely illustrates what she saw as the displacement of politics by purely 'social' concerns.

Critical Assessment

Arendt's views on democracy have had a critical reception both from defenders and from opponents of Western liberal democracy, and have also created problems for her admirers. Defenders of the status quo have found it offensive that despite her experience of Nazism and her studies of totalitarianism, she gave so little recognition to the benefits of liberal representative systems. For (as George Kateb put it) without representative democracy 'there would be more of the things she dreads and fewer of the things she celebrates.'[39] In particular, the kind of spontaneous, informal, public-spirited politics that she did celebrate – movements for civil rights and against the Vietnam War, for instance – finds its most hospitable setting within the framework of those same liberal democracies that are disfigured by materialistic voters and sound-bite politics.

At the same time, those who have sympathized with Arendt's critique of liberal democracy have often been equally discontented with her views, particularly with her category of 'the social'. Many on the left have been used to thinking of revolution in terms of social forces and outcomes, and have been interested in radical democracy chiefly as a means to enable the poor to achieve social justice. To such readers, her claim that politics has been corrupted by the incursion of 'social' concerns has seemed incomprehensible.[40]

Nevertheless, there have always been some political theorists responsive to her reflections on political action at the grassroots, and these have often been people involved in, or responsive to, precisely the kind of spontaneous activity by citizens that she wrote about.[41] Events since her death have tended to confirm their sense that she understood and drew attention to creative aspects of politics that are quite fundamental to democracy, but that mainstream democratic theory had generally ignored. Consider some of the 'Arendtian' events of the past two decades. Dissidents in Eastern Europe, sacrificing private to public interest, spontaneously created spaces of freedom within which they rediscovered the exalted pleasures of action. Trade unionists in Poland literally displayed Solidarity, and demonstrated the power that could be generated by helpless individuals when they found the courage to act publicly in concert. Above all, the awakening of citizens' movements and the crumbling of governments in 1989 have provided vivid examples of 'Arendtian' (and completely un-Marxist) revolutions. In the light of this recent experience, many aspects of Arendt's approach to democracy look more plausible than before, although problems and dilemmas remain, particularly where 'the council system' is concerned.

Among the casualties of 1989 was not only official communism and academic Marxism, but left-wing ideological politics in a broader sense. A whole spectrum of assumptions, formerly made with confidence, no longer appear self-evident. It no longer seems obvious that society and the economy can and should be remade through the seizure of political power, or that the exploited and downtrodden must represent the forces of progress. After 200 years of radical faith in the Golden Age to come, it seems that the future is not mapped out for us after all. Arendt's insistence on the pluralism and uncertainty of politics, on the inability of actors to predict or control the effects of their actions, anticipates the emphasis being placed in these postmodern times on the inherent openness of democracy. In the past (sustained by their insight into the direction of progress) radical democrats could feel confident of the results that must follow genuine popular participation. But nowadays there is a wider audience for those theorists who point, as Arendt did, to the autonomy of politics, whose results theory cannot anticipate. As Benjamin Barber says, 'democratic politics begins where certainty ends.'[42]

To object to Arendt's views on participatory citizenship, then, on the grounds that she did not see it as a road to social justice, seems increasingly inappropriate. Furthermore, her disconcerting stress on the role in radical democratic activity of a self-chosen elite of public-spirited citizens itself looks rather different when seen in the light of recent events, particularly in Eastern Europe. For it is undeniable that although those who engaged in the 'anti-political politics' of the 'parallel polis' may have been careful not to exclude their fellow citizens, they were in fact a minority whose public concerns were not representative of the general population. As a result there is, as Jeffrey Isaac remarks, a genuine tension 'between mass behaviour and meaningful citizenship' which became painfully obvious after 1989.[43] 'The next revolution' to which Arendt had looked hopefully in 1970 did not in fact establish federated participatory republics, and some of those who had built and inhabited 'islands of freedom' under the communist regimes found themselves and their public concerns swamped by the mass democracy and populist politics that followed attempts to assimilate to the West.[44] Are we therefore faced with a choice? Is democracy *either* a heroic republican politics for the few, of the kind admired by Arendt and practised by the dissidents, *or else* the familiar model of liberal democracy, which may be good at protecting civil rights, but which provides materialistic party politics for the masses rather than public freedom?

Jeffrey Isaac has tried to resolve this dilemma by suggesting that the two kinds of democratic politics are in practice complementary rather than mutually exclusive, and, more controversially, that Arendt herself saw them as such.[45] At a practical level, he argues that if democracy is to flourish it needs both aspects: on the one hand the bread-and-butter politics of professional politicians, party competition and the representation of interests, and on the other the informal, Arendtian politics of public-spirited citizens. This is a persuasive point of view, not least because many Western liberal democracies already benefit from this duality, with the informal politics of public-spirited groups and movements acting as a collective conscience that saves the polity from complete corruption.

More controversially, Isaac claims that Arendt was herself thinking along the same lines when she talked about 'councils': that she did not really mean them to replace representative democracy, or really welcome the prospect that a self-chosen elite would rule the rest of the population. All she meant (on this interpretation) was that 'councils' would maintain their vital spaces of freedom alongside the ordinary representative politics that looks after the material interests of the population, just as voluntary organizations of public-spirited citizens do today.

Now, there is no doubt that this is something Arendt *could* coherently

have said. After all, she argued (in a way that may be seen as directly
analogous) that civil disobedience, though illegal by definition, is in a
sense part of the inherited constitutional structure of the American Republic because it represents the citizen's duty to take responsibility for the
body politic to which he or she consents.[46] Nevertheless, although this is
what she could have said, it is not what she did say. Over and over again
when referring to the council system she stresses that she is talking about
a new form of government.[47] It is precisely this that makes offensive her
apparent willingness to countenance the disappearance from politics of the
concerns not only of those who choose to take no interest in public affairs,
but also of those who are unable to do so because they are (for example)
too old, too ill, too inarticulate.

The reason why Arendt herself could find this arrangement plausible
seems to lie in her problematic distinction between 'the political' and 'the
social', especially her separation of politics from what she called 'administration'. She was able to deny that the economic concerns of the general
population were appropriate subjects for political debate, because she
believed that these were matters of 'administration' on which an objectively based consensus existed. This seems to have been a view formed in
the heyday of Keynesian interventionism, when it could be plausibly
argued that socialism and liberalism had converged towards a common
model of government planning of the economy.[48] Since then, of course, a
quite different hegemonic consensus in political economy has become
established, and if the free-marketeers of the new right had their way it
could even be argued that Arendt was right to believe that questions of
prosperity lie outside politics, since well-meaning efforts by governments
do more harm than good. But this paradigm shift from Keynesian to
Hayekian economic models is enough in itself to demonstrate that these
are highly contentious matters. There can be no doubt that at the present
time there is room for plenty of reasonable debate (between citizens as well
as between professional economists) about the precise balance to be struck
between global competitiveness and national or regional protectionism, or
between social rights for workers and reducing unemployment. To suggest
that democratic citizens should not concern themselves with such matters
is indefensible, as is the notion that the interests of those most at risk could
be safely left out of the debate.

Some aspects of Arendt's thinking about democracy therefore remain
deeply problematic. Nevertheless, democrats can learn a great deal from
what she had to say about the plural nature of politics and the unpredictable creativity of political action. Furthermore, in the chastened atmosphere of postmodern scepticism, we might be wise not to dismiss too easily
the tension she pointed to between participatory citizenship and mass

democracy. If progress and enlightenment cannot be counted on; if we have no grounds for believing that reason must triumph; if democracy is genuinely open and its outcomes genuinely unpredictable, then it may not be only 'new democracies' that find themselves faced with the problem of populism. Successful appeals to the voters at the grassroots may send shudders down the spines of those who value public freedom. The relations between populism and democracy are complex, and cannot be discussed here. But any evaluation of Arendt's thinking about democracy would do well to bear in mind not only her visions of public-spirited citizens, but also her reminders of the political implications of starving mobs, consumerist voters, and mass support for Hitler.

Notes

1 She has indeed been accused of failing to appreciate their advantages. See, for example, G. Kateb, *Hannah Arendt: Politics, Conscience, Evil* (Oxford, Martin Robertson, 1983), p. 115.

2 As Richard Bernstein points out, she was already thinking along these lines in the 1940s, in her interventions in Zionist controversies. R. Bernstein, *Hannah Arendt and the Jewish Question* (Cambridge, Polity, 1996), pp. 11–12, 117–18, 127–30.

3 According to Adam Michnik (speaking at a conference on Arendt in Rome in December 1995) he and others involved in the long struggle for democracy in Poland were directly sustained by Arendt's writings about political action. Michnik's own writings are markedly Arendtian in tone. See, for example, A. Michnik, *Letters from Prison and Other Essays* (Berkeley, CA, University of California Press, 1985).

4 See R. H. King, *Civil Rights and the Idea of Freedom* (Oxford, Oxford University Press, 1992).

5 Hannah Arendt, 'Hannah Arendt on Hannah Arendt', in M. A. Hill (ed.), *Hannah Arendt: The Recovery of the Public World* (New York, St Martin's Press, 1979), p. 336.

6 E. Young-Bruehl, *Hannah Arendt: For Love of the World* (New Haven, CT, Yale University Press, 1982), p. 109.

7 Hannah Arendt, *Rahel Varnhagen: The Life of a Jewish Woman*, tr. Richard and Clara Winston (New York, Harcourt Brace Jovanovich, 1974).

8 Hannah Arendt, *The Origins of Totalitarianism*, rev. edn (London, Allen and Unwin, 1967), p. 353.

9 Arendt, *Totalitarianism*, p. 458.

10 Arendt, *Totalitarianism*, p. 466.

11 On the complex relationship between her theory of totalitarianism and her more general political theory, see M. Canovan, *Hannah Arendt: A Reinter-*

pretation of her Political Thought (Cambridge, Cambridge University Press, 1992), esp. ch. 3.

12 Hannah Arendt, *The Human Condition* (Chicago, University of Chicago Press, 1958), p. 7.
13 Arendt, *Human Condition*, p. 246.
14 On the differences between Arendt's views and those of Rousseau and Habermas, see my articles, 'Arendt, Rousseau and human plurality in politics', *Journal of Politics*, 45:2 (1983), 286–302; 'A case of distorted communication: A note on Habermas and Arendt', *Political Theory*, 11:1 (1983), 105–16.
15 Arendt, *Human Condition*, p. 222.
16 Hannah Arendt, *On Violence* (London, Allen Lane, Penguin, 1970), p. 44.
17 'What is freedom?', in *Between Past and Future: Eight Exercises in Political Thought* (New York, Viking, 1968), p. 169.
18 Hannah Arendt, *On Revolution* (London, Faber and Faber, 1963), pp. 53–110.
19 Arendt, *On Revolution*, p. 28.
20 Arendt, *On Revolution*, p. 173.
21 Arendt, *On Revolution*, p. 135.
22 Arendt, *On Revolution*, p. 136.
23 Arendt, *On Revolution*, p. 223.
24 Arendt, *On Revolution*, pp. 271–2.
25 Arendt, *On Revolution*, p. 134.
26 Arendt, *On Revolution*, p. 256.
27 Arendt, *On Revolution*, p. 222.
28 Arendt, *On Revolution*, p. 247.
29 Arendt, *On Revolution*, p. 249.
30 Arendt, *On Revolution*, p. 266.
31 Arendt, *On Revolution*, p. 258.
32 Hannah Arendt, 'Thoughts on politics and revolution', in her *Crises of the Republic* (New York, Harcourt Brace Jovanovich, 1972), p. 232.
33 Arendt, *Crises of the Republic*, pp. 231, 233.
34 Arendt, *On Revolution*, p. 273.
35 Arendt, *On Revolution*, p. 279.
36 Arendt, *On Revolution*, p. 280.
37 Arendt, *On Revolution*, pp. 283–4.
38 Arendt, *On Revolution*, pp. 277–8.
39 Kateb, *Hannah Arendt*, p. 115.
40 See, for example, H. F. Pitkin, 'Justice: On relating private and public', pp. 261–88, and J. F. Sitton, 'Hannah Arendt's argument for council democracy', pp. 307–29, both in L. P. Hinchman and S. K. Hinchman (eds), *Hannah Arendt: Critical Essays* (Albany, NY, State University of New York Press, 1994).
41 See, for example, King, *Civil Rights*, pp. xiii, 219 n. 24.
42 B. Barber, 'Foundationalism and democracy', in V. Gerhardt, H. Ottmann

and M. P. Thompson (eds), *Politisches Denken Jahrbuch* (Stuttgart, Metzler, 1993), p. 29; J. Keane, 'Democracy and the media – without foundations', in D. Held (ed.), *Prospects for Democracy, Political Studies*, XL (1992), pp. 116–29, esp. pp. 124–7; C. Lefort, 'The question of democracy', in *Democracy and Political Theory* (Cambridge, Polity, 1988), pp. 9–20.

43   J. C. Isaac, 'Oases in the desert: Hannah Arendt on democratic politics', *American Political Science Review*, 88:1 (March 1994), 156–68, esp. 156–8.

44   A. Bozoki and M. Sukosd, 'Civil society and populism in the Eastern European democratic transitions', *Praxis International*, 13:3 (October 1993), 224–41.

45   Isaac, 'Oases in the desert', p. 165.

46   Hannah Arendt, 'Civil disobedience', in her *Crises of the Republic*, pp. 82–102.

47   Arendt, *On Revolution*, pp. 253, 259, 262, 265, 268, 271, 282, 284; 'Thoughts on politics and revolution', pp. 230–3.

48   Canovan, *Hannah Arendt*, p. 121.

3

Václav Havel: Civil Society, Citizenship and Democracy

April Carter

Václav Havel is best known as a dramatist, as a prominent opponent of the Communist Party regime in Czechoslovakia after the Soviet Union had crushed the Prague Spring of 1968, and since 1990 as the President of his country.[1] But he is also recognized as an original and significant social thinker and much of his work has been translated into English. His plays are an important source for his political views, but since the 1970s he has formulated his philosophical and social ideas primarily in essays, letters and speeches reflecting the different stages of his life. Central themes in his thought are the need for individual moral and political responsibility, the value of autonomous civil society and the necessary linkage between culture and politics. His understanding of a good society is defined partly in response to two negative models. One model, elaborated in his best known essay 'The power of the powerless', is the pervasive system of ideological and political control exercised by the 'post-totalitarian' communist regimes of the 1970s. The second negative model – influenced by Heidegger – is the spiritual and social alienation of contemporary technological mass society, in the West as well as in Eastern Europe.

Havel is primarily a social critic rather than a political theorist, but his continuing stress on both responsible citizenship and a pluralist civil society can be seen as central to a commitment to democracy embedded in his thought. His specific interpretation of democracy, however, varies in three different stages of his life. He developed his initial concept at the time of the Prague Spring, when in the context of a cultural and moral critique of reform communism he stressed the need for an opposition party. The second theory of democracy as 'anti-political politics' (expressing distrust of party politics) developed during the long years in opposition. The partial revision of this 'anti-political' stance after 1990 in the context of the practical tasks of creating liberal democratic institutions and exercising power has resulted in a third version of democracy. His second theory, which he developed in association with other East European intellectuals in opposition in the 1980s, and which seeks an alternative to the practice of Western liberal democracy, is the most original. It is arguable, however, that its impracticality is demonstrated by Havel's own later modification of it. Havel's third theory does not altogether abandon the hope of improving on the practice of liberal democracy in the West. In examining how Havel's present views on democracy relate to liberal democratic theory I suggest that there are interesting parallels with de Tocqueville.

Havel's understanding of politics therefore has evolved from a politics of resistance to concern with the problems of transforming a society corrupted by the experience of communism into a democracy that is not corrupted in turn by the negative social effects of capitalism and consumerism. This chapter argues that Havel's most important contribution to democratic theory is his focus on the cultural and social context of politics, and in particular his willingness to assert the importance of ethical values.

Background: Life in Political and Intellectual Context

Havel's thought has been crucially shaped by the political inheritance of the interwar Czechoslovak First Republic and by his experiences under the post-1948 communist regime. His political views have reflected the influence of the democratic and non-violent commitments of Thomas Masaryk, the President of newly independent Czechoslovakia.[2] 'I grew up in the spirit of Masarykian humanism,' Havel has commented. 'The first books I found in our library at home and read were books from that tradition.'[3] He was born in 1936 into an affluent and well-connected family, and his 'bourgeois origins' were a barrier to his gaining a proper university education in the Stalinist regime of the 1950s. But he has noted that this disadvantage was a benefit to him as a writer: 'I had the opportunity, right from the start, of seeing the world "from below", that is, as it really is.'[4] This perspective helped him to see through and avoid ideological illusions and alerted him to 'the absurd and comic dimensions of the world'. His early plays written for the avant-garde Theatre of the Balustrade in Prague, *The Garden Party* (1963) and *The Memorandum* (1965), do indeed expose the absurd elements in the Communist Party regime. *The Memorandum*, for example, centres on the introduction of an invented bureaucratic language and comments on the nature of authentic language as opposed to dehumanized jargon. Havel participated as a writer in the debates of the later 1960s which led up to the Prague Spring of 1968. He criticized misuse of words and 'pseudo-ideological thinking' in a 1965 speech to the Writers' Union and demanded greater internal democracy within the Union at its June 1967 meeting.[5] In 1968 he also became an editor of the revived magazine *Tvar*, an independently minded young writers' journal banned in 1966, and also helped to establish the Circle of Independent Writers.

After the Soviet invasion in August 1968 Havel struggled to maintain the Circle and to keep *Tvar* alive, until Dubček, who had presided over the Prague Spring, was replaced by Husák in 1969 and the new regime cracked down on all open non-Party activity.[6] Havel was charged with 'subversion' in 1969 for signing a petition protesting against the suppression of freedom, and although the case was dropped his plays were then banned in Czechoslovakia. He went to live in the countryside, and when money was short he worked in a local brewery. He used this experience as the basis for a one-act play, *Audience*, one of three brief plays centred on the experience of an intellectual dissident.

Havel was prompted into renewed public political activity in the mid 1970s. He wrote an open letter to Husák in April 1975 commenting on the effects of 'stabilization', which had resulted in increasing corruption at the top, and widespread public apathy based on despair and growing materialism, and 'hypocrisy as the main form of communication'.[7] In September 1976 he attended the trial of a young rock band, The Plastic People of the Universe, and was moved by the extraordinary sense of community and mutual trust that grew up among the diverse people in the courtroom. He felt challenged to take his own stand: 'Suddenly, I felt disgusted with a whole world, in which – as I realized then – I still have one foot: the world of emergency exits.'[8] He became one of the leading representatives of Charter 77, when it published its initial manifesto calling on the government to uphold the human rights commitments it had endorsed at Helsinki. During 1977 and 1978 Havel was arrested several times and seriously harassed by the police, who were trying to force him to emigrate.

The 1970s were, however, a period of fruitful speculation for Havel. Intellectuals from the Central European countries of Czechoslovakia, Poland and Hungary thought deeply about the nature of politics and morality and exchanged ideas through *samizdat* (letters and essays circulated underground). Their ideas had an originality and idealism that sprang from shared commitments and from their perspective as 'dissidents' or outsiders. Havel's essay 'The power of the powerless' was an influential contribution to this dialogue, and Polish Solidarity activist Zbigniew Bujak has commented that, when he and his fellow activists in the factories had begun to despair, this essay gave them a theoretical justification for their activity and 'maintained our spirits'.[9]

Havel was sentenced in 1979 to four and a half years in prison for his human rights stand, but was released early because of severe illness. He then began to comment more explicitly on problems facing the West as well as Eastern Europe. When given an honorary doctorate by the University of Toulouse, he wrote a speech (later published as 'Politics and conscience') which is a critique of scientific hubris and its impact on both the natural and the social world. He also became an increasingly important figure inside Czechoslovakia in the late 1980s and in November 1989 was central in setting up Civic Forum. When the Communist Party regime fell in December in the face of mass demonstrations, the Forum became the basis for the new government. Timothy Garton Ash, who was an eyewitness to the developing revolution in Prague, comments on Havel's role: 'It was extraordinary the degree to which everything ultimately revolved around this one man.'[10]

Havel has since the 1970s resolutely refused to place himself on either the left or the right of politics. He was prepared in the 1960s to endorse the goal of democratic socialism and he labelled himself a socialist in his 1975 interview with Jiří Lederer.[11] But by 1984 he was commenting sardonically on the questions put to him by Western visitors who wanted to know if he supported socialism or the reintroduction of capitalism: 'these thoroughly ideological and often semantically confused categories have long since been beside the point.'[12] As he explained in 1986, his commitment to socialism was 'more a human, a moral, an emotional category' than a specific ideological stance (a position reminiscent of Masaryk's moral socialism which rejected Marxism) and he had ceased to use the term because it had become meaningless.[13] Havel had since the 1960s been deeply critical not only of Stalinist forms of communism but of all versions of reform communism, thus standing outside the major debates within the Eastern bloc. But at the same time he rejected the extreme ideological anti-communism of the Western right and many East European émigrés.[14] His reluctance to accept ideological labels is an intrinsic element in his own conception of a politics based on personal responsibility, careful judgement and individual conscience. This also made him critical of the practices of normal politics in the West, where parties exercise a technology of power in competing for votes.

Philosophy and Social Thought

Havel learned philosophy by reading and later listening to Jan Patočka, who had studied under Husserl and Heidegger, and was to become a colleague in Charter 77.[15] The attraction to Heidegger is in some ways puzzling, especially as Havel's sense of the importance of individual moral choice and political responsibility is in striking contrast to Heidegger's much debated accommodation with Nazism. Unlike Arendt or Habermas, Havel does not appear troubled by this question.[16] Patočka's own moral and political integrity may have been one reason why Heidegger's politics may have seemed unimportant to Havel, and he continued to draw on Heidegger in his speeches as President.[17] Heidegger's influence is, however, especially evident in the letters to Olga from prison, in which he muses on philosophical issues and books he has read and uses Heideggerian terms like the 'Voice of Being' that is 'the unuttered in the language of the world'.[18] Since Havel is not explicitly religious and does not believe in a personal God,[19] Heidegger appears to give him a vocabulary in which to express his conviction that humanity needs a sense of transcendence to create a balanced and meaningful social life. Havel's desire for a more specific moral commitment than can be found in Heidegger is, however, suggested by his enthusiastic response to the essay 'Sans identité' by Levinas, the Jewish Lithuanian philosopher who was a key interpreter of Heidegger, but developed an alternative moral philosophy rooted in individual responsibility and an inescapable ethical obligation. Havel senses that Levinas offers 'a storehouse not only of the spiritual traditions and millennial experiences of the Jewish people, but also the experience of a man who has been in prison'.[20]

Heidegger's influence can be clearly seen in Havel's political writings, such as 'The power of the powerless' and 'Politics and conscience', which attack the dangers and aridity of the modern world dominated by science and technology.[21] Havel also appears to accept that both the Soviet and American systems reflected the dominance of 'planetary technology' and so share significant characteristics.[22] Havel sees a global tendency towards a technologically controlled industrial-consumer society, and refers to Heidegger's comments on the 'crisis of democracy' in the context of what Havel calls 'This planetary challenge to the position of human beings in the world'.[23] Havel's distrust of scientific exploitation of nature, and his emphasis on reasserting human control, arise directly out of his horror at the industrial contamination of Czechoslovakia and the depredations of collectivization compared with the husbanding of nature by the small family farms before 1948.[24] Similarly his commitment to individual responsibility springs from his moral rejection of communist society. But Jean Bethke Elshtain is correct when she comments that, although a casual reader may be tempted to dismiss Havel's philosophical framework 'as unnecessarily cumbersome', this would be a mistake, because Havel wishes to emphasize the spiritual crisis of humanity.[25]

Havel is most impressive when engaging in precise analysis and using specific examples to illuminate his original view of the world, as in his depiction of 'post-totalitarianism' in Eastern Europe in 'The power of the powerless'. Post-totalitarian society was maintained by an omnipresent, though by then almost meaningless ideology, fear of punishment for non-conformity, widespread apathy and cynicism and material incentives for conformist behaviour. Havel starts his essay with the example of the greengrocer who supports the ruling ideology by unreflectingly putting among the vegetables in his window the slogan 'Workers of the World Unite'. He next shows how in a regime built on lies and conformity the individual can exercise power by refusing to conform and by 'living in truth', whether by refusing to display a slogan, or requiring standards of quality in the workplace, or acting independently as an artist, or openly resisting injustice.

Dissidents engaging in apparently hopeless protests can appear to be unrealistic. They are necessarily in some sense 'heroic dreamers' engaging in the folly of tilting at windmills. Havel carefully distinguishes, however, between upholding basic principles and prescribing elaborate plans which seem unattainable.[26] He is also acutely aware of the political dangers of utopian thinking, especially when applied dogmatically and arrogantly with the intention of refashioning society as a whole. But he is now concerned that disillusion with grand visions after the fall of communism should not result in people abandoning hope for a better society, or attempting to achieve it, provided they do so step by step. He endorses Karl Popper's distinction between holistic and piecemeal social engineering.[27]

Havel adheres to the view that means and ends are related. Utopianism is particularly dangerous if it justifies ruthless means. He claims in 'Politics, morality and civility' that 'violence, as we know, breeds more violence.'[28] He also rejects calls that he, as President, should be tougher in promoting a good cause, because it is impossible to create 'truth through lies, or the democratic spirit through authoritarian directives'.[29] He also sees the development of a good society (rejecting the selfish and corrupt tendencies fostered by post-totalitarianism) as a prerequisite for genuine democracy. It is to his changing interpretations of democracy that we now turn.

Havel's Initial View of Democracy

Havel's first concept of democracy is based on a rejection of the language and ideas of reform communism, which avoided coming to grips with real issues. The communists seeking to reject Stalinism and create 'socialism with a human face' had not abandoned the ideological mode of thinking and speaking, which Havel had caricatured in his plays and attacked in his 1965 speech to the Writers' Union. In this speech he castigated 'the ritualization of language' to obscure reality, so that personal guilt is hidden behind the 'the abstract category called "the atmosphere of the cult of personality"'.[30] He also noted the difficulty writers had experienced in Czechoslovakia in speaking plainly and in disentangling their literature from ideological formulas. Havel argues that the failure to speak concretely means that people lose touch with reality, and so lose the ability to influence reality.

Havel's most direct contribution to the debate about democratic reform during the Prague Spring was his April 1968 essay 'On the theme of an opposition', in which he criticized the inability of the reform communists to deal properly with the idea of an opposition. He began by dismissing the various ideas which had been put forward to promote restraints on power within a one-party context: freedom of public debate, internal party democracy, coalitions of independent individuals in parliament and other political bodies, and the autonomy of interest groups such as trade unions or student unions. He argued that whilst free speech is a prerequisite of democracy, it is not a substitute for organized opposition, because 'power only really listens to power.'[31] Internal party democracy will wither unless bolstered by democracy in the wider society. Individuals forming *ad hoc* coalitions will lack effective resources compared with the Party organization. Interest groups also cannot be genuinely independent since many Party members belong to them, and in any case they are based on common interests not common policies, and are not suited to sharing power. Therefore, what is needed is an effective opposition party with its own programme which offers a genuine choice and can replace the ruling party in an election. He conceded that an opposition should operate within the framework of a national programme agreed with the Communists, formulating key principles of foreign policy as well as requirements of social justice and democratic socialism. He did, however, also emphasize that for such an opposition to work, the Communist Party must accept the validity of non-communist views, and redress the wrongs that people have suffered in the past for opposing the Party.

The essay is an incisive (if slightly oversimplified) critique of reform proposals and was considered important within Czechoslovakia at the time. What is particularly interesting, in the light of his later views, is the hard headed emphasis on the need to oppose power with power, his sense of the importance of appropriate institutions and the concessions to political realism. Havel did in fact partially repudiate the views in this

1968 essay when he was interviewed by John Keane in 1987: 'I've come to be rather sceptical about the very principle of mass political parties. I suspect that involvement in government inevitably leads to parties' bureaucratization, corruption, and loss of democracy.'[32] It is not cooperation between those with similar views that troubles him, but the rewards of power which go to those who serve parties.

Given the purist and uncompromising attitude to politics which Havel held after 1968, when he was being persecuted by those in power for witnessing to the truth, did he have a coherent theory of democracy in this period? The answer is 'yes', for he sees the experience of opposition as a basis for an ideal of 'post-democracy' that challenges the conventional assumptions underlying the practice of liberal democracy in the West.

Democracy as 'Anti-Political Politics'

The basis of Havel's thinking about democracy in the 1970s and 1980s is his critique of post-totalitarianism and his experience as a 'dissident'.[33] The key concept relevant to his aspiration to a new form of democracy is 'anti-political politics', which is contrasted with Western parliamentary democracy. His view on democracy also draws on the attitudes and practices embedded in Charter 77.

The concept of the 'anti-polis' is not unique to Havel; the Hungarian opposition intellectual Gyorgy Konrad developed the idea.[34] In Czechoslavakia Václav Benda, a mathematician and Catholic thinker, imprisoned with Havel for his human rights activities, elaborated the idea of the 'parallel polis'. In 'Politics and conscience' Havel designates 'anti-political politics' as politics from below: 'Politics of man, not of the apparatus. Politics growing from the heart, not from a thesis.' He also suggests that this concept, born out of opposition within the Soviet bloc, has relevance too for the West.[35] Anti-political politics has a bearing on democracy for several reasons. Firstly, it is practised primarily by people who are not professional politicians. Havel noted that great political changes in Soviet bloc countries were usually initiated not by politicians but by 'mathematicians, philosophers, physicians, writers, historians, ordinary workers', precisely because they were not bound by orthodox modes of political thinking and political habits.[36] Anti-political politics therefore claims that those who are not experts in politics have an invaluable role to play in public life.

Secondly, anti-political politics embodies a concept of responsible and courageous citizenship. During the Velvet Revolution of 1989 Havel was

asked at a press conference about the lessons of Charter 77. He replied:
'When a person tries to act in accordance with his conscience, when he
tries to speak the truth, when he tries to behave like a citizen, even in
conditions where citizenship is degraded, it won't necessarily lead any-
where, but it might.'[37] When addressing the criticism by novelist Milan
Kundera that intellectuals signing public petitions were exhibitionists
seeking to persuade themselves that they could influence history, Havel
commented that such petitions could not only be a significant expression
of solidarity for those in prison, but also have inherent importance as part
of a process in which 'people's civic backbones' begin 'to straighten
again'.[38] His response to the student demonstrations which began the
Velvet Revolution is to marvel where they learned their commitment to
freedom, 'their civic courage and civic prudence'.[39] This emphasis on
citizenship rejects apathy and despair and asserts that responsible individual action is the basis for creating a living democracy.

Thirdly, anti-political politics promotes a sense of community
with like-minded people, which fosters political activity. Havel notes in
'The power of the powerless' how citizens' initiatives such as Charter 77
promote a 'living sense of solidarity and fraternity' and of personal
trust, and 'renew the feeling of higher responsibility in an apathetic
society'.[40] In 'Politics and conscience' he quotes Patočka on the Charter,
where Patočka coined the phrase 'the solidarity of the shaken', of
those who resisted impersonal power with their own humanity and conscience.[41] This community need not be limited to one country or to those
from similar regimes. Havel looked to an international solidarity which
ignores official boundaries or power blocs and exists outside orthodox
politics.

Fourthly, anti-political politics illustrates how organizations may arise
which avoid becoming alien and bureaucratic, but do constitute a network
of effective institutions. Havel noted that 'a certain amount of organization and institutionalization' is 'a natural development'.[42] He cites Benda
on the evolution within East European societies in the 1980s of a parallel
polis which, in addition to protest groups, comprised alternatives to the
official communications system, parallel trade unions, parallel forms of
education and culture, and even parallel foreign relations.

Finally, anti-political politics provides a glimpse of what a future democratic society might look like. Havel coined the term 'post-democracy'
for his ideal, but refused to attempt a blueprint, because such a democracy could only come into being out of specific experience. But he did
think that the informal communal groups springing up to oppose post-
totalitarianism, which were the antithesis of bureaucratic hollow
institutions, could prefigure the spirit and organizational forms of 'post-

democracy'.[43] Although he was aware that the spirit of the Charter might not survive the ending of a shared threat, this did not alter the validity of the model for a better society.

Havel gave a number of reasons why parliamentary democracy based on competition between several parties is not the true opposite of post-totalitarianism. Parliamentarianism fails to confront the supremacy of technology over human needs and the corrupting effects of consumer society. Indeed, the appearance of democratic forms may help to mask the subtle totalitarianism of technological civilization.[44] He also made more specific criticisms of the Western model. Mass parties are run by professional politicians and encourage the electors to abandon their sense of political responsibility. Political parties also encourage selfish competition for power and the promotion of sectional interests over the public interest, resulting in a corruption and trivialization of politics. He has referred to the 'stifling party squabbles in the First Republic' in Czechoslovakia.[45]

Rejection of a party system was encouraged by the experience of Charter 77 and the heady days of Civic Forum. The Charter stood outside left–right labels and was open to all who agreed with the basic demand that human rights should be respected. This principle of non-exclusivity was a rejection of the Communist Party's narrow exclusiveness.[46] It was also an intrinsic aspect of the feeling of solidarity created by the Charter, and was possible because there was no desire to formulate political pro-grammes or to achieve political power.[47] Civic Forum, influenced by members of the Charter, was also a broad coalition of those opposed to the communist regime and committed to non-violent non-partisan action. The Forum remained in existence after the revolution to contest the first elections and to guide the country towards a new political system.[48]

Both the Charter, and the Forum in its early days, operated in a non-hierarchical and participatory fashion. Members of Charter 77 agreed on public statements through a process of negotiations. The Forum initially made decisions after extended public debates, and the plenary meetings selected smaller commissions to discuss strategy and elected individual spokespeople. Ash commented: 'the meetings of the plenum were almost absurdly democratic . . . At one point an assembly of perhaps 200 people was editing the latest Forum communiqué, line by line.'[49] It is unsurprising that this radical democracy was abandoned. But Havel has presided over the defeat of most of the Forum ideals, and the creation of a parliamentary system with multiple competing parties. So it is important to know how far his own views have changed. I will suggest that there is a shift in emphasis, rather greater than he acknowledges, but that there are nevertheless important continuities in his theory of democracy.

Havel's Current Thinking on Democracy

When confronting the problems arising after Civic Forum had come to power, Havel had to pay more precise attention to institutional questions. For example, in his 1991 essay 'A time of transition' he notes that, whereas it is understandable for a people accustomed to the meaninglessness of communist constitutions to think that any constitution is unimportant, they should now realize that a constitution divides and allocates powers which vitally affect their daily lives.[50] Later in the same essay he discusses in some detail the advantages of moving away from the 1990 electoral law, which created a form of proportional representation in which some electoral districts had over thirty members of parliament, towards much smaller constituencies and an electoral system closer to that of West Germany (a mix of the majority system and proportional representation). As early as September 1990 *La Repubblica* reported that Havel favoured a maximum of five parties.[51]

Havel was challenged to clarify his views on political parties, since some of his comments had suggested great scepticism about a party system. He addressed this issue in 'A time of transition', where he claimed that to be against parties would be to oppose democracy, since citizens must be able to join a wide variety of associations including parties, which are 'integral' to contemporary parliamentary democracy.[52] What he is against is excessive partisanship and the 'dictatorship of parties' which occurred in the First Republic in Czechoslovakia. Havel hopes these expressions of partisanship might be curbed by suitable electoral laws and (it is implied) by a mature electorate. Nonetheless, 'partisanship' is so closely linked to the operations of a party system that it might be argued that Havel remains sceptical about party politics, but is resigned to trying to minimize the harm it causes, for example where electoral considerations distort political decision-making.

Havel's wider vision of a good democracy is set out in 'Beyond the shock of freedom', where he dreams of a Czechoslovakia in which political power is highly decentralized, local elections are more gripping than national ones, and there is scope for variety and experiment to create towns and a countryside which meet human needs. Towns should be able to develop distinctive neighbourhoods, and historic centres should be brought back to life. He advocated the demolition of giant housing estates (a symbol of dehumanization for Havel) and their replacement with houses and low rise flats. Small shops and pubs ought also to be encouraged. Agriculture should be in the hands of family farms or small cooperatives, able to join in processing and marketing networks. Ecological pollution would be tackled by planting trees, reducing industrial emissions, cleaning up the rivers. Havel stresses the value of voluntary associations: 'The whole country will be crisscrossed by a network of local, regional, state-wide clubs, organizations and associations with a wide variety of aims.'[53]

Havel reiterated his belief in the importance of pluralism and local initiative in a 1995 debate with Prime Minister Václav Klaus. Collective action promotes 'citizen pride' and 'such positive traits as "love thy neighbour"'.[54] Havel also regrets that 'instead of learning from the West about civic and political culture, we have been quick to acquaint ourselves with the empty world of inane commercials and even more inane television series, allowing them to plunder . . . our lives and souls.'[55]

For the economy Havel urges that state ownership should be retained for appropriate services, such as transport and communications, and he sees a role for planning – especially in the transition to a market economy.[56] He also believes that the state should guarantee social welfare and promote social justice. But he takes for granted the necessity of the market, because he sees it as the opposite of state control, promoting individual responsibility for economic actions and allowing expression of individual initiative. There is room for both private enterprise and co-operatives, but his earlier belief in workers' self-management seems to have disappeared.

Continuities and Conflicts in Havel's Democratic Thought

There are clear continuities in Havel's democratic thought. He stresses in all his writings the need for a politics imbued with morality, and for individuals to have a commitment to the public good. He has a concept of citizenship as responsibility to think and act so as to promote that good and he condemns apathy. This citizenship may be demonstrated by protest or by active participation in a democratic context, but either way it requires commitment. His belief in the need for plain language in order to confront things as they really are, and to avoid the pitfalls of ideology and propaganda, is reminiscent of another satirist of totalitarianism, George Orwell. In addition, Havel as a playwright, as well as a political theorist and political actor, is intensely aware that politics cannot be divorced from other aspects of society, in particular cultural and spiritual life.

One connecting theme between Havel's writings in the 1970s and the 1990s can be summed up in the phrase 'civil society'. This is not a term Havel himself usually used in his opposition period – his preferred concept then was anti-political politics – but it was widely used by East European

intellectuals in the 1980s and taken up in the West to denote a distinction
between state power and the creative possibilities inherent in a plurality of
groups and organizations developing autonomously from below. In liberal
democracies civil society is envisaged as a network of associations creating
social ties between individuals and fostering organizational and political
skills. It is therefore both a source for political initiatives and a check on
state oppression.[57] In the context of post-totalitarianism, where all social,
intellectual and cultural life tended to be politically controlled, 'civil
society' inevitably tended to be defined as political opposition.[58] But in a
parliamentary system civil society can develop and remain generally non-
political (though its existence has implications for the health of democracy). In his 1995 debate with Klaus, Havel defended civil society as 'a
society with a large measure of self-government . . . a social space that
fosters the feeling of solidarity between people'.[59]

Despite these continuities, and Havel's tendency to deny any major
shift in his views, there is a significant change in tone and emphasis after
1990. Apart from a greater stress on formal institutions and acceptance of
the inevitability of a party system, the latest writings lack the radicalism
expressed during the opposition years. In particular, he has shifted from
proposing an alternative to Western liberal parliamentarianism to urging
a version of liberal democracy.

There is also a significant shift in his view of the economy from 'self-
management' by workers in a socialist economy (in 'The power of the
powerless') to acceptance of a private enterprise economy with large elements of foreign investment, although modified by some degree of state
control. The move here is from a form of humanist socialism to social
liberalism. His critiques of extreme commitment to the free market and
privatization as ideological fanaticism,[60] and political disputes with the
Prime Minister, Václav Klaus, identified with Friedmanite economics, are
quite compatible with espousing social liberalism.

Havel's Relationship to Liberal Democracy

Havel's oppositional concept of democracy, based on a heroic version of
citizenship as resistance, awareness of the importance of the public realm,
distrust of mass political parties and aspirations to 'post-democracy', suggests comparisons with Hannah Arendt's belief in participatory democracy, which is also the direct antithesis of totalitarianism. They also share,
as Elshtain has noted, a reluctance to accept left or right labels.[61] But
Havel's concept of civil society suggests the value of plural spheres as
opposed to an overriding commitment to the public sphere of politics. His

later acceptance of parliamentary procedures and a role for parties led by professional politicians further distances him from Arendt. He is not an unqualified participatory democrat, though he certainly rejects elitist versions of liberal democracy of the sort recommended by Schumpeter, which seek to minimize political activity by ordinary people.[62] Havel strongly favours a degree of responsible citizen participation.

The comparison that springs to mind is with de Tocqueville, who also celebrated decentralization of power to local government, valued a network of voluntary associations fostering variety and initiative, and had a view of responsible citizenship which required a degree of participation. They also share a sense of the interrelations between the character of a society and its culture and the character of its politics. Finally, there are parallels with de Tocqueville in Havel's criticism of mass society.[63] (This comparison does not extend to the economic views of de Tocqueville, who was a much more unqualified market liberal than Havel.) It is interesting to observe Havel reaching these conclusions independently in such a different political and social context, although the experience of Soviet-style communism may make social thinkers receptive to Tocquevillean ideas.[64] Although the comparison throws doubt on the distinctiveness of Havel's contribution to democratic theory in his latest writings, it is also arguable that key political insights have to be reformulated and applied in contemporary settings.

One obvious criticism of Havel's democratic thought (except in his 1968 writings) is that he has been reluctant to address institutional questions and organizational power. This was especially obvious in his celebration of anti-political politics, which failed to define alternatives to a parliamentary and party system. But it is not at all clear how he hopes now to avoid the worst effects of partisanship in a multi-party system. Havel still tends to be somewhat imprecise about institutions, despite some specific proposals he has made as President, and to fall back on moral exhortation. His views on the economy (where he recognizes he lacks expertise) were ill-defined in his socialist self-management phase, and he does not explore how he expects to maintain a decentralized economy in a Czech Republic integrated into Western capitalism.

It is pertinent that Petr Pithart, former opposition intellectual and Prime Minister between 1990 and 1992, who is sympathetic to Havel's views, thinks that Havel moralizes too much and should focus more on institutional issues.[65] His criticism chimes with a critical review of *Summer Meditations* by Steven Lukes, who suggests that in these essays Havel resorts to 'high minded moralism' rather than looking squarely at reality. Lukes queries the possibility of adhering to a pure morality when holding a position of political power. Lukes also notes that President Havel uses words to promote 'uplift and exhortation' rather than to 'illuminate' or 'pierce' as he had advocated earlier in opposition.[66]

Nevertheless, although the essays in *Summer Meditations* are less rich and illuminating than Havel's earlier writings as a critical observer, it is easy (as Havel himself is aware) to be cynical about apparently naive views on morality and politics expressed by someone in power. Havel's 'naiveté' can be seen as a reminder of important truths which sophisticated commentators on politics learn to overlook. George Kennan, reviewing *Summer Meditations*, comments that Havel is right to question whether the dominance of party machines and a trivializing electoral politics is an inevitable component of a free political system. He asks whether, at the turn of the century, we can still afford to leave 'the great affairs of state so extensively dependent upon the outcomes of struggles among political factions more immediately concerned with their own competitive fortunes than with the major problems of national interest'.[67]

Conclusion

Havel poses important moral questions for the long-established liberal democracies, in which people are demonstrably losing confidence in the integrity and public spirit of politicians, and in which many voters seem to act as privatized consumers rather than as concerned citizens. He calls on both those in power and ordinary individuals to accept an inescapable moral responsibility for their role in shaping the nature of their own society.

Havel is one of the most distinctive voices among those theorists who have revived concern about the social and cultural context in which liberal democratic institutions operate, a concern crystallized round the concept of 'civil society'. American theorists who have resuscitated Tocquevillean prescriptions include Elshtain and Robert Putnam. Elshtain in *Democracy in Crisis* laments the loss of civil society, and later cites Havel's moral stance as a source of democratic hope.[68] Putnam is best known for his 1993 study of the long-term positive effects of civic traditions in northern Italy, *Making Democracy Work*.[69] In a 1995 article 'Bowling alone: America's declining social capital', he uses a survey indicating that more Americans go bowling than vote in elections, and that most of them go alone, as an image of the privatized nature of contemporary American society.[70] Michael Walzer has given qualified support to the argument for civil society, as a 'necessary achievement' in the context of 'violence, homelessness, divorce, abandonment, alienation and addiction', noting that forms of local association and action 'imply an understanding of civility'.[71] Havel's insistence on the importance of culture in the widest sense and the quality of relationships between people therefore has relevance not only for the fractured society of his homeland but for modern societies in general.

Notes

1   I am grateful to participants in the seminar of the Centre for Democracy at the University of Westminster for helpful comments on an earlier version of this chapter, and in particular to John Keane for sharing with me his detailed knowledge of Havel. In this chapter I have relied on the English translations of Havel's writings, which have been quite extensively translated and published in the West.

2   See A. van den Beld, *Humanity: The Political and Social Philosophy of Thomas G. Masaryk* (The Hague, Mouton, 1975). Masaryk's belief in social justice, parliamentary democracy, non-violence and a cultural and political nationalism which is linked to internationalist ideals can all be found in Havel. So can the emphasis on morality and the moral foundations of democracy.

3   V. Havel, *Open Letters: Selected Prose 1965–1990* (London, Faber and Faber, 1991), p. 98.

4   Havel, *Open Letters*, p. 4.

5   His 1965 speech 'On evasive thinking' is reprinted in *Open Letters*, pp. 10–24. The June 1967 Fourth Writer's Congress was one of the key events in the unfolding of the Prague Spring. An account of the congress and references to Havel's role can be found in D. Hamšik, *Writers Against Rulers*, tr. D. Orpington (London, Hutchinson, 1971).

6   Havel wrote a personal letter to Dubček urging him to uphold publicly the principles of the Prague Spring: *Open Letters*, pp. 36–49.

7   Havel, *Open Letters*, p. 62.

8   Havel, *Open Letters*, p. 107.

9   Bujak cited in Havel, *Open Letters*, p. 126.

10   T. Garton Ash, *We the People: The Revolutions of '89 Witnessed in Warsaw, Budapest, Berlin and Prague* (Cambridge, Granta, 1990), p. 89.

11   Havel, *Open Letters*, p. 97: 'I consider myself a socialist. I even think that I have taken something from Marxism.'

12   Havel, *Open Letters*, p. 263.

13   V. Havel, *Disturbing the Peace*, tr. Paul Wilson (New York, Knopf, 1990), p. 9.

14   See for example his comments on 'relentless anti-communist warhorses' writing in émigré magazines, *Disturbing the Peace*, p. 170; and see also his sensitive reflection on the life of Communist Party leader František Kriegel, courageous defender of the Prague Spring, who became a signatory of Charter 77, *Open Letters*, pp. 363–72.

15 Jan Patočka, 1909–77, was a spokesperson for Charter 77 and died of a heart attack after prolonged police interrogation. Havel speaks of him with great respect and affection. Patočka's philosophical writings have only recently been translated into English: see E. Kohan (ed.), *Jan Patočka: Philosophy and Selected Writings* (Chicago, University of Chicago Press, 1989).

16 It is natural that German philosophers should be particularly concerned about Heidegger's initial support for Nazism and his reticence on this topic after 1945, but other philosophers have also been concerned about his behaviour and whether support for Nazism was inherent in his thought. Both issues have been widely debated since the 1980s. See J. Habermas, 'Work and *Weltanschauung*: The Heidegger controversy from a German perspective', in H. L. Dreyfus and H. Hall (eds), *Heidegger: A Critical Reader* (Oxford, Basil Blackwell, 1992), pp. 186–208.

17 See A. Tucker, 'Václav Havel's Heideggerianism', *Telos*, 85 (1990), 63–78.

18 V. Havel, *Letters to Olga*, tr. Paul Wilson (London, Faber and Faber, 1988), p. 354.

19 See Havel, *Letters to Olga*, p. 269 on the problems of faith in a personal God, and pp. 345–6 on Havel's preference for the term 'Being'.

20 Havel, *Letters to Olga*, p. 312.

21 M. Heidegger, 'The question concerning technology', in D. F. Krell (ed.), *Martin Heidegger: Basic Writings*, rev. and expanded edn (London, Routledge, 1993), pp. 307–42.

22 G. Steiner, *Heidegger*, 2nd edn (London, Fontana, 1992), p. 138.

23 Havel, *Open Letters*, p. 207.

24 Havel, *Open Letters*, p. 253.

25 J. B. Elshtain, 'Politics without cliché', *Social Research*, 60:3 (Fall, 1993), 441–2.

26 Havel, *Open Letters*, pp. 320–2. These comments are made in the context of remarks on the Western peace movement.

27 V. Havel, 'The responsibility of intellectuals', *New York Review of Books* (22 June 1995), 36–7.

28 V. Havel, *Summer Meditations*, tr. Paul Wilson (New York, Knopf, 1992), p. 5.

29 Havel, *Summer Meditations*, p. 7.

30 Havel, *Open Letters,* p. 15.

31 Havel, *Open Letters*, p. 27.

32 Havel's interview with 'Erica Blair' in the *Times Literary Supplement*, 23 January 1987, quoted in Havel, *Open Letters*, p. 25.

33 Havel has commented on the misleading connotations of the Western terms 'dissident' or 'opposition', but it is hard to avoid them when denoting his resistance to the Husák regime.

34 G. Konrad, *Anti-Politics*, tr. Richard E. Allen (London, Quartet, 1984).

35 Havel, *Open Letters*, p. 271.

36 Havel, *Open Letters*, p. 160.

37 Havel, *Disturbing the Peace*, p. xvi.

38   Havel, *Disturbing the Peace*, p. 175.
39   Havel, *Open Letters*, p. 393.
40   Havel, *Open Letters*, pp. 212–13.
41   Havel, *Open Letters*, p. 271.
42   Havel, *Open Letters*, p. 160.
43   Havel, *Open Letters*, p. 203.
44   Havel, *Open Letters*, pp. 161, 208.
45   Havel, *Open Letters*, p. 99.
46   Havel, *Open Letters*, p. 156.
47   Havel, *Open Letters*, p. 156.
48   The Forum did, in early 1990, embrace eight small parties, but they were
     promoted under the Forum umbrella, and the Forum resisted becoming a
     party itself. See Jan Urban, 'Czechoslovakia: The power and the politics of
     humiliation', in G. Prins (ed.), *Spring in Winter: The 1989 Revolutions*
     (Manchester, Manchester University Press, 1990), p. 124.
49   Ash, *We the People*, p. 90.
50   Havel, *Summer Mediations*, pp. 24–5.
51   M. Bankowicz, 'Czechoslovakia from Masaryk to Havel', in S. Berglund and
     J. Ake Dellenbrant (eds), *The New Democracies in Eastern Europe: Party
     Systems and Political Cleavages*, 2nd edn (Aldershot, Edward Elgar, 1994),
     p. 159.
52   Havel, *Summer Mediations*, p. 53.
53   Havel, *Summer Mediations*, p. 104.
54   V. Havel and V. Klaus, 'Civil society after communism: Rival visions',
     Journal of Democracy, 7:1 (January 1996), 19.
55   Havel and Klaus, 'Civil society after communism', p. 21.
56   Havel, *Summer Mediations*, p. 104.
57   The term 'civil society' has a complex history, defined in somewhat different
     ways in early liberal thought, by Hegel and by Marx, before acquiring new
     significance in the 1980s. See for example J. Keane (ed.), *Civil Society and the
     State: New European Perspectives* (London, Verso, 1988) which explores the
     background and covers the contemporary East European usage.
58   The prosecution of the rock band, The Plastic People of the Universe, in
     1976 illustrated how cultural autonomy could become political protest.
59   Havel and Klaus, 'Civil society after communism', p. 18.
60   Havel, *Summer Mediations*, p. 65.
61   J. B. Elshtain, 'A performer of political thought: Václav Havel on freedom
     and responsibility', in I. Shapiro and J. Wagner DeCew (eds), *Theory and
     Practice, Nomos XXXVII* (New York, New York University Press, 1995), pp.
     469–79.
62   See J. A. Schumpeter, *Capitalism, Socialism and Democracy*, 3rd edn
     (London, Allen and Unwin, 1950), chs 21 and 22. For other versions of
     elitism and criticisms of them see H. S. Kariel (ed.), *Frontiers of Democratic
     Theory* (New York, Random House, 1970) .
63   See in particular A. de Tocqueville, *Democracy in America*, 2 vols, but also

A. de Tocqueville, *The Ancient Regime and the French Revolution*, which explores the centralized autocracy and loss of local civic pride under the monarchy.

64 One of the last essays by Ferenc Fehér, exiled Hungarian opposition theorist, was entitled 'The evergreen de Tocqueville'. See J. Caroll, 'Democracy', *Quadrant*, 39 (April 1995), 26.

65 Havel and Klaus, 'Civil society after communism', pp. 22–3.

66 S. Lukes, 'President as preacher', *Times Literary Supplement* (25 September 1992), 9.

67 G. F. Kennan, 'Keeping the faith', *New York Review of Books*, 39:15 (24 September 1992), 3.

68 J. B. Elshtain, *Democracy on Trial* (New York, Basic Books, 1995): on civil society see pp. 5–21, and on Havel see pp. 133–5.

69 R. D. Putnam, *Making Democracy Work: Civic Traditions in Modern Italy* (Princeton, NJ, Princeton University Press, 1993).

70 R. D. Putnam, 'Bowling alone: America's declining social capital', *Journal of Democracy*, 6:1 (January 1995), 65–78.

71 M. Walzer, 'The civil society argument', in C. Mouffe (ed.), *Dimensions of Radical Democracy* (London, Verso, 1992), pp. 106–7.

4

Jürgen Habermas and Deliberative Democracy

Martin Leet

Jürgen Habermas has always been committed to radical democracy. This chapter aims to interpret his theoretical work as an articulation of the meaning of radical democracy, its place within a critical theory of society, and its role in society itself. Indeed, in the intellectual context of the post-war period, Habermas has been described as 'the first German theorist of democracy'.[1] It may seem paradoxical, then, that much of Habermas's contribution does not systematically address the issue of democracy. Democracy is a background feature because Habermas's focus is on the weighty question of the sustainability of modern society and culture as a whole. Nonetheless, democracy of a 'deliberative' kind is a central component of Habermas's response to this question.

Habermas belongs to the tradition of the Enlightenment and its associated aspirations to progress and freedom. He believes that human beings are capable of rising above self-interest, prejudice and dogma through the exercise of reason. Habermas's confidence in reason endures despite the fact that much has happened in Western society to undermine Enlightenment optimism. Humans have certainly exercised reason but it is precisely this exercise which is now often criticized, as the cause of contemporary human problems.[2] Questions have arisen as to whether there is *any* basis at all for reason to be used so as to further the interests of all.

Habermas's work provides a positive response to these questions. It seeks to establish that human reason is essentially an ethical and moral force. In Habermas's abstract framework of analysis, however, the concrete problems that daily confront modern societies often seem to fade. It is sometimes argued that Habermas's theory is too distant from the requirements of practice. And yet, if an insistence on linking theory and practice can be regarded as a distinctively Marxist concern, then Habermas firmly situates himself within this tradition. Indeed, in response to recent criticism on this point, Habermas has claimed for himself the title 'the last Marxist'.[3]

While it is possible to approach the trajectory of Habermas's work from different perspectives, an attempt is made here to understand it as a consistent endeavour to link theory's philosophical and practical dimensions. In many ways, Habermas's efforts to do this intersect around the concept of democracy. For this reason, it is important to explore first the motivational context of his commitment to democracy. The second and third sections of the chapter deal with the two basic levels of abstraction in Habermas's concept of democracy. The second section sets out the emphatically philosophical justification of democracy, in terms of a theory of rationality and history. The third section indicates how Habermas complements this philosophical approach with an understanding of its institutional implications. The fourth section analyses his contribution to radical democratic theory. Finally, a discussion of persisting problems in the relation of theory to practice is raised. For reasons of space, each section limits itself to only a brief examination of key concepts and themes.

Background: Political and Theoretical Context

Habermas suggests that 'What really determined my political views was the year 1945.'[4] In that year, at the age of sixteen, he was a member of the Hitler Youth and was sent to the western defences of Germany. Habermas describes the end of the war as an experience of 'liberation'.[5] There was a general culture of optimism among the youth, even though the political culture in Germany remained inhibited for some time, preventing an open confrontation with the past.[6] Reflecting upon these events Habermas has written: 'We believed that a spiritual and moral renewal was indispensable and inevitable.'[7] Even though Habermas overestimated the possibilities, he gained a tangible sense of what democracy meant. There was, for example, 'the deep, everyday experience we lived through after 1945: things got better with the reintroduction of democracy'.[8] Habermas felt, existentially, the meaning of democracy and its significance as a historical achievement. He has translated this, at the philosophical level, into a commitment to defend the benefits of modernity against those who focus either exclusively on the losses, or on a still-to-be-conquered future. Habermas writes, 'the fact that one only becomes aware of these acquisitions when they are threatened is a circumstance which merits philosophical attention.'[9]

Habermas's commitment to democracy can also be traced back to this post-war German 're-education'. It kindled an enthusiasm for the prospects of the Federal Republic catching up with the stable, democratic political cultures of England, France and the United States.[10] A keen sensitivity to ambivalence and ambiguity also developed, however, as it soon became clear that democratic transformation was not occurring as rapidly as he had hoped. To begin with, there was an 'essential continuity' in both the universities and the political system, producing 'the fear that a real break with the past had not been made'.[11] Habermas suggests that it was the student movement of the late 1960s which finally broke through stubborn authoritarian tendencies.[12] It served to make obvious the 'life fiction' of the Adenauer period that 'we are all democrats now.'[13]

As early as 1977, however, Habermas was again disturbed by the vulnerability of German political culture. A pretext for abandoning democratic values developed with the return of economic crisis, the rise of terrorism and the exploitation of the situation by conservative elites to maintain 'a feeling of anxiety and induce a sense of "realism"'.[14] More recently, he has spoken of a 'second life fiction'.[15] This is the politically influential idea that the German reunification process has relieved a once separated nation of the responsibilities of democracy. Habermas believes that a widespread belief prevails that the old Federal Republic had been crippled with liberal democracy in light of the Holocaust. Emerging from this is a second life fiction, that a renewed Germany can now continue its former quest for a national identity separate from Western Europe.

Habermas insists that an adequate theoretical perspective must be capable of embracing these ambivalent tendencies. In this respect, his contact with the critical theory of the Frankfurt School has been crucial. A key insight that Habermas has obtained from this tradition, especially from Herbert Marcuse, is that we always need to reflect on

> the extent to which we all unconsciously share the conventional resignation that reinforces existing conditions in our thoughts, without testing the 'conception' lying behind those conditions, the objective possibility that they can undergo historical development.[16]

A one-sided, unbalanced theoretical approach cannot possibly do justice to *both* 'existing conditions' and the 'conception' lying behind them. With this in mind, Habermas has been keen to avoid 'the philosophy of hope and despair'.[17] Although deeply influenced by Theodor Adorno, who exemplified this philosophy, Habermas does not wish to take up this aspect of his thinking. Habermas is convinced that philosophy cannot accomplish much and that it is only by thinking otherwise that one can get caught up in the cycles of hope and despair. Philosophy can merely identify the reason, however distorted and suppressed, that is latent within the world, and can possess no certainty about the possibilities of its future realization.

It is important to stress the significance of this *reconstructive* approach to philosophy for Habermas's attempt to link theory and practice. This approach puts strict limits on what Habermas can say, as a philosopher, about the substantive problems facing modern societies. Reconstruction serves only to identify (in a fallible way) the necessary conditions and presuppositions (the 'conception') underlying the everyday practices in which we engage.[18] These conditions specify what we are ideally trying to achieve in expressing ourselves, even if we are unaware of it. At most, reconstruction can make us more aware of *why* we are acting but it cannot tell us how to act. Thus, in Habermas's development of a theory of democracy, there is only a reconstruction of the conditions that make possible the democratic regulation by citizens of their existence together. Substantive questions cannot be addressed other than through democracy itself.

While the reconstructive approach places limits on what Habermas can say as a philosopher, he has still been active in the roles of citizen and intellectual. In doing so, he has provided an example of the practice his theory implies. From the 1950s, when he published articles discussing philosophical and sociological issues in newspapers and journals aimed at the general public,[19] to his more recent interventions on issues such as the Gulf War and German unification, Habermas has often engaged in political controversy. Indeed, he has played a considerable part in establishing a certain kind of public role for the intellectual in Germany.[20] Habermas seeks to find a middle ground between, on the one hand, the elitist and impractical intellectual who claims to possess objective truth and, on the other hand, the intellectual with pretensions to power, who wishes to play a role in organizational politics. In between these two roles, Habermas finds a place for the intellectual as a catalyst for critical debate within the political public sphere. Here the intellectual adopts the 'normative self-understanding of democratic will-formation'.[21] That is, he or she adopts an egalitarian and fallible attitude and places faith in the capacity of a public sphere to open itself and its attitudes to the critical force of arguments, whatever their source.

This selection of a few elements of the interpretive context which informs Habermas's work is not intended to reduce his theoretical efforts to a series of socio-psychological experiences. It is designed only to provide a general background to his engagement with democratic theory. An important part of that contribution has been an attempt to demonstrate that partisanship for democracy is not merely an individual, psychological issue. In accordance with his reconstructive approach, Habermas wants to show that a specific form of democracy underlies the social and political practices of Western, liberal societies. This means that democracy is not simply an individual or even a collective *preference*, but is something we are already implicitly advocating in our attempts to live together peacefully.

The Philosophical Justification of Democracy

Habermas's concept of democracy finds its place within a comprehensive theory of modernity. Habermas says that from an early stage in his career his central problem 'was a theory of modernity, a theory of the pathology of modernity, from the viewpoint of the realization – the deformed realization – of reason in history'.[22] To answer this problem, Habermas argues we must first investigate the very basis of human life, to see what capacity for reason exists. It is then possible to see how modernity represents an inconsistent application of the emancipatory potential of reason. Habermas's analysis begins from the foundations of human existence and gradually works its way up into an understanding of the place of democracy in the modern world.

Rationality and Communicative Action

Human cognition, speech and action always involve an attempt to realize something. The pursuit of our various purposes in life also entails the use and application of knowledge. Habermas argues that the concept of 'reason' or 'rationality' is connected with the quality of our knowledge, its capacity to enable us to realize our purposes. Nonetheless, reason should not be identified with the *content* of knowledge. What is important, according to Habermas, is that we *necessarily claim* that our acquisition and use of knowledge is appropriate and adequate. In actions and expressions, we raise what Habermas calls 'validity claims'. These claims are the criteria to which we refer in evaluating our attempts to realize our purposes. Expressions and actions satisfy the *precondition* for rationality when they are susceptible to being criticized and argued for. Reason, itself, becomes operative when it is possible to engage in a discursive process of testing, revising and affirming validity claims.[23]

Habermas's work traces the far-reaching consequences of the linguistic nature of human reason. For Habermas, the human species is distinguished from other forms of life in that 'at the socio-cultural stage of development animal behaviour is reorganized under imperatives of validity claims.'[24] This means that the form of social reproduction, at any particular time and place, is *in principle* tied to the kind of rational process of criticism and revision mentioned above. The knowledge contained in methods of reproducing life is open to contestation. It is this hypothetical quality of openness which makes learning possible. 'In virtue of their criticizability,' writes Habermas, 'rational expressions also admit of improvement; we can correct failed attempts if we can successfully identify our mistakes.'[25] He argues that this potential for learning was relatively restricted in premodern communities. Methods for satisfying the requirements of human life were sanctified in an unproblematic consensus. Fixed religious and metaphysical world views justified everyday practices as natural and immutable. The taboos of this 'authority of the sacred' prohibited the criticism of knowledge. Habermas says that recognition of the sacred produces a feeling of *moral obligation* in the individual because 'it is surrounded with an aura that simultaneously frightens and attracts, terrorizes and enchants.'[26]

The authority of sacred knowledge was gradually displaced with the onset of modern societies. Thus, the possibility arose of developing new methods of creating and maintaining social order. These developments, which are still manifesting themselves according to Habermas, open up scope for more rational forms of social reproduction. They make possible human cooperation on the basis of knowledge susceptible to criticism. Habermas's theory of modernity is designed to explain the general ways in which this opportunity presents itself. It indicates, also, the other, less rational paths that can be taken. 'Communicative action' and 'lifeworld' are the key, complementary notions used to understand the potential for more rational forms of social order. While Habermas's analysis of these concepts is complex, it will suffice, for the purposes of this essay, to explain the basic role they perform in Habermas's theoretical framework.

The idea of the lifeworld expresses the insight that a kind of sacredness never completely disappears from modern social life. The sacred denotes values, beliefs and practices that, having 'passed through' linguistic formulations, solidify and become fixed. They confront individuals 'from the outside'. The freeing up of rationality is equivalent to the openness to interrogation of these sorts of beliefs and norms. Nevertheless, discursive examination is never entirely free of unquestioned norms. There is another set of preconceptions, which lie 'behind' our explicit discussions. Habermas says that without a 'sprawling, deeply set, and unshakeable rock of background assumptions, loyalties and, skills',[27] even the most simplistic of our utterances would lack meaning.[28] We would also lack motivation to act and possess no 'natural' orientation to things, others or ourselves. The concept of the lifeworld, although complex, is simply meant to indicate that humans cannot exist in a cultural, social or personality vacuum. A complete destruction of this type of 'sacredness', of our preconceptions and know-how, would amount to an undermining of linguistic communication and therefore the human way of life as such.

The concept of communicative action is complementary to that of the lifeworld. Habermas defines it as action 'oriented to achieving, sustaining, and renewing consensus'.[29] Consensus is important because, along with Durkheim, Habermas insists that a certain proportion of individual beliefs and norms needs to be held in common if society is not to implode. Communicative action, by orienting the action plans of participants in a consensual manner, preserves the fund of social morality. It obliges speakers and hearers to take seriously into account the claims of each other in formulating their individual aims and intentions. It seeks to harmonize individually defined goals and aspirations with a shared understanding of collective purposes and beliefs. Communicative action is only able to do this within the context of a lifeworld. 'The lifeworld forms both the horizon for speech situations and the source of interpretations, while it in turn reproduces itself only through ongoing communicative actions.'[30]

Democracy and Reason

The scope for communicative action grows tremendously with the onset of modern, pluralistic societies. In more traditional societies it was limited, on the one side, by the sacredness of institutions and, on the other, by a relatively homogeneous set of background assumptions and skills. As far as disagreements did occur, they could be easily resolved in relation to a solid, overarching agreement on the way life should be lived. This alters, first, with what Habermas calls the 'linguistification of the sacred'.[31] Societies are less and less held together by the 'spellbinding power' of the sacred and rely more and more upon the process of communicative action for producing explicit agreements. Secondly, as ways of life multiply for various reasons, there is no longer a singular lifeworld encompassing the whole of society. Modernity denotes a time and space in which 'Individuals, groups, and nations have drifted far apart in their backgrounds of biographical and social-cultural experience.'[32]

These trends mean that disagreements and lack of orientation become more routine in everyday practice. A heightened responsibility is placed on individuals to cooperate and explicitly produce shared certainties. The 'rationality potential'[33] ingrained in communicative action makes possible a constructive response to this predicament. The freedom to engage in reason means, however, a corresponding increase in the burdens individuals must shoulder. In fact, at a certain stage, lifeworlds can cease to overlap one another sufficiently for communicative action to be successful. The ways of life of individuals and groups may become so different that the minimum level of shared understanding required cannot be reached. Habermas describes a predicament in which we 'still argue about moral judgements and beliefs with reasons [but] an encompassing value-consensus on basic moral norms has been shattered'.[34]

In this situation, the rationality of communicative action can still assert itself by pointing to 'the practice of argumentation as a court of appeal'.[35] Argumentation is defined as a reflective form of communicative action. Once participants no longer agree on basic moral norms, the only thing they share is a belonging to 'some communicative form of life'. That is, as human beings, they all reproduce their lives through language. Since these life forms 'have certain structural aspects in common' the participants can rely only on the 'normative contents' of these common aspects as a basis for 'shared orientations'.[36] These normative contents are structures of 'reciprocal recognition' built into ordinary language communication. The only thing that can rationally motivate every participant to keep trying to resolve his or her conflicts consensually is if they can be assured that their needs and interests will be recognized. Habermas describes this idea as the principle of discourse or argumentation or 'D': 'Just those action norms are valid to which all possibly affected persons could agree as participants in rational discourses.'[37]

Discourse or argumentation is an attempt to restore the loss of an erstwhile consensus. Habermas defines it as 'that type of speech in which participants thematize contested validity claims and attempt to vindicate or criticize them through arguments'.[38] According to Habermas, there are three *universal* validity claims: truth, rightness, and truthfulness or sincerity. In communicating with another, a speaker claims that what they say is true if they are referring to the objective world. If they are referring to the social world shared with the hearer, they claim that it is right. If they refer to their own, inner world of subjective experience then they are claiming that they are truthful or sincere. While all three validity claims may come into play in the attempt to resolve a single issue, it is especially in disputes over the *normative rightness* of a claim that the regulation of personal interactions is placed in jeopardy.

The question arises, however, whether impartiality can really solve persistent moral disagreements. Can we expect 'all those possibly affected' to agree on something when they have only resorted to argumentation because of disagreement on everything else? It is this very difficulty that Habermas exploits in his philosophical specification of democracy. If argumentation cannot be expected to routinely produce *outcomes* in the form of agreements, participants can rely on nothing other than the norms embodied within the process of argumentation itself. That is, if they still insist on regulating their life in a consensual fashion, they must accord one another the rights and duties necessary for the practice of argumentation to continue. Habermas's argument culminates in the specification of democracy as the project of institutionalizing these basic rights and duties.[39]

It is with this dynamic concept of democracy that Habermas hopes to preserve the fundamental idea of Enlightenment. That is, while the factual reproduction of social life takes place haphazardly under constraints and necessities, it nevertheless contains the ideal of a 'conscious conduct of life' as a modifying force. The reciprocal recognition of validity claims means that we can deal with substantive issues and conflicts under universal points of view. We persist in searching for truth, rightness and sincerity despite the conservative weight of existing conditions. Theory and practice are already connected at the same time as they contradict one another. Thus, amidst the plurality, conflict and change of modern life is a communicative drive towards resolution. Without this drive, says Habermas, we would have no rational alternative to violence and coercion as methods of collective will formation and conflict resolution.[40] Of course, 'with this comes the problem of having to explain how the reproduction of society can possibly proceed on such fragile ground as that of context-transcending validity claims.'[41] Habermas deals with this problem in the institutional analyses discussed below.

The Institutional Features of Democracy

Habermas's attempt to link theory and practice takes place at different theoretical layers, the above account providing a sketch of the most abstract level. This section explores its more concrete, institutional manifestations after describing a number of difficulties facing democracy in modern society. It should be remembered, too, that even at the institutional level, Habermas proceeds only reconstructively. He limits himself to a clarification of the *conditions* of democratic *procedure*.

There are a series of obstacles confronting the democratic response to the disintegration of traditional ways of life. The violent class, ethnic and religious conflicts that have recurred in modern societies are examples of a different approach. They are instances of what Habermas calls 'strategic action'. Strategic action is an alternative to communicative action in situations of disagreement. It involves an actor viewing others only in terms of their degree of usefulness for achieving a preconceived end.[42] One reason why human beings may prefer strategic action over communicative action arises from *internal* inadequacies in lifeworld structures. They may lack the appropriate resources and motivations (cultural, social and personality) allowing them to transcend their own point of view and recognize another.[43] More important than this, argues Habermas, are those factors which *externally* prevent the capacities of modern lifeworlds from releasing their communicative potential. Here, he says, the 'systems' of modern societies force modes of strategic action upon individuals.

The notion of 'system' refers to entire domains of social life in which strategic action has been legally institutionalized.[44] That is, actors are legally freed from the requirements of communicatively coordinating their actions. This does not mean anarchy because systems provide an alternative mechanism of coordination. Habermas argues that the two central systems of modern society are the economy and the state, whose coordinating mechanisms are money and power respectively. Money and power, as 'steering media', regulate action by providing a reference point for all participants involved. They are the common currency used to negotiate claims and conflicts within systemic contexts.[45] Problems arise, according to Habermas, when these media break out of their legal domains and literally invade the lifeworld.[46] Individuals and groups are prevented from autonomously regulating their collective existence owing to the systemic 'colonization' of the lifeworld. Money and power then define issues and problems in their own terms and lock out communicatively generated interpretations. From the sphere of industrial life to that of the environment, decisions can be made according to predetermined criteria rather than via the impartial standards of democratic discussion. Importantly, this phenomenon not only prevents democratic generation of agreements, it also damages lifeworld structures of reciprocal recognition which are the very basis of democracy.

One more significant trend in modernity compounds the difficulties for democracy. The consensual working out of interpretations becomes more arduous with the separate institutionalization of validity claims. The scientific enterprise, the legal system and institutions of art criticism make questions of truth, rightness and sincerity a matter for experts. Validity claims are cut off not only from one another but also from everyday orientations. Citizens must confront a bewildering complex of expertise which challenges their understanding of reality. Not only may they disagree among themselves over what is true, right and sincere, but specialists devoting their lives to these questions also have their interpretations.

In the context of all this, we may ask whether Habermas offers a practical concept of democracy. Political parties, trade unions and other formal organizations have been the traditional basis of progressive movements. For citizens, however, this set of potentially democratic footholds into systems is lost according to Habermas. He subsumes them under a systemic logic of action incapable of radical democratization. Critics have argued, therefore, that the analysis of the conflict between system and lifeworld offered in *The Theory of Communicative Action* failed to provide a practically enlightening theory.[47] Habermas acknowledges that he does not offer a socialist concept of democracy in contrast to earlier formulations.[48] He places out of the question a radical democratic regulation of economy and state. Instead, the task for radical democracy now is to 'erect a democratic dam against the colonializing *encroachment* of system imperatives on areas of the lifeworld'.[49] The task is a defensive one, to *protect* structures of reciprocal recognition. And the responsibility for this lies in *informal* public spheres and civil associations within the lifeworld.

Apart from legitimate queries about Habermas's acceptance of key tenets of systems theory, we may simply question whether the informal associations of citizens can be expected to take up even this more limited radical democratic project. In effect, Habermas's analysis in *The Theory of Communicative Action* left few clear answers to the possible efficacy of 'fragile validity claims'. His latest major work, *Between Facts and Norms*, offers some possible solutions. Here, there is a clearer account of the circulation of power in modern society and the role democracy plays within it.

There are two interrelated keys to Habermas's argument. The first concerns a revision of his understanding of modern law, while the second involves an elaboration of the concept of 'power'. The starting point remains the fact that systems need to be legally justified. This requirement of legality opens up a channel between system and lifeworld through which either one can influence the other.[50] While Habermas's earlier concern was with the influence of systems on the lifeworld, he reverses his focus in the latest work. For the sake of brevity, I will deal only with the arguments regarding law.

The first stage in Habermas's approach to law consists of the thesis that modern law embodies the core dynamic of democracy. Habermas argues that 'From the standpoint of *legal theory*, the modern legal order can draw its legitimacy only from the idea of self-determination: citizens should always be able to understand themselves also as authors of the law to which they are subject as addressees.'[51] Habermas insists that only the discursive concept of democracy can convincingly articulate this idea.[52] We saw above that this concept involves subjects mutually according one another the basic rights and duties required for rational discourse. Habermas argues that when this process takes place within modern positive law, the result is a 'basic system of rights'. This system is the *threshold* of constitutional rights required to make possible the idea of self-determination. The system of basic civil rights is as follows:

1   Basic rights that result from the politically autonomous elaboration of the
    right to the greatest possible measure of equal individual liberties.
2   Basic rights that result from the politically autonomous elaboration of the
    status of a member in a voluntary association of consociates under law.
3   Basic rights that result immediately from the *actionability* of rights and from
    the politically autonomous elaboration of individual *legal protection.*
4   Basic rights to equal opportunities to participate in processes of opinion and
    will formation in which citizens exercise their *political autonomy* and through
    which they generate legitimate law.[53]

The first three rights refer to the addressees of law, and 'guarantee what
we now call the *private* autonomy of legal subjects'.[54] They can only be
described formally because their actual *content* must be the result of a
democratic practice of will formation by citizens as authors. The fourth
basic right follows from this requirement. Democracy is defined as the
heart of this system of basic rights[55] as well as the project of realizing these
rights in the specific circumstances of modern societies.[56] In short, the
system of rights *legalizes* the core dynamic of democracy. Habermas suggests that the 'first act of a constitution-making practice already drives the
wedge of an expansive idea into societal complexity.'[57]

It should be noted here that the discursive concept of democracy, while
involving a reciprocal conferral of rights, does not enforce the strong
duties of discourse. Citizens have a right *not* to take on such obligations.
They are free to remain private individuals in strategic domains.[58] For this
reason, Habermas argues that constitutional democracy ultimately depends on the internal motivations of its citizens. At the same time, once
activated, these motivations can have far-reaching effects. To substantiate
this claim, we must look at the second stage of Habermas's approach
to law.

Habermas argues that because law plays a crucial role in tasks of social
integration, the dynamic of democracy, like a 'spider's web',[59] can extend
to the whole of society. Habermas draws on the accounts provided by
Durkheim and particularly Talcott Parsons of the way law replaces the
sacred as a centripetal force in modern societies.[60] As already seen, the
dissolution of the sacred makes communicative action responsible for
producing shared orientations. In turn, this power of communicative
action is limited in the context of complex societies. Habermas argues that
law compensates for this by acting as a sociological 'transformer'[61] of
agreements reached in the lifeworld. The key sociological feature of law is
that it 'stabilizes behavioural expectations'. It lets 'members of a social
collectivity know what behaviour they may demand of one another when
and in which situations'.[62] Because law has this large-scale regulatory
influence and because law is tied to discursive review, it also effectively

extends in time and space the abstract features of communicative action. In short, validity claims overcome their fragile character.

With this understanding of law, Habermas has had to revise an earlier distinction made between law as *institution* and law as *medium*.[63] That distinction largely excluded law's democratic potential from systemic contexts in which it functioned without need of substantive interrogation. The result was a tripartite account of how law operated. First, as medium, it helped internally regulate systemic contexts of action. Second, as medium, it legitimized the colonization of the lifeworld by legalizing the expansion of systemic media. Third, as institution, it formally protected the structures of modern lifeworlds. Habermas dispenses with this approach in his latest formulation and insists that law is always an institution. Whatever it regulates, it remains tied to communicative processes.[64] This means that he conceptually allows for more democratic regulation of the systems of state and economy.

Connecting the revised and expanded concepts of law and power allows Habermas to draw out several political recommendations. For example, he argues that 'procedural law must be enlisted' to democratize the administration by means of a 'legitimation filter'.[65] He suggests that the state can play a more democratic role in neo-corporatist arrangements by protecting the public interest from secretive deals among large organizations.[66] The same goes for democratic party leaders in relation to holders of administrative power.[67] The judiciary's expertise over questions of rightness needs to remain linked with 'enlarged critical forums'.[68] Discursive democracy has the potential, also, to affect the existing regulation of the workplace.[69] These opportunities arise because the institution of law develops procedures of legitimate law-making which, largely irrespective of the context or the competencies of actors, assert a democratizing influence. Individuals and groups are 'forced' through democratic filters 'at the social level of institutionalized processes'.[70] Habermas characterizes these processes as a 'higher-level intersubjectivity' that screens subjective inputs.[71]

These revisions in the concepts of law and power mean that the formal political system is not democratically legitimate unless it has considerably opened up its internal workings to broader processes of opinion and will formation. In Habermas's approach, the 'strong publics' of the formally organized political system *make* decisions and serve as a 'context of justification', while the 'weak publics' of the lifeworld are effective as a 'context of discovery'.[72] In the final instance, democracy begins and ends in the much larger and more diffuse communicative practices of the lifeworld.

Habermas argues that these communicative practices are based in 'civil society' whose 'institutional core comprises those non-governmental and non-economic connections and voluntary associations'.[73] While the public space for this informal democracy is constitutionally guaranteed, it cannot be organized or institutionalized. The public sphere is a 'wild', 'anarchic' structure which 'resists organization as a whole'.[74] Compared with the political system, the associations of civil society are more sensitive to social issues and are best suited to developing appropriate interpretations and problem solutions. Thus, Habermas insists that a 'constitutionally regulated circulation of power' is maintained only on condition that the 'core' political system remains responsive to the 'periphery' of the public sphere.[75]

Despite the above revisions of, and extrapolations from, his earlier work, we may still question whether Habermas's concept of democracy is realistic. Habermas himself admits that the 'normal business of politics' cannot satisfy the strong conditions of this 'two-track' model of 'deliberative democracy'.[76] Thus, he argues that the public sphere must be able to detect social problems, sharpen them into 'a consciousness of crisis' and thereby introduce them into the parliamentary context 'in a way that *disrupts* the latter's routines'.[77] The reconstructive approach to theory can do no more than point to this possibility. The prospects for democracy depend, in the last instance, on citizens *choosing* to exercise their communicative capacities. The dynamic of democracy must, in the final instance, be generated and regenerated by citizens themselves.

Contribution to Democratic Theory

It was noted in the introduction that the connection between theory and practice is only one perspective from which to approach Habermas's work. The tension, rather than opposition, between the two provides a dynamic for learning processes and is incorporated into the concept of democracy. In fact, Habermas has, throughout his career, consistently used his notions of communicative action and discourse ethics to overcome a multitude of 'dualisms' in theory. His 'dialectical' approach seeks to overcome the one-sidedness of competing theoretical frameworks and integrate their respective truths within his own, more encompassing point of view. This is no less evident in Habermas's contribution to democratic and legal theory. Here, the central offering is, perhaps, the attempt to reconcile the long-standing competition between liberalism and communitarianism. For reasons of space, I can only touch on it tangentially by focusing on Habermas's contribution to the concept of radical democracy. For it has been that project which has motivated his work from its beginnings.

We have already seen how Habermas's acceptance of key theses of systems theory limits the project of radical democracy. It is also constrained by the pluralistic character of the lifeworld which cannot be reduced to a common good. This leads Habermas to reconstruct radical democracy in terms of a proceduralist concept of 'deliberative politics'. The essence of deliberative politics is that the preferences and opinions of citizens brought forward into debate need to be *publicly justifiable*. Policy formulation and will formation are democratic only if citizens do not simply aggregate privately formed preferences, but also engage in discourses that open those preferences to reasoned consideration. Deliberative democracy shifts the focus from final outcomes to the quality of the processes via which they are achieved.[78] It is obvious that this goes beyond the liberal model which is only concerned with providing rules which guarantee a fair compromise of given interests. It also, however, revises the republican model. Habermas seeks to retain the thrust of radical democracy without understanding it as a citizenry expressing a common way of life. Habermas replaces any notion of a 'macrosocial subject' with the idea of 'subjectless communications'.[79]

With this approach, Habermas shifts the focus of radical democracy away from the substantive realization of a goal to a *procedural framework* for responding to social problems which raise the question: 'What should we do?' The need to express a common good is then subsumed as only one element in a comprehensive approach to problem solving in which the analytically distinct aspects of problems need to be dealt with separately.[80] There are, firstly, those aspects of a problem which admit of consensus and must be resolved through discourse. *Pragmatic* discourse deals with finding the most suitable means for achieving ends that are already given. *Ethical* discourse refers to the classical task of radical democracy, of clarifying and rationally shaping a shared way of life. *Moral* discourse involves determining what is in the equal interests of all human beings. It specifies the values which act as parameters and limiting conditions for the other two types of discourse. Discursive democracy also caters for those aspects to problems which cannot be consensually resolved. This requires processes of bargaining which seek a fair compromise of interests. Nevertheless, discourse still has an indirect connection with bargaining because it must specify the conditions under which a *fair* compromise can be reached.

Habermas argues that the outcomes of discussions about problems, and the policies developed to solve them, are legitimate when this procedure is followed within the institutional framework described earlier. It is also important, he says, that policies be subjected to judicial review to ensure 'their fit with the existing legal system'.[81] Habermas argues that this is the only way we can conceive radical democracy today. He claims to provide a more balanced concept of democracy in which elements of the liberal and republican traditions find their respective places. But, is this 'radical democracy' in name only?

Martin Leet

Criticisms

Habermas's attempt to sustain the project of radical democracy might be likened to swimming against the tide. The discursive concept of democracy retains radical normative ideals while incorporating all those trends of modernity which have undermined fundamental assumptions of socialist thinking.[82] We may ask whether this results in an 'unbalanced' concept of radical democracy. Here I want to mention only one line of criticism that has been raised against Habermas in this respect.

The issue involves Habermas's justification of democracy in the strong normative terms of the theory of communicative action. We have already noted that Habermas sees democracy arising from an insistent need by citizens to pursue collective goals and regulate their conflicts *consensually*. If democracy did not have its roots in validity claims it would not be distinguishable from violent or strategic methods. Thus, while the formal political system must constantly *make* decisions, decisions that may not be agreed to by all who are affected, the crucial point for Habermas is that only the motivation for consensus exerts a stubbornly *democratizing* influence. Some critics argue, however, that Habermas prescribes overly demanding requirements for democracy which jeopardize its capacity to provide an alternative to violence.[83]

At first, the discursive concept of democracy may not appear onerous to citizens since it relies on no prior substantive consensus. It depends only on recognition of the validity of the principle of impartiality (or 'D'). Nonetheless, it has been argued that even this formal principle demands too much. In the context of modern pluralism, citizens cannot always agree on what impartiality involves. One group can see another's definition of impartiality as inimical to their interests and vice versa. Habermas's claim that impartiality is a shared, universal principle is designed to rise above these sectarian points of view. Thomas McCarthy, however, makes the point that 'The separation of formal procedure from substantive content is never absolute: we cannot agree on what is just without achieving some measure of agreement on what is good.'[84] If this is so, then it is unlikely that any principle, no matter how formal, can possess universality.

The concepts of consensus and impartiality are critical in Habermas's account. Citizens need to distinguish impartially between the moral, ethical and pragmatic aspects of political problems in order to embark upon the requisite types of discourse and bargaining. If they cannot overcome reasonable disagreements at this preliminary stage, then discursive democracy must fail in practical terms. Instead of 'spurring on'[85] democratic processes, the motivation for consensus may well produce disappointment and disaffection.

The apparently interminable nature of contemporary moral and ethical debates testifies to the above predicament.[86] From this point of view, it may be argued that the very legitimacy of democracy derives from its superior ability to resolve problems that *do not* admit of consensus. Thus, Habermas's identification of the willingness of citizens to resolve conflicts non-violently with the motivation for consensus seems misplaced. Critics insist that even on explicitly moral and ethical questions, discourse must often give way to bargaining and fair compromise if democracy is not to become unworkable. If this is a practical exigency of modern democracies, then the 'normative account of legitimacy' needs to be broadened 'to recognize forms of compromise that are not simply based on strategic calculations'.[87] Otherwise, Habermas's radically normative concept of democracy may undermine the legitimacy of the general notion of democracy as such.

Conclusion

Habermas's contribution to theory as a whole is a reconstruction of the unfinished project of modernity. His contribution to democratic theory must be understood in this context. The proceduralist concept of deliberative democracy is designed to clarify the vision lying at the heart of those political cultures of liberal origin, as well as the permanent and not so permanent obstacles confronting its realization. That vision is of a societal organization produced through discursive opinion and will formation alone.

Habermas has remained impervious to those who seek concrete political recommendations from a critical theory of society. While not prescribing what we should do, he provokes, questions, and seeks to assist us to grow in self-consciousness about the tension between theory and practice in which we are already enmeshed. With this self-limiting approach, Habermas keeps open the possibility that we, as citizens of democratic societies, may in fact become more rational and responsible.

Notes

1 David Roberts, *Reconstructing Theory: Gadamer, Habermas, Luhmann* (Carlton South, Victoria, Melbourne University Press, 1995), p. 3.
2 For a recent but more popular statement of this argument, see John Ralston Saul, *Voltaire's Bastards* (New York, Vintage, 1993).

3 Jürgen Habermas in 'Concluding remarks', in Craig Calhoun (ed.), *Habermas and the Public Sphere* (Cambridge, MA, MIT Press, 1992), p. 469.

4 Peter Dews (ed.), *Autonomy and Solidarity: Interviews with Jürgen Habermas* (London, Verso, 1992), p. 77.

5 Dews, *Autonomy and Solidarity*, p. 77.

6 Dews, *Autonomy and Solidarity*, pp. 77, 188.

7 Dews, *Autonomy and Solidarity*, p. 43.

8 Dews, *Autonomy and Solidarity*, p. 189.

9 Dews, *Autonomy and Solidarity*, pp. 138–9.

10 Dews, *Autonomy and Solidarity*, p. 79.

11 Dews, *Autonomy and Solidarity*, pp. 43–4, 47, 78–80.

12 Dews, *Autonomy and Solidarity*, pp. 229–36.

13 Jürgen Habermas, 'The second life fiction of the Federal Republic: We have become "normal" again', *New Left Review*, 197 (1993), 63.

14 Dews, *Autonomy and Solidarity*, p. 48.

15 Habermas, 'The second life fiction'.

16 Habermas in Rolf Wiggerhaus, *The Frankfurt School: Its History, Theories and Political Significance*, tr. Michael Robertson (Cambridge, Polity, 1994), p. 545.

17 See Agnes Heller, 'Habermas and Marxism', in John Thompson and David Held (eds), *Habermas: Critical Debates* (London, Macmillan, 1982), pp. 21–2.

18 See for example Jürgen Habermas, *Moral Consciousness and Communicative Action*, tr. Christian Lenhardt and Shierry Weber Nicholsen (Cambridge, Polity, 1990), pp. 21–2.

19 Wiggerhaus, *The Frankfurt School*, p. 539.

20 Habermas notes that it was not until after the Second World War that a German tradition of intellectual participation in the public sphere developed. See Jürgen Habermas, 'Heinrich Heine and the intellectual in Germany', in *The New Conservatism: Cultural Criticism and the Historians' Debate*, tr. Shierry Weber Nicholsen (Cambridge, Polity, 1989), pp. 71–99.

21 Habermas, 'Heinrich Heine', p. 93.

22 Dews, *Autonomy and Solidarity*, p. 98.

23 Jürgen Habermas, *The Theory of Communicative Action, Volume One: Reason and the Rationalization of Society*, tr. Thomas McCarthy (Boston, Beacon, 1984), pp. 8–10.

24 Jürgen Habermas, *Legitimation Crisis*, tr. Thomas McCarthy (Boston, Beacon, 1975), p. 10.

25 Habermas, *Theory of Communicative Action One*, p. 18.

26 Jürgen Habermas, *The Theory of Communicative Action, Volume Two: Lifeworld and System, A Critique of Functionalist Reason* (Cambridge, Polity, 1987), p. 48.

27 Jürgen Habermas, *Between Facts and Norms: Contributions to a Discourse Theory of Law and Democracy* (Cambridge, Polity, 1996), p. 22.

28 Habermas, *Theory of Communicative Action One*, p. 336.

29   Habermas, *Theory of Communicative Action One*, p. 17.

30   Habermas, *Between Facts and Norms*, p. 22.

31   Habermas, *Theory of Communicative Action Two*, pp. 77–111.

32   Jürgen Habermas, 'Questions and counterquestions', in Richard Bernstein (ed.), *Habermas and Modernity* (Cambridge, Polity, 1985), p. 192.

33   Habermas, *Theory of Communicative Action Two*, p. 77.

34   Jürgen Habermas, 'On the cognitive content of morality', in *Proceedings of the Aristotelian Society* (London, Aristotelian Society, 1996), p. 352.

35   Habermas, *Theory of Communicative Action One*, p. 17.

36   See Habermas, 'On the cognitive content', pp. 352–3.

37   Habermas, *Between Facts and Norms*, p. 107.

38   Habermas, *Theory of Communicative Action One*, p. 18.

39   Habermas, *Between Facts and Norms*, pp. 110–11. The third section of the chapter goes further into what these rights and duties are.

40   See, for example, Jürgen Habermas, 'Remarks on the discussion', *Theory, Culture and Society*, 7 (1990), 127.

41   Habermas, *Between Facts and Norms*, p. 8.

42   Habermas, *Theory of Communicative Action One*, pp. 285–6.

43   For criticisms of Habermas's neglect of internal deficiencies in the lifeworld, see Jeff Livesay, 'Habermas, narcissism, and status', *Telos*, 64 (1985), 75–90; as well as Nancy Fraser, 'What's critical about critical theory? The case of Habermas and gender', in Seyla Benhabib and Drucilla Cornell (eds), *Feminism as Critique: Essays on the Politics of Gender in Late Capitalist Societies* (Cambridge, Polity, 1987), pp. 51ff.

44   Habermas argues that systems require legal institutionalization in the lifeworld: see Habermas, *Theory of Communicative Action Two*, pp. 172–9. The significance of this is considered further below.

45   There are, however, significant differences between the two media. The notion of 'power' cannot be entirely reduced to a 'steering medium' in Parsons's sense. See Habermas, *Theory of Communicative Action Two*, pp. 267–72. Habermas relies particularly on Hannah Arendt to emphasize that administrative power must be constantly legitimated by the 'communicative power' of the public sphere. See *Between Facts and Norms*, pp. 146–50.

46   Habermas, *Theory of Communicative Action Two*, pp. 301–73.

47   See, for example, Fraser, 'What's critical'; Carol Johnson, 'Applying Habermas to Australian political culture', *Australian Journal of Political Science*, 27 (1992), 55–70; Dieter Misgeld, 'Critical hermeneutics versus neoparsonianism?', *New German Critique*, 35 (1985), 55–82; Thomas McCarthy, 'Complexity and democracy, or: The seducements of systems theory', *New German Critique*, 35 (1985), 27–53.

48   See Jürgen Habermas, *The Structural Transformation of the Public Sphere: An Inquiry into a Category of Bourgeois Society*, tr. Thomas Burger and Frederick Lawrence (Cambridge, Polity, 1989).

49   Jürgen Habermas, 'Further reflections on the public sphere', in Calhoun, *Habermas and the Public Sphere*, p. 444.

50   Habermas, *Theory of Communicative Action Two*, p. 185.

51   Jürgen Habermas, 'Postscript (1994)', in *Between Facts and Norms*, p. 449.

52   Habermas's critique of alternative articulations is considered in the next section.

53   Habermas, *Between Facts and Norms*, pp. 122–3.

54   Habermas, *Between Facts and Norms*, p. 123.

55   Habermas, *Between Facts and Norms*, p. 121.

56   Habermas, *Between Facts and Norms*, pp. 125–9.

57   Habermas, 'Postscript', p. 462.

58   Habermas, *Between Facts and Norms*, pp. 119–20.

59   Habermas, *Between Facts and Norms*, p. 437.

60   Habermas, *Theory of Communicative Action Two*, pp. 77–87; *Between Facts and Norms*, pp. 73–6.

61   Habermas, *Between Facts and Norms*, p. 81.

62   Habermas, *Between Facts and Norms*, p. 177.

63   Habermas, *Theory of Communicative Action Two*, pp. 362–5.

64   Jürgen Habermas, 'Remarks on the discussion', p. 130. Habermas still recognizes that law can be instrumentalized for non-democratic purposes. However, this is an empirical question rather than a matter of conceptualizing two different types of law.

65   Habermas, *Between Facts and Norms*, pp. 440–1.

66   Habermas, *Between Facts and Norms*, pp. 350–1, 441.

67   Habermas, *Between Facts and Norms*, p. 443.

68   Habermas, *Between Facts and Norms*, pp. 439–40.

69   Habermas, *Between Facts and Norms*, pp. 413–14.

70   Habermas, *Between Facts and Norms*, pp. 340–1.

71   Habermas, *Between Facts and Norms*, p. 299.

72   Habermas, *Between Facts and Norms*, p. 307. Habermas adopts these terms from Nancy Fraser, 'Rethinking the public sphere: A contribution to the critique of actually existing democracy', in Calhoun, *Habermas and the Public Sphere*, pp. 109–42.

73   Habermas, *Between Facts and Norms*, p. 366.

74   Habermas, *Between Facts and Norms*, p. 307.

75   Habermas, *Between Facts and Norms*, pp. 354–6.

76   The meaning of 'deliberative democracy' is considered further below.

77   Habermas, *Between Facts and Norms*, pp. 356–9.

78   A short bibliography is provided on the concept of deliberative politics in the first note of the translator's introduction to Habermas, *Between Facts and Norms*, p. 517.

79   Habermas, *Between Facts and Norms*, p. 299.

80   Habermas, *Between Facts and Norms*, pp. 151–68.

81   Habermas, *Between Facts and Norms*, p. 167.

82   See also Jürgen Habermas, 'What does socialism mean today?', *New Left Review*, 183 (1990), 3–21. For one example of the argument that Habermas effectively cuts his ties from Marx and socialism, see Nancy Love, 'What's

left of Marx?', in Stephen White (ed.), *The Cambridge Companion to Habermas* (Cambridge, Cambridge University Press, 1995), pp. 46–66.

83 Thomas McCarthy, 'Practical discourse: On the relation of morality to politics', in Calhoun, *Habermas and the Public Sphere*, pp. 51–72; William Rehg and James Bohman, 'Discourse and democracy: The formal and informal bases of legitimacy in Habermas' *Faktizität und Geltung*', *The Journal of Political Philosophy*, 4 (1996), 79–99.

84 McCarthy, 'Practical discourse', p. 62.

85 Habermas, 'Postscript', p. 462.

86 See also Alasdair MacIntyre, *After Virtue: A Study in Moral Theory* (London, Duckworth, 1981).

87 Rehg and Bohman, 'Discourse and democracy', p. 94. These authors reconstruct a weaker set of epistemic conditions for democratic deliberation, pp. 94–9. For other suggestions along these lines, see McCarthy, 'Practical discourse', pp. 66–8, as well as the special section on his work in *Philosophy and Social Criticism*, 22 (1996).

5

Richard Rorty: Postmodernism and a Pragmatic Defence of Democracy

Katherine Welton

Since the publication of *Philosophy and the Mirror of Nature*, Richard Rorty has earned a reputation as something of a philosophical iconoclast. His fondness for overturning conventional assumptions about knowledge, selfhood and language has attracted much critical attention. Never explicitly a democratic theorist, he nevertheless exhibits a strong interest in democracy in much of his writing. Rorty locates this interest within the context of the intellectual challenges raised by postmodern theory, combining a postmodern claim about the contingency of knowledge with a strong defence of the procedural framework of liberal democracy. The manner in which Rorty reconciles his particular regard for American democracy with his postmodern scepticism and anti-universalism constitutes a provocative contribution to the debates over the defence, critique and justification of Western liberal democracy.

The relationship between philosophical knowledge and democracy provides one of the main themes of Rorty's work. His purpose is to criticize how intellectuals in the developed nations choose to write about democracy. More specifically, his objection is to the idea that any general theory of human nature or universal principles of knowledge are necessary to provide a foundation or justification for the social practice of democracy. He offers no detailed critique of the problems that face present democracies, nor does he suggest much in the way of proposals to overcome them. Nonetheless, Rorty's work offers a theory of democracy that emerges not only from his critique of other theorists, but also from articles that are explicitly about democracy.[1] Some of Rorty's most unequivocal claims about democracy appear in shorter papers, such as his review of Habermas's work, or interviews such as that in the *Times Literary Supplement*.[2]

The key to Rorty's argument lies in the claim that, if we accept that our knowledge is at best uncertain, then we must think and talk about democracy in a different way. Rorty argues that if our values and beliefs about democracy are contingent, then the best we can do is to establish a procedural framework which enables tolerant conversation about these values and beliefs. In several respects this argument is unexceptional. What is distinctive, however, is his argument for the uncertainty of our knowledge and the character of the response to this which focuses upon conversation. Rorty places great emphasis upon 'conversation' as a central dynamic of democracy. This emphasis is also reflected in Rorty's famous willingness to engage in debate, which has led to exchanges with prominent political theorists such as Jürgen Habermas, Richard Bernstein and Sheldon Wolin.

This chapter begins with a brief discussion of the intellectual context of, and influences upon, Rorty's work. Here the focus is his theory of knowledge because this provides the foundation for his treatment of democracy and his critique of democratic theorists. I then canvass a few issues that Rorty nominates as significant for democratic theory. I argue, following Bernstein, that there seem to be two different strands in Rorty's claims about democracy.[3] The first strand emerges from his theory of knowledge and is based on the claim that we can dispense with philosophical foundations for democracy.[4] The second strand consists of Rorty's claims for the centrality of liberal democracy for our own Western communities. I will examine the claims that Rorty makes in support of liberal democracy, and outline the kind of procedural model of democracy that emerges from Rorty's work. I maintain there is a tension between these two strands, as one stresses the primacy of contingency, and the other relies on the empirical reality of strong political attachments. Rorty argues that his loyalty to liberal democracy is based not upon a claim for its inherent truth or goodness, but rather upon pragmatism and tradition. I aim to show how Rorty combines these disparate arguments, and also indicate what it is that he finds particularly valuable and defensible about liberal democracy.

I argue that Rorty is constrained to offer only a limited procedural outline for his democratic model, because he argues that any substantive claim entails the kind of philosophical justification he would reject. Rorty refuses this justification of democracy, not only because he cannot see the relevance of it, but also because he sees actual harm in the process. This harm, he claims, stems from the fact that such strong justification risks jeopardizing liberal tolerance, and also deflects attention from the key purpose of liberal democracy, which is to prevent suffering. But Rorty's model of democracy is problematic in this regard. In the final section of

the chapter, I examine whether Rorty's model can guarantee either tolerance or the elimination of suffering. I contend that it cannot, because
Rorty's rigid conception of the public/private dichotomy leads to a limited
conception of what is politically possible in the public sphere. Rorty's
main defence of liberal democracy rests on the assertion that, at present, it
is the only procedural 'vocabulary' available that enables everyone to be a
citizen. Nevertheless, members of oppressed groups, such as women and
ethnic minorities, argue that liberal democracy has not delivered upon this
promise of citizenship. I suggest that by limiting the possibilities of debate
over the central values and procedures of democratic communities, Rorty's
own conception of democracy provides a meagre substitute for the richer
tradition of democratic theory of which he is so critical.

Background

Context and location are integral parts of Rorty's philosophy. Given the
emphasis Rorty places upon community in his work, one might expect a
clear indication of Rorty's ideological and philosophical context. His own
self-location, however, is somewhat ambiguous. Rorty's writings are lit-
tered with allusions to 'we', referring to those various intellectual and
political groups to which he nominates himself as belonging. These references include 'postmodern bourgeois liberals',[5] 'we ironists',[6] and occasionally, 'fellow social democrats'.[7] There is also evidence from his own
biography, such as 'we leftist intellectuals in the rich democracies',[8] and
'left-wing Democrat professors like myself'.[9] Many of these categories
seem contradictory, and although Rorty might not necessarily find this a
problem, these contradictions have been the source of disagreements with
other theorists. Bernstein, for example, challenges Rorty to identify just
exactly what he meant by 'we', arguing that Rorty's 'we' generally means
'all those who agree with [him]'.[10]

   Born in 1931, Rorty has been a teacher and writer of philosophy in the
United States for the past thirty years. As an undergraduate he studied at
the University of Chicago, and completed a doctorate at Yale. He taught
at Princeton University, where he completed *Philosophy and the Mirror
of Nature*. Rorty is now Professor of Humanities at the University of
Virginia. He has written directly about his biography in a candid piece
designed to address his numerous critics from the left and right. In this
short essay, he claims that the left criticizes him as 'complacent', and the
right as 'irresponsible'. His aim is to rebut the charge that his views are the
result of a frivolous adoption of deliberately controversial positions.[11]
Discussing his political development, he reveals that his parents were both

Trotskyists, and he grew up with an awareness of the profound injustice of capitalist America. Nevertheless, Rorty claims that his youth was also shaped by his own 'private, weird, snobbish, incommunicable interests', including a passion for the study of wild orchids.[12] Rorty argues that his subsequent theoretical concerns can be directly linked to the failed attempt to reconcile his parents' politics with what seemed to be the useless, aesthetic character of his horticultural obsession.

Some of these concerns can be clearly observed throughout his work, and emerge as significant elements of his more recent discussions of democracy. His first book, *Philosophy and the Mirror of Nature*, was a critique of the foundationalist approach to major problems in philosophy, such as the mind/body dichotomy and theories of knowledge.[13] Rorty's stress on the contingency of knowledge is one of the recurring themes of his writing, and provides the basis for many other components of his work. An example of this is Rorty's conception of the limited role that a philosopher can play in society and politics. This is a familiar theme that can be detected in his early publications, but continues to be of interest to him. Rorty suggests that it is a mistake to assume or to claim that philosophers have anything relevant to offer on questions of social policy.[14] The most a philosopher can hope to contribute is limited advice on the best way to combine or understand certain traditions of thought, but not any single vision of what is valuable or right.[15] The idea that philosophers should reject the role of social critic is the central theme of *Contingency, Irony and Solidarity*. Rorty argues that the central thesis of the book – that philosophical speculation is an essentially private matter – opened the way for his argument that no reconciliation is necessary between one's private philosophical attachments and public obligations.[16] The call to 'privatize' philosophy is also interwoven with Rorty's later writing on democracy.

Rorty's conception of the contingency of knowledge is also responsible for his identification as a postmodernist. Even in this, however, he remains ambiguous. He defines his version of postmodernism, via the work of Lyotard, as a 'distrust of metanarratives',[17] but elsewhere claims that he finds postmodernism 'philosophically right though politically silly'.[18] Rorty expresses a distaste for those aspects of postmodern theory devoted to identifying and deconstructing ideological contradictions, or what he calls 'cultural politics'. Rorty is postmodernist, in so far as he is prepared to question all philosophical foundations. Nevertheless, he does not align himself with what he sees as the postmodernist urge for 'transgressive' thinking, which Rorty identifies as an over-focus on 'cultural politics', at the expense of attempts to mobilize democratic institutions in order to address existing problems of oppression.[19]

Despite the ambiguous and contradictory nature of Rorty's self-characterizations, they signal the importance that he places upon belonging to particular communities, and with this, the shared meanings, vocabulary and dialogue that accompany that belonging. The metaphor of inquiry as an ongoing public conversation forms a central part of Rorty's epistemology.[20] His work on democracy, for example, is often written in response to issues that others, such as Dewey or Rawls, have raised. His most explicit analysis of democracy, the essay 'The priority of democracy to philosophy', is in part a commentary on Rawls's *Theory of Justice*.[21] Rorty acknowledges other influences that include the poet Harold Bloom and the philosopher of language, Donald Davidson.[22] It is Dewey's influence, however, that is particularly significant for the way Rorty theorizes the links between democracy, pragmatism and justification.

Rorty's Philosophical Approach and the Implications for Democracy

Rorty has maintained an interest in the work of American pragmatist John Dewey from his earliest writings to the present day.[23] Rorty inherited from Dewey a pragmatist argument against the need for secure foundations of knowledge. Rorty also draws upon Dewey's argument against the necessity to justify liberal democracy using foundationalist standards, on the pragmatic grounds that it is simply not a particularly useful thing to do. Rorty defines pragmatism as 'antiessentialism applied to notions like "truth" . . . and similar objects of philosophical theorizing'.[24] Rorty says of Dewey that he would accept happily that the only possible justification of democracy will be a 'circular justification of our practices . . . which makes one feature of our culture look good by citing still another, or comparing our culture invidiously with others by reference to our own standards'.[25] Rorty argues that, for pragmatists, 'the pattern of all inquiry – scientific as well as moral – is deliberation concerning the relative attractions of various concrete alternatives.'[26] This is opposed to inquiry or justification directed by the idea that what we see corresponds with truth or reality, or what Dewey disparaged as 'the spectator theory of knowledge'.[27]

This claim about the relationship between representation and reality is central to Rorty's theory of knowledge. For Rorty, an anti-representationalist is one who can ignore the question 'Are we representing reality accurately?' and instead focus on asking 'Are there more useful conceptual instruments at our disposal?'[28] In this instance, the term 'useful' signals the pragmatic basis of the justification, but Rorty does not go into detail about what is meant by 'useful'. Elsewhere, he seems to equate the 'usefulness' of knowledge with efficiency. He suggests that, instead of inquiring into whether our beliefs are contradictory, we should concern ourselves with the question of whether or not 'our use of [linguistic] tools is inefficient'.[29] Furthermore, in *Consequences of Pragmatism*, Rorty argues that adopting a pragmatic approach to knowledge means viewing different branches of inquiry, for example science and art, as different ways in which to ask the 'questions about what will help us get what we want (or about what we *should* want)'.[30] Thus 'useful', in Rorty's terms, can signify something that is efficient, as well as instrumental. What is not significant is whether or not knowledge can be said to correspond to objective 'fact'.

According to Rorty, this anti-representationalism is not the equivalent of complete epistemological scepticism. Rorty claims that we should make a distinction 'between the claim that the world is out there and the claim that truth is out there'.[31] This is not the same as claiming that thought determines reality. It serves, rather, to deny the significance of terms like 'reality' and 'truth' and to replace them with the idea that if our vocabularies seem to be coherent and appropriate to our own circumstances, then we should be content to use them until convinced otherwise.[32] This constitutes a pragmatic commitment to the utility of knowledge and an examination of the consequences of that knowledge, as opposed to judgements based upon the supposed truth-value of any one way of talking about something.

Rorty does not pretend to isolate his own beliefs from this fundamental epistemological uncertainty. This is reflected in the emphasis that he places on the concept of contingency. Rorty argues that we have to be able to accept that our beliefs about our selves and our communities are subject to revision at any time, should our circumstances or vocabularies change.[33] Contingency means that any of our dearly held beliefs or practices always remain open to question, or subject to what Rorty calls redescription.

The term 'redescription' is used by Rorty to explain what he thinks of as the new 'method' of philosophy, as opposed to the main foundationalist Enlightenment tradition. Redescription basically refers to the practice of installing a new vocabulary to replace an old, worn-out one. Rorty argues that redescription is the process by which our old vocabularies switch over to new ones. The move from one vocabulary to another does not come about (as it might in foundationalist terms) because the latter vocabulary is carefully tested and eventually found to have a closer relationship to the truth. Instead, Rorty argues that the shift 'works holistically and pragmatically', as people come to see, in a new vocabulary, things that are more useful and coherent to them than those in the old.[34]

This sort of anti-foundationalism is often criticized as the first step towards a moral relativism that is incapable of condemning great evils such as Nazism. That spectre is raised to argue against the idea that community standards of behaviour, meaning and knowledge are only contingent, and are decided upon the basis of communal agreement, or solidarity. Rorty, however, denies that he is a relativist. His argument is that there is no way of knowing whether our beliefs correspond to reality, not that all beliefs have an equal claim to being true or false. This is a fine distinction, but important in the context of Rorty's treatment of democracy. A relativist position, besides being self-refuting, does not allow the relativist to criticize other beliefs. Rorty's approach, as I will outline later, enables him to be consciously ethnocentric, and thus to argue that Western liberal democratic norms are the best, at present, for our own communities.

Rorty applies the same anti-foundationalism to his theory of human nature, which is again central to his critique of democratic theorists such as Walzer and Taylor. This theory of human nature emerges from Rorty's theory of knowledge and, in particular, his argument on the contingency of our language, knowledge and selfhood. Rorty argues that 'there is nothing deep inside each of us, no common human nature, no built-in human solidarity, to use as a moral reference point.'[35] As a consequence, he thinks that theorists who construct models of democracy based upon the concept of a shared selfhood that extends beyond the bounds of local community are engaged in the wrong kind of thinking. Rorty nominates his own theory of the self as 'a centerless web of historically conditioned beliefs and desires'.[36] Nevertheless, he is content to acknowledge that this model of the self will not suffice for anyone with metaphysical persuasions that differ from his own. Rorty's point is that just as people's religious convictions do not, for the most part, prevent them being good and useful citizens of liberal democracies, so too may their philosophical convictions be regarded as equally private in a liberal democracy.

The Critique of Democratic Theorizing

It is possible to see, therefore, how Rorty's critique of democratic theory derives from his theory of knowledge. Rorty argues against foundationalist justifications of democracy because he regards them not only as pointless, but also as genuinely harmful. Rorty argues that they can be harmful because asking those kinds of question could distract us from the real business of liberal democracies, which he suggests ought to be the prevention of suffering and cruelty.[37]

Rorty's main query about democracy, therefore, is largely concerned with whether foundationalist democratic theory offers a better route towards preventing suffering and cruelty than non-foundationalist theory. Rorty approaches this issue through the question of whether we really need to theorize about or justify the philosophical foundations of democratic institutions. It is fundamentally an argument about the relationship of a certain kind of theory to the practice of democracy.

Rorty argues that we can get along by 'benignly' ignoring the philosophical justifications, crude or complex, that Bernstein, Walzer, Taylor, MacIntyre and others want to provide. These justifications are largely motivated, in Rorty's view, by the idea that liberal democracy 'either should not or cannot survive the collapse of the philosophical justification that the Enlightenment provided for [it]'.[38] For Rorty, these attempts at justification, with their attendant conceptions of the citizen, or theories of rights, human nature, the good, or the just, are entirely unnecessary. From the standpoint of Rorty's anti-representationalist epistemology, any statements about democracy, or prescriptions for it that claim to be based upon truth or morality, will only ever be contingent in any case. The best that Rorty can offer by way of justification is to say, pragmatically, that Western liberal democracy works, upon the basis of comparison with concrete historical alternatives.

It is from this perspective that Rorty asserts that democracy is prior to philosophy. By 'prior', Rorty means that democracy does not need philosophical justification. The successful practice of democracy provides its own justification. Furthermore, Rorty suggests that 'When the two come into conflict, democracy takes precedence over philosophy.'[39] Because Rorty distrusts 'grand theory', he regards the democratic procedure of tolerant conversation as more important than any kind of philosophical foundation. This is a claim about the irrelevance of a certain kind of theory to practice, but also a claim about the proper place of philosophy as being separate from public life. Human solidarity does not emerge from anything philosophers might think or say, but from a shared sense of community, belonging and tradition.

Rorty argues that we do not need conceptions of universal human nature, or human rights, in order to judge whether or not our liberal democratic institutions live up to their promise. A theory of human nature or the self cannot provide liberal democracy with a basis for anything. Rorty claims that 'for purposes of liberal social theory, one can do without such a model. One can get along with common sense and social science, areas of discourse in which the term "the self" rarely occurs.'[40] Rorty does see a need for something to provide the 'communal self-reassurance of the modern democratic societies', but suggests that this job is better performed by those he calls 'superficial dreamers', and he nominates, for example, Martin Luther King and H. G. Wells, amongst others. Rorty suggests that these thinkers are valuable because they can 'supply local hope, not universal knowledge'.[41]

Rorty claims that the proper role for philosophers is not to provide expert knowledge for the public realm; philosophy should be a private activity. In *Contingency, Irony and Solidarity*, he indicates the political significance of his approach:

> the compromise advocated in this book amounts to saying: *Privatise* the Nietzschean–Sartrean–Foucauldian attempt at authenticity and purity, in order to prevent yourself from slipping into a political attitude which will lead you to think that there is some social goal more important than avoiding cruelty.[42]

What Rorty is suggesting is that philosophical deliberation is not a particularly 'useful' activity for a democratic society. Speculation about what is true or just or right becomes a pursuit to be indulged in at one's leisure, having no purpose beyond individual reassurance or self-gratification, and no consequences beyond those of any other private pursuit.

Rorty argues that attempts to justify liberal democratic theory by recourse to transcendental conceptions of human nature should be regarded in the same way that previous democratic theorists regarded religious beliefs. That is, they have no place in providing foundations for democracy. Rorty gives an example of someone who might have an objectionable Nietzschean world view with which they indulge themselves 'philosophically' in private, while they remain publicly 'loyal' to their liberal democratic society. This is possible because such individuals recognize that one of the virtues of a liberal democratic state is that it is indifferent to their private philosophical belief.[43]

Rorty's Defence of Liberal Democracy

Rorty's argument about the strength of the procedural framework of liberal democracy leads to the second theme in his writing about democracy. Despite the emphasis upon contingency in his theory of knowledge, Rorty rejects the label 'relativist', and does not argue that 'anything goes' when deciding on an appropriate democratic procedure and framework. He makes a strong defence of Western liberal democracy. Occasionally, this slides into a more specific defence of American democracy, although he never establishes clearly his own position in respect to the many American democratic traditions.[44] He has argued, for example, that

> I see America pretty much as Whitman and Dewey did, as opening a prospect on illimitable democratic vistas. I think that our country – despite

its past and present atrocities and vices . . . is a good example of the best kind of society so far invented.[45]

This is an unequivocal defence of American democracy, which he must then reconcile with his anti-foundationalism. Rorty chooses to argue that his liberal vocabulary should have priority because it is the only one that allows us, at present, to be fully inclusive. In an interview, Rorty was asked to explain the difference between justifying something on the grounds that it is the will of God, and justifying something by simply saying that it is a central part of the liberal vocabulary. Rorty replied that the difference is 'that it's not just crucial to your liberal vocabulary, it's crucial to the vocabulary that got us all in the public square as citizens of a democracy. It's not just my vocabulary, it's one which we all have to use when we get together.'[46] In other words, Rorty will defend a secular, liberal democracy, because he sees it as the only vocabulary that will enable everyone to participate in the public sphere.

It is here that Rorty's postmodernism, defined as a distrust of foundations, seems to be inconsistent with his strong defence of liberal democracy. He argues that 'the vocabulary of Enlightenment rationalism, although it was essential to the beginnings of liberal democracy, has become an impediment to the preservation and progress of democratic societies.'[47] Rorty's postmodernism is of a very specific and rather peculiar kind that is directed largely against what he sees as the foundationalism of our metaphysical hangovers from the Enlightenment tradition. As Bernstein suggests, this target is questionable, for sometimes it appears as if Rorty is attacking only the most crude foundationalist.[48]

The tension between epistemological uncertainty and what seems to be a more conservative commitment to community produces two different strands in Rorty's writing on democracy. Much of his critique of democratic theorizing derives from his postmodernist epistemology, while his defence of North American liberal democracy relies on tradition and on the solidarity of the community voice. The two strands seem to run counter to each other, as one is a claim about contingency, and the other constitutes a definite attachment to one particular model of democracy.

Rorty tries to reconcile the tension between contingency and attachment in two ways. First, he argues that what democratic societies need is not the kind of justifications provided by philosophers, but only a procedural framework that enables tolerant conversation about the ends and means of that society. This can be accompanied, if desired, by private philosophical deliberation over substantive commitments. But Rorty argues that the public framework ought to be limited to establishing the procedural guidelines under which conversation can take place. In the following section, I indicate how Rorty establishes a sharp distinction between procedural and substantive claims, in order to make this argument. The second way to resolve the tension between Rorty's postmodernist epistemology and his allegiance to liberal democracy is through the notion of solidarity. This is the idea that only community beliefs and values can provide (non-foundational) justification for a democratic society.[49] This argument is based on a deliberate ethnocentrism that enables Rorty to claim that a certain model of liberal democracy is better for us, because it is part of our tradition.

Procedure and Substance

As argued above, Rorty suggests that the procedural framework of liberal democracy is that which enables the 'conversation' of liberal democracy to continue without philosophical justification. To explain this further, Rorty has also used the metaphor of a bazaar, where people of all beliefs meet and contract their business, despite the fact that there might be violent philosophical disagreements between participants. But the philosophy is left till after the bazaar has closed, when the participants retire to the equivalent of an exclusive 'English gentleman's club' and enjoy philosophy privately to their heart's content.[50] For Rorty, this presents itself as the only solution to the problem of the collapse of our belief in the foundational standards of the Enlightenment, and the necessity for some framework within which to conduct the ongoing 'conversation' of liberal democracy.

Rorty is adamant that this procedural framework can stand alone without philosophical justification. Instead of relying on philosophy for reassurance, Rorty argues that democratic society needs only a process of 'reflective equilibrium'.[51] He borrows the phrase 'reflective equilibrium' from Rawls, who defines it as the 'mutual adjustment of principles and considered judgments'.[52] It is the process of ensuring that principles and judgements concur, and that the source of these principles has been the subject of reflection. Rorty argues that what democracy needs is not a ' "philosophical framework" of concepts', but rather a procedural framework, such as reflective equilibrium, with no substantive content.[53] Rorty's objection to nominating substantive goals seems to be only that it leads to justifying things by using philosophy. Rorty objects because he regards this kind of justification, as I indicated earlier, either as pointless and condescending, or as a harmful distraction.[54] For Rorty, notions of procedural justice and equality can be understood as 'parochial, recent, eccentric cultural developments', but still be understood as worth preserving.[55] They are to be defended by comparisons with concrete alternatives, however, on the pragmatic grounds that these concepts help us to understand and achieve the kind of society we want, not by appeals to foundational concepts or universal truths.[56]

Rorty acknowledges that his argument for an appropriate procedural framework resembles Habermas's model of communicative action. He thinks that he agrees with Habermas that 'A liberal society is one which is content to call "true" (or "right" or "just") whatever the outcome of undistorted communication happens to be, whatever view wins in a free and open encounter.'[57] According to Rorty, at least in respect to the procedural form that the public sphere should take, there is little to choose between his own position and that of Habermas. Their main point of difference, according to Rorty, lies in the realm of the 'merely philosophical', because Habermas retains a commitment to establishing universalist and rationalist norms.[58] Rorty writes that he finds it possible to 'go along with Habermas up to the point at which he opts for universalism, and then swerve off'.[59] In response to Habermas opting for a grounded rationalism, Rorty replies that he is content to 'go intersubjective . . . [but not] universalist'.[60] This is easy enough to do, he argues, simply by accepting that philosophy is not, in itself, particularly relevant to politics, whereas community and intersubjectivity are.

Rorty recognizes that there is a danger that the outcome of a tolerant, rational procedure might not always be tolerant itself. He suggests that liberal democracies already have the means for avoiding this by 'lending an ear to the specialists in particularity'.[61] Rorty contends that bourgeois liberal democracy can 'reassure' itself by employing what he calls 'connoisseurs of diversity and guardians of universality'.[62] 'Reassure' may seem a peculiar choice of word, but Rorty uses it to indicate a kind of moral justification for community that is not linked to universal values. He identifies 'agents of care' (for example, sociologists, journalists, and anthropologists, but, predictably, not philosophers) who bring diversity to the attention of the 'agents of justice'. Rorty argues that liberal democracies already function by adhering to tenets of procedural justice, but also by employing 'specialists in particularity . . . [whose function is to] . . . continue to expand our moral imagination'.[63] Their purpose is to balance the universalist nature of procedural justice, by reminding the community of the existence and significance of diversity.

Deliberate Ethnocentrism

Rorty's deliberate ethnocentrism allows him to prioritize liberal tolerance, or at least to do so until another vocabulary emerges that seems more useful than the procedures of liberal democracy. In this case, 'useful' might refer to the ability of a particular vocabulary to serve people's interests. According to Rorty's method of 'redescription', the supporters of a new vocabulary would seek to redescribe present liberal procedures and past and future conceptions of representation, participation and justice. For example, one of the key goals of feminism could be outlined in Rortyan terms as the need to redescribe our understanding of the public/private split, to enable women to be seen as full citizens.

But even if such a redescription were to take place, the whole process still remains a fundamentally liberal procedure. Rorty's model of democracy could compel people to submit tolerantly and openmindedly to all conversation designed to convince them to use other vocabularies, whether they were provided by a Rortyan liberal or by a feminist. So Rorty never moves away from this liberal procedural framework that he maintains is the only guarantee of free debate in the public sphere. Rorty tries to escape the criticism that he, in effect, universalizes liberal democratic norms and procedures by arguing that his model should be read as deliberately ethnocentric.

Rorty suggests that Western liberals who have not 'gone postmodern' are virtually forced to be ethnocentric, because the concept of human equality, upon which criticism of ethnocentrism is based, is a 'Western eccentricity'.[64] In other words, those who argue against ethnocentrism often do so on the basis of a set of moral concepts that are themselves a product of a particular culture and historical moment. The postmodern liberal, according to Rorty, can accept that liberal procedures are ethnocentric, but they still provide the best framework for all the different cultures of the world to coexist, even those that would reject the principles of tolerant liberalism.

Critique

The democratic theory that emerges from Rorty's work is not always a coherent or convincing one. Rorty has attracted much criticism, both for perceived contradictions in his anti-foundationalist approach to knowledge, and also for what some regard as his conservatism in championing Western liberal democracy. Bernstein, for example, argues that Rorty's work is 'an ideological *apologia* for an old-fashioned version of cold war liberalism dressed up in fashionable "post-modern" discourse'.[65] Although maintaining a strong critique of Rorty's epistemology and politics, in a later essay Bernstein allows that Rorty's work poses important challenges, and his controversial style helps to enliven the discipline of philosophy by questioning some of our most dearly held beliefs.[66] Wolin, in an otherwise critical essay, suggests that perhaps there is a distinctive merit in Rorty's work that stems from the juxtaposition of postmodern theory with democracy. As Wolin sees it, explicit treatment of democratic issues is a rare occurrence in postmodern theory.[67]

Unfortunately, Rorty does not elaborate on which of the many different forms of democracy he supports, beyond nominating basic institutions such as 'the vote, the newspapers, the community organizations' as important.[68] As Bernstein argues, he seems to operate with a nominalist assumption that the meaning of 'liberal democracy' is fairly obvious to all.[69] Rorty does occasionally refer separately to liberalism and democracy but more commonly combines them as one political model. This is not entirely unreasonable, for there is a strong convergence between liberalism and Western democracy.[70] Nevertheless, the two are not identical, and the differences between them remain a source of contention. Wolin, for example, suggests that Rorty's focus on the privatization of philosophy is not democratic at all, and argues that a rigid distinction between the public and private spheres 'is not what democracy is importantly about', citing instead 'equality and the belief that public power should be devoted to common endeavors'.[71] On the other side of the political spectrum, theorists of the new right such as Friedrich Hayek also reject too close an association of democracy with liberalism, from the perspective that the value of liberty should take precedence over democracy, in the sense of the will of the people.[72]

Rorty's theory of liberal democracy is of a specific kind. His conception of liberty is a negative one, and therefore the role of the public sphere is deliberately kept to a minimum. Because there can be no certain knowledge, public intervention or direction always has the potential to destroy unnecessarily the liberty of an individual. It is not clear, however, why Rorty has to reject substantive claims in favour of a procedural framework. Indeed, his philosophy contains substantive commitments to principles of tolerance, accommodation, anti-cruelty and human equality.

Nonetheless, Rorty suggests that the substantive content of democracy will be worked out in the process of public debate, but this assumes a fully inclusive and equal public space. Rorty's theory of democracy is based on the assumption that citizens are equal, and that the liberal public sphere is fully inclusive for all participants. Feminists, for example, would want to argue that this is demonstrably not the case. It also assumes a free private sphere, another common liberal assumption that is equally problematic. As Nancy Fraser argues, this assumption ignores the lessons of the social movements of the past century that 'have taught us to see the power-laden, and therefore political, character of interactions that classical liberalism considered private'.[73] Wolin is also critical of the way that Rorty's notion of 'private identity is, by definition, severed from public obligations to others'.[74] Wolin questions the sharp distinction between the two in Rorty's work, and suggests that he shields the public/private distinction from the contestability and contingency that he would ascribe to most other beliefs.

By arguing that differences between participants in the public sphere can be reduced to the 'merely' philosophical and thus relegated to the private sphere, Rorty evades the question of whether procedural justice and liberal institutions might contain biases. In Rorty's account, these procedures seem to all intents and purposes to be neutral, a claim that is open to dispute. Such an assumption could lead to a dangerous compla-cency on the part of liberal democratic communities. The political conse-quences of such complacency might be that as long as the procedural requirements of discussion were taking place, widespread inequalities need not be addressed.

The further danger of a complacent reliance on the procedural justice of the public realm is evident when one examines the kind of philosophy that Rorty says should be 'privatized'. On the one hand, Rorty talks about the need to 'privatize' universalist philosophy such as theories of human nature and theories of foundational knowledge. On the other hand, he also urges the privatization of the selfish, anti-democratic beliefs of the 'ironist', that contravene the tolerant and utilitarian character of Rorty's public sphere. But there are other kinds of theory that do not conform to either of these characterizations. Feminist theorists, for example, seek to examine the gendered power relations embedded in both the public and the private spheres.[75] Rorty imposes a rigid dichotomy between the Enlightenment rationalist philosopher on the one hand, and the postmodern liberal ironist on the other. Both are invited to confine their philosophical concerns to the private sphere, and to leave the public sphere free for liberal procedural justice. Unfortunately, what seems then to be lost is the opportunity for genuine critique of these procedures and insti-tutions, and the substantive values that shape them. According to Rorty, those who wish to provide critical perspectives on procedures and values either can do so in the non-political private sphere, or will have to engage in the process of 'redescription' persuasively enough to ensure a shift in the 'vocabulary' of that particular community.

Wolin criticizes the concept of redescription as being deeply apolitical, arguing that Rorty subscribes to a theory of history that attributes all social change to the manipulation of language.[76] The claim that language has a constructive function is not unique to Rorty. Indeed, it could be said to be one of the few defining features of postmodern theory as a whole. But in Rorty's model of democracy, it seems to be regarded as a relatively benign process. Rorty even describes it as the newest philosophical method whereby change comes about by redescribing existing practices so that they conform properly to the self-image of a community. Rorty uses the terminology of historian of science Thomas Kuhn, who identified revolutionary breakthroughs in science as 'paradigm shifts'. Kuhn suggested that once such a breakthrough had been made, there could be no return to the previous way of viewing something.[77] To use Rorty's terms, the 'vocabulary' of science permanently changes. This comparison becomes problematic, however, when Rorty extends Kuhn's theory to explain shifts in a community's self-perception. To apply this as a theory of social change ignores the deep political struggles, both material and ideological, that accompany such shifts. One of the key goals of the feminist movement, for example, has arisen out of the struggle to articulate women's experiences. Part of the project has been to uncover gaps in political and epistemological theory caused by the prior neglect of these experiences.[78] This is more than a linguistic manoeuvre; there is real power at stake in this kind of redescription. If viewed only as shifts in vocabulary, these struggles are stripped of their political importance, and their implications for power in both the public and private spheres.

Conclusion

I have argued that Rorty's interest in democracy is, for the most part, a concern with criticizing how democracy itself is treated by philosophers and political theorists. In his own terms, it is a theory about the vocabulary of democracy. Accordingly, it is largely a negative critique. Rorty makes few positive prescriptions for the theory or practice of democracy. Those writers he does cite with approval are often novelists, such as Orwell or Nabokov, or popular political leaders like Martin Luther King, not philosophers.

Norman Geras suggests that because of the stress that Rorty places on continuing debate, his postmodern bourgeois liberalism is more radical and more humane than previous forms of liberalism. In other words, at least in a liberal utopia where almost everything is contingent, this means that everything is up for public discussion.[79] But Rorty's work plainly relies on some claims that are not treated as contingently as some of his other commitments. Not everything is up for question. For example, Rorty prioritizes the procedure of tolerant conversation, which is essentially communicative action without foundations. He advocates tolerance and anti-cruelty as central values, but it is not clear why and on what grounds. Those values are unjustifiable, according to his own epistemology. Nonetheless, it is not clear why Rorty is prepared to accept these as legitimate because they are part of our liberal democratic tradition. He is not prepared to examine any of the other substantive values that are part of that same democratic tradition, or recognize some of our other competing or complementary traditions. Rorty's desires to eliminate cruelty and suffering are laudable and challenging aims, but they can be no more than arbitrary commitments. Rorty suggests that we should accept these commitments because they have resonance with familiar ways of talking about things within our communities. Even in Rorty's own terms, however, the vocabularies of Western democracies, not to mention those of other parts of the world, seem richer and more complex than this.

These criticisms should not detract entirely from the significance of Rorty's work on democracy. Postmodernism has offered a major challenge to the way in which theorists approach the issues of the foundations of political theory and practice. Postmodern claims about the contingency of knowledge are often castigated as being the first step along the road to relativism, which leads to an inability to act politically. Rorty's vigorous defence of 'postmodern bourgeois liberalism' is an attempt to reconcile what are often regarded as the opposing positions of politics and postmodernity. Rorty's theory of democracy challenges the conventional wisdom that there can be no robust politics without the certainty of foundational knowledge. Nonetheless, the endpoint of his model is a politics where the exercise of power is redescribed as a linguistic shift, and nearly all opportunities for critique and change in liberal democracy are relocated to the individual private sphere, where they effectively disappear. Unfortunately, with them goes the opportunity for a genuine questioning of the procedural, substantive and philosophical values that make up Rorty's conception of contemporary liberal democracy.

Notes

1 For example, see articles by Rorty in the final section of his *Objectivity, Relativism, and Truth: Philosophical Papers Volume One* (Cambridge, Cambridge University Press, 1991). See also R. Rorty, 'Thugs and theorists: A reply to Bernstein', *Political Theory*, 15:4 (1987), 564–80.
2 Martyn Oliver, 'Towards a liberal utopia: An interview with Richard Rorty', *Times Literary Supplement* (24 June 1994), 14, and also R. Rorty, 'Posties', *London Review of Books* (3 September 1987), 11–12.
3 Bernstein has suggested that there are three interwoven motifs in Rorty's writing; Rorty's critique of philosophical foundations, an aesthetic strand which incorporates the attitude of irony and lightmindedness, and his

defence of liberal democracy. See R. J. Bernstein, 'One step forward, two steps backward: Richard Rorty on liberal democracy and philosophy', *Political Theory*, 15:4 (1987), 538–63, esp. pp. 541–2. In this chapter, I take the approach that some of the major components of the 'aesthetic strand' can be understood as mechanisms to resolve the tension between the other two approaches.

4   Rorty, *Objectivism, Relativism, and Truth*, p. 192.

5   Rorty, *Objectivity, Relativism, and Truth*, p. 197. Rorty has since indicated that the phrase 'postmodern bourgeois liberals' was not meant entirely seriously, and should merely be understood as the idea that it is possible to be 'an extreme anti-foundationalist in philosophy and be a perfectly conventional bourgeois liberal in politics without feeling any strain'. From Oliver, 'Towards a liberal utopia', p. 14.

6   R. Rorty, *Contingency, Irony and Solidarity* (Cambridge, Cambridge University Press, 1989), p. 79.

7   Rorty, 'Thugs and theorists', p. 564.

8   R. Rorty, 'Feminism, ideology, and deconstruction: A pragmatist view', in S. Zizek (ed.), *Mapping Ideology* (London, Verso, 1994), p. 228.

9   R. Rorty, 'Trotsky and the wild orchids', *Common Knowledge*, 1:3 (Winter 1992), 140–53, esp. p. 150.

10 Bernstein, 'One step forward', p. 554.

11 Rorty, 'Trotsky and the wild orchids', p. 141.

12 Rorty, 'Trotsky and the wild orchids', p. 143.

13 R. Rorty, *Philosophy and the Mirror of Nature* (Princeton, Princeton University Press, 1979).

14 R. Rorty, 'What are philosophers for?', *The Center Magazine*, XVI: 5 (1983), 40–51, esp. p. 43.

15 Rorty, 'Trotsky and the wild orchids', p. 152.

16 Rorty, 'Trotsky and the wild orchids', p. 147.

17 Rorty, *Objectivity, Relativism, and Truth*, p. 199.

18 Rorty, 'Trotsky and the wild orchids', p. 151.

19 See R. Rorty, 'Intellectuals in politics: Too far in? Too far out?', *Dissent* (Fall 1991), 483–90, esp. p. 489.

20 Rorty, *Contingency, Irony and Solidarity*, p. 67.

21 Rorty, *Objectivism, Relativism, and Truth*, pp. 175–96. Bernstein takes issue with the way Rorty ignores significant components of Rawls's theory, in order to present him as agreeing with Rorty on the question of foundations. See Bernstein, 'One step forward', pp. 545–6.

22 Nancy Fraser argues that there is a tension in Rorty's work between a romantic impulse and a pragmatic one. See N. Fraser, 'Solidarity or singularity? Richard Rorty between romanticism and technocracy', in her *Unruly Practices: Power, Discourse and Gender in Contemporary Social Theory* (Cambridge, Polity, 1989), p. 93. This same tension can be seen in whom Rorty chooses to read and write about.

23 Bernstein takes exception to Rorty's reading of Dewey, arguing that he

misinterprets him on important points. See Bernstein, 'One step forward', p. 541. This is significant, but not, I think, central to determining how Rorty's own democratic model might look. It might be one way of providing a better alternative to Rorty, but that is a different project.

24 R. Rorty, *Consequences of Pragmatism: Essays, 1972–1980* (Minneapolis, MN, University of Minnesota Press, 1982), p. 162.

25 Rorty, *Contingency, Irony and Solidarity*, p. 57. He refers also to Oakeshott and Rawls in the same context.

26 Rorty, *Consequences of Pragmatism*, p. 164.

27 Dewey quoted in Rorty, *Consequences of Pragmatism*, p. 164.

28 R. Rorty, 'We anti-representationalists: A review of Terry Eagleton's *Ideology: An Introduction*', *Radical Philosophy*, 60 (1992), 40–2, esp. p. 40.

29 Rorty, *Contingency, Irony and Solidarity*, p. 12.

30 Rorty, *Consequences of Pragmatism*, p. xliii.

31 Rorty, *Contingency, Irony and Solidarity*, pp. 4–5.

32 Rorty, *Contingency, Irony and Solidarity*, pp. 178–9.

33 Rorty, *Contingency, Irony and Solidarity*, p. 9.

34 Rorty, *Contingency, Irony and Solidarity*, p. 9. Rorty likens 'redescription' to Thomas Kuhn's idea of a revolutionary paradigm shift in scientific knowledge. See T. Kuhn, *The Structure of Scientific Revolutions*, 2nd edn (Chicago, University of Chicago Press, 1970).

35 Rorty, *Contingency, Irony and Solidarity*, p. 177.

36 Rorty, *Objectivity, Relativism, and Truth*, p. 192.

37 Rorty, *Contingency, Irony and Solidarity*, p. 63.

38 Rorty, *Objectivity, Relativism, and Truth*, p. 177.

39 Rorty, *Objectivity, Relativism, and Truth*, p. 192.

40 Rorty, *Objectivity, Relativism, and Truth*, p. 192.

41 Rorty, 'Posties', p. 12. This seems a little disingenuous, given the reliance that many of Rorty's 'superficial dreamers', such as Martin Luther King, would place upon universalist assumptions.

42 Rorty, *Contingency, Irony and Solidarity*, p. 65.

43 Rorty, *Objectivity, Relativism, and Truth*, p. 192.

44 See Margolis for an account of some of the more recent traditions, in particular the pluralist and elitist debates. M. Margolis, 'Democracy: American style', in G. Duncan (ed.), *Democratic Theory and Practice* (Cambridge, Cambridge University Press, 1983).

45 Rorty, 'Trotsky and the wild orchids', p. 141.

46 Oliver, 'Towards a liberal utopia', p. 14.

47 Rorty, *Contingency, Irony and Solidarity*, p. 44.

48 Bernstein, 'One step forward', p. 546.

49 Rorty, *Objectivity, Relativism, and Truth*, p. 200.

50 Rorty, *Objectivity, Relativism, and Truth*, p. 209.

51 Rorty, *Objectivity, Relativism, and Truth*, p. 184.

52 J. Rawls, *A Theory of Justice* (Cambridge, MA, Belknap Press of the Harvard University Press, 1971), p. 20.

53 Rorty, 'Posties', p. 12.

54 See Rorty, 'Posties', p. 12, and Rorty, *Contingency, Irony and Solidarity*, p. 63, respectively.

55 Rorty, *Objectivity, Relativism, and Truth*, p. 208.

56 Rorty, *Objectivity, Relativism, and Truth*, p. 211.

57 Rorty, *Contingency, Irony and Solidarity*, p. 67.

58 Rorty, *Contingency, Irony and Solidarity*, p. 67.

59 Rorty, 'Posties', p. 12.

60 Rorty, 'Posties', p. 12.

61 Rorty, *Objectivity, Relativism, and Truth*, p. 201.

62 Rorty, *Objectivity, Relativism, and Truth*, p. 206.

63 Rorty, *Objectivity, Relativism, and Truth*, p. 207.

64 Rorty, *Objectivity, Relativism, and Truth*, p. 207.

65 Bernstein, 'One step forward', p. 556.

66 R. J. Bernstein, 'Rorty's liberal utopia', *Social Research*, 57:1 (Spring 1990), 31–72, esp. p. 72.

67 Sheldon Wolin, 'Democracy in the discourse of postmodernism', *Social Research*, 57 (Summer 1990), 5–30. For further discussion of postmodern approaches to democracy, including Rorty, Heller and Feher, and Laclau and Mouffe, see M. Saward, 'Postmodernists, pragmatists and the justification of democracy', *Economy and Society*, 23:2 (1994), 201–16.

68 Rorty, 'Intellectuals in politics', p. 489.

69 Bernstein, 'One step forward', p. 547.

70 D. Held, *Models of Democracy* (Cambridge, Polity, 1987), p. 5.

71 Wolin, 'Democracy in the discourse of postmodernism', p. 25.

72 Hayek in Held, *Models of Democracy*, p. 248.

73 Fraser, 'Solidarity or singularity?', p. 102.

74 Wolin, 'Democracy in the discourse of postmodernism', p. 14.

75 Fraser, 'Solidarity or singularity', p. 104.

76 Wolin, 'Democracy in the discourse of postmodernism', pp. 19–20.

77 Kuhn, *The Structure of Scientific Revolutions*, p. 111.

78 N. Hartsock, *Money, Sex and Power: Toward a Feminist Historical Materialism* (New York, Longman, 1983).

79 N. Geras, *Solidarity in the Conversation of Humankind: The Ungroundable Liberalism of Richard Rorty* (London, Verso, 1995), p. 88.

6

John Rawls: Liberal Democracy Restated

Jonathan Wolff

Contemporary English-language political philosophy began in 1971,[1] with the publication of John Rawls's *A Theory of Justice*,[2] and the announcement of a new journal *Philosophy and Public Affairs*. No doubt (to adopt Rawls's own idiom) this puts things too strongly, but for many Rawls is the defining figure for late-twentieth-century English-language political philosophy. I say 'political philosophy' rather than 'political theory' for Rawls writes as a philosopher turning his attention to matters of politics, rather than as an activist in politics looking for philosophical underpinnings for a political view. Rawls's influence – both as inspiration and as object of criticism – is beyond measure. A flood of books and journal articles followed the publication of *A Theory of Justice*, and if anything the pace has subsequently increased in response to the publication of his second book, *Political Liberalism*, in 1993.[3]

It is his theory of justice, and not any doctrines about democracy, for which Rawls is celebrated, and while he says that he writes to address problems that occur in the context of modern democratic societies, there is in his work little direct defence, or even discussion, of the institutional and procedural requirements of a democratic state. Nevertheless, as we shall see, Rawls mounts a short but powerful defence of the idea of a liberal constitutional democracy. While the system he advocates may in broad outline seem little different to those already to be found in many modern democracies, we shall also see that he is very far from an uncritical advocate of the status quo.

First I shall present the general outlines of Rawls's theory of justice, and then summarize some of his main thoughts about democracy. The following three sections pick up three major themes in Rawls's thinking here: how to ensure that everyone's rights to vote and to stand for office do not become devalued (what Rawls calls ensuring the 'fair value of political liberty'); the grounds on which people should vote; and why majority rule is valuable. Through consideration of these issues I hope to show why we should come to see liberal constitutional democracy as a profound philosophical and political achievement, rather than as the commonplace fact of life it so often seems to be.

Background

John Rawls was born in 1921 in Baltimore. His first teaching post was at Princeton and he was a Fulbright Fellow at Oxford in 1952. He taught philosophy at Cornell and the Massachusetts Institute of Philosophy before moving to Harvard in 1962, where he has spent the great part of his working life as Professor of Philosophy. He has lived the life of an academic philosopher, rather than that of a public figure, and has not been tempted to play a more active role in politics, despite the wide influence and dissemination of his views. Clearly he feels that his contribution – his life's work – is through his published ideas, which should be allowed to speak for themselves. He has published little about his motivations or inspirations. Indeed, Rawls's only published memoir accompanies his photograph in a book *Philosophers*, by Steve Pyke, and reads in its entirety:

> From the beginning of my study of philosophy in my late teens I have been concerned with moral questions and the religious and philosophical basis on which they might be answered. Three years spent in the US Army in World War II led me to be concerned with political questions. Around 1950 I started to write a book on justice, which I eventually completed.[4]

That book was *A Theory of Justice*, often regarded as the most important work of moral or political philosophy of the twentieth century.

Justice as Fairness

Why has Rawls's theory of justice proved so influential? The brief answer is that he puts forward a clear theory, briefly statable though requiring lengthy articulation, together with a novel, intriguing and highly plausible argument. Rawls's theory has provoked three separate, though related, issues for discussion: whether the theory was acceptable; whether the argumentative method was sound; and whether the method justified the

theory. Thus, three types of political philosopher were immediately drawn
into debate with Rawls: those interested in substantive political theory;
those interested in methodology; and those interested in detailed, intricate
argument. Such debates go some way to explaining Rawls's importance,
although it must be added that his theory is highly attractive in its own
right, and backed by deep reflection and impressive research. But it should
not be overlooked that Rawls was writing at a time in which political
philosophy seemed to have become exhausted. Rawls was little less than a
liberation.

It has been said that before Rawls there were only two options in
political philosophy: utilitarianism, or no theory at all. This perfectly sums
up how Rawls too saw the position. As *A Theory of Justice* opens, Rawls
immediately sets himself against two opponents. The first is the utilitarian
who believes that to bring about the good society we should maximize
total or average happiness. The second is the intuitionist who believes that
there are many values but no principled way of settling the matter if we
find that they clash. For example, if we can increase the general standard
of living but only by reducing liberty, the intuitionist suggests we must
simply rely on our strongest feelings on a case by case basis. Rawls's project
is to find a path incorporating the theoretical rigour of utilitarianism and
the value pluralism of intuitionism, while avoiding utilitarianism's pre-
paredness to sacrifice the individual and intuitionism's failure to provide a
rational decision-making procedure. These are the demanding conditions
he sets out to satisfy, by means of a revival of a Kantian approach to
politics.

Rawls calls his theory of justice 'justice as fairness' and at its heart are
what he calls his 'two principles of justice':

First principle
Each person is to have an equal right to the most extensive total system of
equal basic liberties compatible with a similar system of liberty for all.

Second principle
Social and economic inequalities are to be arranged so that they are both:
(a) to the greatest benefit of the least advantaged . . . and
(b) attached to offices and positions open to all under conditions of fair
     equality of opportunity.[5]

The first principle is the *liberty principle*. Of the second principle, part (a)
is the *difference principle*, and part (b) is the *fair opportunity principle*.
According to Rawls the *liberty principle* has 'lexical priority' over the
second principle. What this means, for Rawls, is that considerations of

liberty should have absolute priority over matters of economic advancement, or equality of opportunity. On this account, for example, it is no defence of slavery that it makes the slaves better off than they would be with their freedom. For enforced slavery is inconsistent with equal liberty, and so must give way even if it has economic advantages for the slaves. The only exception to lexical priority is that in conditions of grave material scarcity or crisis it may be acceptable to limit liberty if this is necessary in order to produce enough material goods to keep us all alive and well. Nevertheless, once society has reached a sufficient level of material well-being, liberty must always take further priority.

We can see how this position satisfies the demands Rawls sets for an acceptable theory, and thus combines the advantages of both utilitarianism and intuitionism while avoiding their pitfalls. Theoretical rigour and rational decision-making are ensured by incorporating the idea of lexical priority, which gives an answer in every case, while value pluralism is guaranteed by the inclusion of each of liberty, satisfaction of material need (by means of the difference principle) and equality of opportunity. Finally, the potential victimization allowed by utilitarianism is avoided by guaranteeing the liberty of every individual.

I mentioned above the originality of Rawls's method of arguing for these principles. In general terms he uses what is known as a 'hypothetical contract' method, derived, Rawls says, from thinkers in the social contract tradition, especially Locke, Rousseau and Kant. Rawls's idea is that people hypothetically placed in a certain position – what he calls the *original position* – would come to agree upon these principles, and this shows that they are the correct principles of justice.

The basic idea behind the use of this methodology is the thought that people often disagree about issues of justice because they are biased by their own point of view. If you expect a decision to affect you in a particular way, your appraisal of its justice may well be coloured by these expectations. Accordingly, we should expect far fewer disputes about the requirements of justice if the interests of those making the judgements are not involved. Similarly, if your own interests are involved, but you do not know how they would be affected, you would be much more likely to be able to overcome many of the problems of bias. Thus, ignorance about your interests can generate impartial reasoning. For this reason Rawls argues that if people were placed behind a 'veil of ignorance', not knowing their strengths, abilities, talents, social status, sex, race or personal values, then they would find it rational to agree to his principles of justice. This, he claims, shows that his principles are the correct principles of justice. His method merely requires us to abstract from those factors which bias us in our own interests.

One question often raised is the scope of these principles. Are they intended to be universal and ahistorical, applicable in all times and places, or do they have more limited application? Conventional wisdom has it that in *A Theory of Justice* Rawls had universalistic ambitions, and that, under the pressure of criticism, his view changed during the next decade, and by 1985, with the publication of 'Justice as fairness: Political not metaphysical',[6] Rawls had become much more of a relativist.[7] For Rawls himself, though, this interpretation badly distorts his intentions in *A Theory of Justice*, for he had, he claims, always been addressing only those societies in the modern democratic tradition. His current self-interpretation is that he is drawing on ideas implicit within the political culture of modern democracy to provide principles of justice to regulate such democracies. What exactly he means by 'modern democracy', though, is not always clear. The wide interpretation is that this would include any state which finds it important to claim that it has democratic status, however dubious that claim seems in practice. This would, then, include the former Soviet Union and satellites even in their communist phase. On the other hand, upon reading *Political Liberalism*, one increasingly has the suspicion that Rawls is concentrating almost exclusively on problems and public ideas within the United States of America. This inevitably brings with it a charge of triviality: that Rawls is simply recounting what Americans already believe. What this objection overlooks, however, is that contemporary USA is very far from embodying Rawls's two principles of justice. So it would be a tremendous achievement even to show that ideas latent in its public culture provide strong support for Rawls's form of liberal egalitarianism. In any case, whatever the truth about his earlier views, Rawls is now clear that this theory is not intended to have universal scope, and for the purposes of this discussion I shall assume that *Political Liberalism* clarifies and extends some of the ideas of *A Theory of Justice*, but does not introduce any substantial new ideas which conflict with the earlier work.

Clearly a great many further questions could be (and have been) asked about Rawls's argument.[8] But the question for us is, what has any of this to do with the defence of democracy?

Rawls and Democracy

What is liberal democracy? Notoriously two separate ideas are connected with the term 'democracy': firstly, majority voting procedures; and secondly, the protection of certain rights of the individual. Equally notorious is the view that these ideas are in tension: granting too much power to the majority can lead to an oppressive state in which the rights of the minority are ignored or overturned, while granting too many constitutionally protected rights leads to a shrinking sphere of democratic decision-making. The first threat, of course, is the tyranny of the majority. The second, very important but far less discussed threat, we could call the 'enfeeblement of the political'.

I take the idea of a liberal democracy to be that of a system in which something like a correct balance is struck between the two ideas of majority rule and the protection of the minority. Thus one would typically find a constitution, written or unwritten, together with flourishing debate and decision-making in the wide areas of politics left undetermined by the constitution. Constitutionally protected rights safeguard the basic liberties of the citizen, but society can make its own decisions about less fundamental matters.

Is Rawls a liberal democrat? No one could doubt his commitment to liberalism. The desire to protect individual rights was one of the motivating forces behind *A Theory of Justice*. Indeed, in their early advertisement for the book, Harvard University Press chose to represent the message of the book by quoting the phrase: 'in a just society the rights secured by justice are not subject to political bargaining.'[9] These rights are given by Rawls's two principles of justice, with particular emphasis given to the basic liberties set out in the first principle.

Thus, one half of the idea of a liberal democracy – a liberal constitution – is strongly in evidence in *A Theory of Justice*. Where is the other half? Critics of Rawls have sometimes hinted that it is barely to be found,[10] so a truly Rawlsian society would suffer from what I have termed the enfeeblement of the political. And, indeed 'democracy', 'voting' and 'political parties' do not appear in the index. This is more a defect of the index than of the book, however, and a cross-reference to 'majority rule' solves the problem. When we examine the relevant sections of the book we find Rawls defending a fairly conventional constitutional democracy in which individuals vote for representatives in local constituencies; the representatives are assumed to belong to political parties. Despite the familiarity of this picture there are, however, a few twists of great theoretical and practical interest.

Before the twists, the basics. Rawls starts from what he terms the *principle of equal participation*. All citizens have an equal right to take part in, and to determine the outcome of, the constitutional process that establishes the laws with which they are to comply.[11] 'All sane adults, with certain generally recognized exceptions' should have the right to vote in fair, free and regularly held elections.[12] People should be free to form political parties, and the idea of a 'loyal opposition' – a party in opposition to whoever is in power, yet which accepts and respects the constitution and political process – is vital to reasonable politics.

Further, the equal right to participation means that each citizen's vote is to have equal weight, which entails in turn that constituency boundaries should be kept constantly under review by an independent body.[13] (If the constituency in which you live grows larger, then your vote is diluted and thus you begin to have a less than equal say.) In addition, all should have equal access 'at least in the formal sense' to public office.

So far this sounds like little more than a textbook description of what we actually find in contemporary liberal democracies. Rawls does go deeper, and there are three points in particular to which I want to draw attention: the 'fair value' of political liberties; voting and motivation; and intrinsic versus instrumental justifications of democracy.

The Fair Value of Political Liberties

The idea of fair value of political liberties takes up the point that all should have equal access 'at least in the formal sense' to public office. The phrase 'a formal sense' seems to indicate no more than that everyone should have the right to stand for office, or, at least, all those over a certain age. And it is true that Rawls believes that all should have such rights. But he does not stop there. He is rightly concerned that inequalities in wealth will, in practical terms, lead to inequalities in access to political power.[14]

In contemporary politics we see this phenomenon in several ways. Most obviously, political parties solicit contributions from business, from trade unions, and from wealthy individuals, and it is reasonable to believe that parties which benefit in this way will treat the interests of their major donors with greater weight in formulating policy. Thus, greater wealth can be translated into greater political influence for personal benefit. Furthermore, wealthy individuals can stand for office, and often have some chance of success, in circumstances where those of lesser wealth would find their position hopeless. The rich can spend their own money on election expenses, or encourage wealthy friends and contacts to support them. The poor may have no chance to compete. And there are many reasons why this may seem to be an undesirable situation. As John Stuart Mill observed, how can we trust anyone prepared to spend their own money on getting elected? Surely they would be looking for some return on their investment?[15]

So it has been argued that as Rawls gives high priority to equality of the basic liberties, including the right to stand for political office, and he recognizes that inequalities of wealth can lead to inequality in the right of political participation, he is logically compelled to prohibit economic inequalities. That is, he should allow no differences of income and wealth in his society.[16] This is a radical and dramatic way of ensuring that the political liberties have the same value for all. There would be no inequalities of wealth to translate into inequalities of political power. Thus we have, in effect, an argument from democracy to absolute equality of income and wealth.

Rawls is not impressed by this argument, however, and wishes to deal with the problem of the effects of differential wealth on political processes another way. After all, inequalities of wealth could be to the economic benefit of all, including the worst-off. Allowing inequalities may well create a system of incentives which would lead to more economic activity and general prosperity than a system of straight equality. This is the point of the difference principle, which says that inequalities are permissible if they make even the worst-off better off than they would be without them. If it is true that inequalities can be to the benefit of all, then it would be a pity to lose the benefits of inequality in order to equalize the right of political participation if another way can be found of doing so. Indeed, Rawls believes an alternative is available: do not allow people to turn economic advantage into political advantage.

The problem, as Rawls sees it, is not so much that people have different amounts of money, but that they are able to spend money helping one party, one person, or even themselves get elected. It is this possibility that must be ruled out. So Rawls makes what for these times is a truly radical proposal: people should not be able to spend money in an attempt to influence the electoral process. Accordingly, political parties should be funded out of taxation revenues.[17] The details of such a scheme do need to be worked out in a fair and practical way, and there are numerous possibilities, but the main point is that if people cannot spend money electioneering, then the inequalities of income and wealth permitted by the difference principle turn out to be compatible with an equal right of political participation. Rawls does not say that he wants to go as far as John Stuart Mill, and suggest that members of parliament should be unpaid (to prevent such posts being 'an object of desire to adventurers of a low class' says Mill[18]), but the logic of Rawls's position is that members of parliament should not be particularly well paid: no one should wish to become a member of parliament for the money.

Voting and Motivation

If we have a representative democracy, as Rawls advocates, then two types of voting take place within the system. First of all, ordinary citizens vote for members to represent them in the parliamentary chamber, and secondly, those representatives vote to make laws. But on what grounds should citizens and representatives vote one way rather than another?

The point, or even the meaning, of this question may seem rather unclear, but it might be best approached through a potential criticism of majority voting which Rawls attempts to defuse. The criticism is that accepting the majority view can be unfair, for members of the minority might passionately prefer their first choice, whereas members of the major- ity might have a relatively weak preference. Hence, majority voting fails to take into account intensity of preference. Rawls's response to this may seem rather dismissive. He says that the objection assumes that the vote concerns the satisfaction of preferences (that the right outcome is the one that satisfies the most preferences), but that assumption is wrong. What we seek is just and efficient legislation. Individual preferences – and therefore the strengths of individual preferences – are irrelevant.[19]

This may seem rather high-handed. After all, if preferences are irrel- evant why bother to take a vote in the first place? Behind this point, though, is a distinction of fundamental importance for democratic theory. There are a number of different ways in which we might conceive of a vote taking place. The simplest would be the thought that a democratic vote simply tells us what the majority prefer. People express their preferences, and in counting the vote we simply work out where the majority prefer- ence lies. If this was the right way of thinking about majoritarian decision- making, then the problem of 'intense preferences' would certainly be a concern. The minority might together have a stronger preference than the opposed majority. This is not, though, how Rawls thinks of democracy.

A second view is that people vote not for their particular preference, but for what they think is right. John Stuart Mill, for example, believed that this was the correct approach, arguing that the citizen's 'vote is not a thing in which he has an option; it has no more to do with his personal wishes than the verdict of a juryman. It is strictly a matter of duty; he is bound to give it according to his best and most conscientious opinion of the public good.'[20] Thus, voters should vote for what they think is the correct outcome. On this view, then, the vote reveals a majority view about what is right. Why pay any special attention to the majority on this point? We will return to this question shortly.

So does Rawls think that people should vote for what they think is right? Well, yes and no. We have to make a further distinction before we can give a proper answer. For Rawls, one of the main features of modern democracies, particularly Western or 'Western-type' democracies, is irre- ducible pluralism between conceptions of the good, or values. People within one society come from varying religions, different cultures and backgrounds, with different values, and may even speak different languages. But this does not mean we are forced into constant disagreement, for the liberal state, according to Rawls, strives to be neutral between competing conceptions of the good. The two principles of justice provide a framework for such a neutral state. Thus, he claims in *Political Liberalism*, it is possible to forge an 'overlapping consensus' among reasonable people to accept the two principles.

Nonetheless, it will be asked, what does it mean to say that people are reasonable? Who are these reasonable people? For present purposes the most important feature of reasonable people is that they accept what Rawls calls 'the burdens of judgement'. This is the idea that reasonable people understand that there are areas of life where reason alone is not sufficient to determine which view is to be preferred. Reasonable people who accept the burdens of judgement also accept that it is wrong to use state power to coerce people to comply with a view that cannot be shown to be correct. To illustrate, even if I am utterly convinced of the truth of a particular religion, I must, if I accept the burdens of judgement, accept that educated, sane, intelligent, mature people can rationally hold other views. Hence, if I am reasonable I must accept that it would be wrong for me to use state power to force my view on others.

So to return to the question. I asked whether Rawls thinks that people should vote on the basis of what they think is right. Part of his answer is that they should not vote on the basis of their own private morality. Even if a majority are absolutely convinced of the truth of, say, the Christian religion, it would nevertheless be wrong for anyone to vote to grant it state privileges, or for the state to discriminate against other religions. The burdens of judgement are too high: it cannot be shown that Christianity is correct, and therefore it would be wrong to make it the state-protected religion. Accordingly, Rawls wants us to vote according to our ideas of what could be justified to our fellow citizens, irrespective of the contents of their private moral beliefs or conceptions of the good. Thus, we should vote as equal citizens, trying to find policies that can be justified to all, and not as theologians or moralists, convinced that we know the truth.[21]

But to return to another question: if we are not interested in the voter's individual preferences, or even the voter's individual values, why bother asking the voter for a view? If we want just an efficient legislation, should we not simply ask philosophers and social scientists, and ignore the views of the majority? It is this query that leads to the claim that the apparent logic of Rawls's system enfeebles the political: that the ultimate principles of the just society are worked out from the original position and there is nothing left for the electorate to do. Our question now is why Rawls declines to follow this apparent logic.

The Values of Majority Rule

If, as Rawls says, 'There is nothing to the view . . . that what the majority wills is right',[22] then why ever bother with majoritarian decision-making? As with so many theorists, Rawls's instinct is to turn the question the other way around. If not majoritarian decision-making, then what? The only alternative is some form of minority decision-making, and what could possibly justify any group's claims to be the privileged decision-makers?

The most obvious way to argue in defence of minority rule would be to return to Rawls's claim that the purpose of democracy is to arrive at just and efficient legislation. If that is so, why should this be done well by a democracy? Surely a highly trained and intelligent elite could do a better job: Plato's philosopher kings, or at least their modern bureaucratic successors.

This argument, however, need not be decisive. Perhaps the best response to it is to follow Rousseau's lead and suggest that we would do better still if the people as a whole had the proper education, and the political virtues, to take an informed, highly active role as citizen self-legislators. Interestingly, Rawls refuses to take up this suggestion, arguing that 'In a well-governed state only a small fraction of persons may devote much of their time to politics. There are many other forms of human good.'[23]

How, then, does Rawls resist Plato's anti-majoritarian argument? It cannot be irrelevant that, in fact, there are no potential philosopher kings, at least given the complexities of modern society. All of us are ill-informed in some or other respects, we are imperfect reasoners, and we have unnoticed blindspots and prejudices. Thus, Rawls likens the majority decision-making procedure to the sort of 'pooling of information' that often takes place in order for a group to reach a collective decision.[24] Different individuals have different experience, expertise, and points of view, and after free and open discussion a group is likely to make a more reliable decision than any individual is likely to have been able to alone. Hence, to arrive at just and efficient legislation, open discussion within a group, followed by majority voting, may be the best way forward.

This is confirmed by the thought that even if it is true that the basic principles of justice are those which would be chosen from the original position, Rawls also suggests that the application of the principles to concrete cases will be far from clear. What type of economic arrangements will make the worst-off better off; what type of education will best further equality of opportunity; what police procedures will best protect freedom of association; are all difficult and contestable issues. Rational and reasonable people can strongly disagree, and so all we can do is vote (after open discussion and debate, of course).

Is this a strong – or indeed, any – defence of majoritarian voting? Unfortunately not. What it argues for is majority decision-making within a legislative body: in a parliament, for example, or a congress. For these arguments are based on the idea that the way to achieve just and efficient legislation is to leave decisions to highly committed groups of people comprising a diversity of backgrounds and experience. Nothing yet answers the question of why ask ordinary citizens, who have no special knowledge or experience, their opinion as to who those legislators should be. After all, in many advanced societies the people have no influence over the question of who should be judges, generals or chiefs of police. Why, then, should they have influence over the question of who should be their legislators?

This question may make us feel rather uncomfortable. It is one of the articles of faith of modern society that a society is gravely deficient if its legislators are not democratically elected. Yet when we come to try to explain why such a system should lead to better legislation than forms of bureaucratic rule we have rather little to say. It may be helpful, though, to set this into a wider context by considering what we should think of as two contrasting approaches to the defence of democracy.

One type of defence argues that there is something about democracy which leads it to produce decisions of particularly good quality. In this case the claim would be that if we allow the people to vote, they will appoint legislators more likely to enact just and efficient legislation than we could expect under any other system. We may call this the 'instrumental' defence of democracy: democracy is the best instrument for achieving the type of outcomes we desire. The trouble is that so far we have been given no reason to suppose that this is true: we will vote for those we find most persuasive, and they may not make the best decisions.

The other type of defence to be considered can be called the 'intrinsic' defence of democracy. On this view, we should value democratic elections not because they will lead to the appointment of the best rulers, but because there is something especially important or good about allowing the whole people to vote. One way of making out this case is to say that giving each individual a vote on this matter is a way of respecting the liberty and equality of all citizens. Of course, there may be other ways of doing this, but in the modern world the most potent sign that all those who live within a country are respected as free and equal citizens is that they are all allowed – even encouraged – to vote in elections. A partial franchise, as, for example, in the recent experience of apartheid in South

Africa, was a way of giving the message that one part of society was inferior to another.

The interesting consequence of contrasting instrumental and intrinsic defences of democracy is that we are now able to formulate quite sharply what some may think to be the central problem of democracy. If we treat everyone as free and equal and give the vote to all, there is no reason to think they will use it to make the best decisions. In other words, the intrinsic and instrumental defences of democracy are in conflict.

To illustrate this argument, consider a contemporary question of political economy: whether the central bank should be independent of the government. In the United Kingdom, until 1997, the Bank of England ultimately had to follow the orders of the Chancellor of the Exchequer. In 1997 the new Labour administration changed this arrangement to bring it closer to the situation in Germany where the central bank is independent of the government. Why make this change? The main argument is that if the bank is under the control of the politicians, then a government may use economic policy for party-political reasons. In particular, in the year or so prior to an election whichever party is in power will be tempted to try to ensure re-election by engineering a 'pre-election' boom. Few Chancellors have been able to resist such temptation and it is often argued that this 'short-termism' will be to the detriment of the economy in the longer term. In Germany, and now in the United Kingdom, this cannot happen, at least not to the same degree. As the central bank is not under political control, it is not part of the democratic process. So it sometimes can be argued that having the central bank under democratic control is bad for the economy. Should we then argue in favour of the independence of the central bank? This may seem the rational solution: yet it will be criticized as undemocratic. And here is our problem. It is argued that if you leave too much to the electorate they will make bad decisions. You can have real democracy or sound economics, but not both. This example illustrates the general worry that if you wish to respect the intrinsic value of a system which gives everyone a say over decisions which affect them, then you should expect that system to be a poor instrument for making just and efficient legislation.

In response, it will be said that the argument so far merely points out that such a reconciliation of the intrinsic and instrumental defences of democracy can be difficult. Nothing has been said to render it impossible. And it is on this point, finally, that we return to Rawls, where a few very brief, and apparently inconsequential, side remarks give the key to how this problem can be solved, at least in theory. Rawls seems to accept that there can be a tension between instrumental and intrinsic defences of democracy. But Rawls adds, 'Of course the grounds for self-government are not solely instrumental.'[25] We have already seen that universal franchise and majority rule can, to some degree, be defended on grounds of liberty and equality. But Rawls takes this further: he argues that giving people a vote gives them a type of responsibility, and a requirement to take others' beliefs and interests into account. In other words, treating people as free and equal in this way will have, Rawls argues, profound effects on their moral development. So, Rawls claims, having a vote will tend to increase not only the sense of self-worth of individuals, but also their political competence.[26]

In effect, Rawls seems to be claiming that the apparent tension between the intrinsic and instrumental justifications of democracy – illustrated by means of the 'central bank' example – corrects itself. If you treat people with the respect due to free and equal citizens, then there is a good chance, Rawls believes, that they will come to earn that respect through responsible and informed action. Rawls has faith that giving people the vote, and a wide range of issues over which they have some influence, will help turn them into good citizens. Showing individuals this degree of regard will have deep effects. It will help them develop their moral and political sensibilities, and the understanding that they must justify their behaviour to others. On this view, although there are possible conflicts between the instrumental and intrinsic justifications of democracy, given time – possibly not even much time – those treated as citizens will act as citizens, informing themselves and acting in a responsible manner.

We may ask how this proposal differs from what I called Rousseau's solution, which is rejected by Rawls. That was the idea that we should all become very active participants in political life, gaining the expertise to make accurate political decisions, by becoming steeped in politics. Rawls's response was that, while some people may choose to spend their lives in political activity, there are many other worthwhile ways of spending one's time. Here, though, the proposal is much more modest. People should keep themselves informed, and bear the interests and views of others in mind in their action, including their voting. This level of activity, although it has significant effects, takes relatively little time, and thus leaves plenty of scope for other pursuits within a single life.

Conclusion

How, in the end, should we assess Rawls's arguments? It seems to me that he has presented a well-measured and well-judged defence of an improved form of representative liberal democracy. The objection of the 'tyranny of the majority' was never a threat for Rawls: our constitutional rights are well protected by his liberty principle, which sets out an area immune from democratic intervention. The converse problem, that there is too little left for the political process to do – the enfeeblement of the political, as I called it – is answered at least in part. The constitution can never do more than set out the broad outlines of the just society, and much work remains to be done to ensure that just and efficient legislation comes into being. This is the role of voters and their representatives.

But what advances has Rawls made in democratic theory? Although theory and practice are not easy to separate in this area, we can note two advances in democratic theory, and one suggestion for practical, institutional, reform. The first theoretical advance is to make clear that in an ideal ballot, whether within government or in an election, people should not vote purely for their private interests or preferences, or even in accordance with their private moralities, but on the basis of what they feel they can justify to others. We should vote as citizens, not as egoists or moralists. The second theoretical claim is that although there can be tensions between the inclusion of all in the electorate and the goal of just and efficient legislation, there is reason to believe that once people are given the vote they will develop into citizens who will use it wisely.

The main institutional improvement that Rawls offers is that individuals should not be permitted to spend their own money in political campaigns, either for themselves, or for others. Given the inexorable rise of 'showbiz' politics, this would make a significant change, but Rawls's point here is that until this reform is carried out the 'fair value of political liberties' is undermined.

The main criticisms of Rawls, I believe, come not so much from doubts about the validity of these arguments, but from questioning the realism of his proposals. To take the last point first, the idea that the state, not individuals, should bear election expenses has to face the practical objection that any such change has to be made convincing to the taxpayer who will end up paying the costs of political campaigns should such reforms be made. Whether many political parties would be willing to make out such a case, and whether it can achieve widespread support, remain highly questionable.

On the proposal that we should vote as citizens, not as moralists or egoists, we must appreciate that unless the very great majority of the electorate are motivated to vote on the same type of ground it is possible that confusion and even harm may result. In the world as it is, there is no agreement on how individuals should vote. Accordingly, some vote from selfish motivations, others from consideration of private morality, still others as citizens, and no doubt there are other forms of motivation too. Under such circumstances we have absolutely no reason to think that those elected to government will be those most likely to generate just and efficient legislation. It may be, for example, the government will have been elected on a platform that serves the self-interest of a minority group. The point is simply that when voters vote from a variety of motives, anything can happen.[27]

This point leads naturally to the next: if people in real life vote according to a variety of motivations, then this undermines Rawls's claim that those given the rights of citizens will tend to act like citizens (or, at least, vote like citizens). Therefore, some will argue that experience shows that democracy's claimed advantages for the moral development of the individual are a massive exaggeration. But on the other hand, how do we explain why democratic voting has led to so few political or economic disasters, especially when compared with non-democratic regimes? Perhaps some will appeal to the corny anarchist slogan, 'if voting changed anything they wouldn't allow it', and certainly there are real questions about how much can be achieved through the ballot box, once a constitution is in place (the problem of the enfeeblement of the political). Rawls, no doubt, would simply wish to retort that there are good reasons to believe that granting individuals citizen rights has increased their moral and political sensibilities. Ultimately, this is an empirical question. What we must concede to Rawls is that, if he is right, then the instrumental and intrinsic justifications of democratic voting do tend to come together, and this would be a significant result. This is indeed a brave suggestion. Opinions will differ as to whether this is too much to hope for.

Notes

1 I am very grateful to Veronique Munoz Dardé, Keith Graham, and especially April Carter and Geoff Stokes for their comments on earlier drafts of this paper.
2 J. Rawls, *A Theory of Justice* (Oxford, Oxford University Press, 1971).
3 J. Rawls, *Political Liberalism* (New York, Columbia University Press, 1993).
4 Steve Pyke, *Philosophers* (New York, Distributed Art Publishers, 1995).
5 Rawls, *A Theory of Justice*, p. 302.
6 J. Rawls, 'Justice as fairness: Political not metaphysical', *Philosophy and Public Affairs*, 14 (1985), 223–51.
7 See, for example, C. Kukathas and P. Pettit, *Rawls: A Theory of Justice and its Critics* (Oxford, Polity, 1990).
8 For a slightly more detailed introduction to Rawls's argument see my *An Introduction to Political Philosophy* (Oxford, Oxford University Press, 1996), pp. 168–94. An excellent collection of papers discussing Rawls's argument is Norman Daniels (ed.), *Reading Rawls: Critical Studies on Rawls' A Theory of Justice* (Stanford, CA, Stanford University Press, 1989).

9   For example, in the inside back cover of *Philosophy and Public Affairs*, 1:2 (1972).

10 See, for example, Benjamin Barber, *The Conquest of Politics: Liberal Philosophy in Democratic Times* (Princeton, NJ, Princeton University Press, 1988).

11 Rawls, *A Theory of Justice*, p. 221.

12 Rawls, *A Theory of Justice*, p. 222.

13 Rawls, *A Theory of Justice*, p. 223.

14 Rawls, *A Theory of Justice*, p. 225.

15 J. S. Mill, 'Considerations on representative government', in H. B. Acton (ed.), *Utilitarianism, Liberty, Representative Government: Selections from Auguste Comte and Positivism* (London, Dent, 1972), p. 310.

16 Norman Daniels, 'Equal liberty and unequal worth of liberty', in his *Reading Rawls*.

17 Rawls, *A Theory of Justice*, p. 226. Rawls's proposal for public financing of elections is already implemented *to some extent* in many countries, sometimes in the form of partial funding for national elections (as in Australia since 1983), or through the provision of free broadcasting time on TV and radio and free postage for candidates, as in Britain. Public funding schemes and legal limits on spending have not, however, been effective in preventing high expenditure on elections, problems of inequality in funds available to parties, and examples of corruption relating to campaign funds. This is particularly true in the USA which broke with tradition and passed laws in 1971 and 1974 which set limits to spending, and provided some public funds for party conventions and for the final presidential campaign. Candidates in the presidential primaries can apply for public funding to match funds they have raised. Numerous devices for evading spending limits through contributions of 'soft money' have, however, meant that in practice money has become increasingly important for winning elections. For further detail see H. E. Alexander, 'American presidential elections, 1976–1992', in H. E. Alexander and R. Shiratori (eds), *Comparative Political Finance among the Democracies* (Boulder, CO, Westview, 1994). *Full* public funding of elections and stricter controls on ancillary spending, for example issue advertising, might have a much greater impact on the conduct of elections.

18 Mill, 'Considerations on representative government', p. 311.

19 Rawls, *A Theory of Justice*, p. 230.

20 Mill, 'Considerations on representative government', p. 299.

21 Rawls, *Political Liberalism*, p. 219.

22 Rawls, *A Theory of Justice*, p. 356.

23 Rawls, *A Theory of Justice*, p. 228.

24 Rawls, *A Theory of Justice*, p. 358.

25 Rawls, *A Theory of Justice*, p. 233.

26 Rawls, *A Theory of Justice*, p. 234.

27 For an illustration of problems in a simple case see my 'Democratic voting and the mixed-motivation problem', *Analysis*, 54:4 (1994), 193–6.

7

Michael Walzer: Pluralism, Justice and Democracy

Mark Kingwell

Michael Walzer's philosophical interests are wide, but they are united in a concern for justice.[1] As a key figure in the deployment of left-communitarian ideas against the neutralist liberal orthodoxy of contemporary American political theory, Walzer's work functions as a rich chorus of dissent within an often austere academic discourse. His arguments are frequently based on subtle readings of cultural history, drawing on sources as diverse as Talmudic parable and Aztec mythology, and the kind of sensitive interpretation of existing political culture that he has advocated as the proper business of professional theorists. These methods, and the conclusions they deliver, evoked a degree of hostility among those who pursue a different and (they would say) more stringent argumentative strategy.

Democratic concerns ground all of Walzer's political theory, especially the theory of 'complex equality' defended in his most important book, *Spheres of Justice*, published in 1983.[2] At key moments in that text, base-level democratic convictions constrain the theory in ways that have proved puzzling to some readers, who occasionally suspect that logic points in another direction. Walzer claims to read the 'inner logic' of various social practices, or 'spheres', ranging from kinship systems to medical care. On the basis of those readings he offers as his central conclusion the idea that the essence of social injustice is *domination*, when the goods of one social sphere infect the distributive patterns of another sphere: when, for example, money buys votes, or social graces secure a high-level job.

The key to social justice, therefore, is not a single principle of distribution, or even a single set of principles, but rather a complex and interpretive social dialogue in which the goods of relatively autonomous social spheres are distributed in such a way that no distributive principle from one sphere dominates distribution in another. This explicit focus on the notion of justice may seem slightly odd to more radical democratic theorists, when the key ideas of democratic decision-making and pluralistic political discourse that give point to Walzer's ideas of socialist justice go largely undefended. And yet Walzer's theory of justice proves to be, at the same time, a theory of social democracy.

Central to this conclusion is Walzer's concept of the role of the social critic. In a truly just society, he suggests, social critics are created as a necessary by-product of a complex and evolving society to prevent its own ossification. He does not insist upon a high degree of democratic participation, in the manner, for example, of Benjamin Barber, or of William Galston and other recent 'virtue-based' liberal thinkers.[3] Walzer does, however, imply that his notion of democratic citizenship is strongly conditioned by the idea that social criticism is everybody's business. It must remain possible in principle for all citizens to take up a critical, that is a suspicious but constructive, stance toward the political culture of which they are a part.

Background: Life and Intellectual Context

Michael Laban Walzer was born in New York City in 1935 into a politically engaged household within a community of radical Jewish thinkers. He completed a PhD at Harvard in 1961, first taught at Princeton, but returned to Harvard in 1966 and remained there, as Professor of both Philosophy and Government, until 1980. In that year, Princeton's Institute for Advanced Study lured him back to New Jersey, where he has remained ever since. As editor of the socialist journal *Dissent* since 1976, and as a contributing editor of the liberal *New Republic*, Walzer has spanned the divide between academic and popular political writing, putting into practice his support for engaged political criticism.

Walzer's academic work covers a range of related topics, from religion to war to social theory, but it exhibited early his ongoing commitment to radical politics and the way communities are shaped by the dialectic between belief and criticism. Whether in writings on religious movements,[4] or in passionate manuals on political practice,[5] Walzer has remained what he once described himself in the subtitle of a book of essays: 'an unreconstructed democrat'.[6] His persistent concern has been how to make political conclusions of a radical kind cogent, without ascending to the rarefied realms of abstract, universalist right, or declining into unexamined Marxism. In the resulting 'intermediate zone' of political writing, he often finds himself opposed to the typical 'thin' moral idea of liberalism: namely, the idea that all persons are bearers of rights and therefore possessed of an equal claim to resources. That approach, Walzer thinks, destroys the 'thick' complexity of real communities for the sake of theoretical simplicity, and likewise underplays the real forms of tyranny that may occur when abstract egalitarianism is put into practice in excessively simple forms – forms which mask various kinds of distortion in the political culture.[7]

Walzer has made himself the kind of critic who meets the three demands of criticism as set out in his 1989 book *The Company of Critics*: 'The critic exposes the false appearances of his own society;' Walzer writes, 'he gives expression to his people's deepest sense of how they ought to live; and he insists that there are other forms of falseness and other, equally legitimate, hopes and aspirations.'[8]

The idea of a just war is an example of Walzer's engagement with political culture. America's involvement in Korea and, later, Vietnam seemed to many to highlight a contrast between unjust and just involvement in war, with the nasty (indeed, partly covert) operations in South East Asia set against the 'good' Second World War. This judgement was often made by reference to classical just-war theory. Yet, for Walzer, the moral judgements of just-war theory become important as a branch of a larger project of social criticism.[9] The condemnation of Vietnam in the 1970s gave way, in the early 1980s, to larger arguments about the dangers of nuclear war.

Not that Walzer is entirely at odds with his own political culture. Roosevelt's New Deal policies in the 1930s fundamentally reshaped American society, making it into the sort of welfarist regime that Walzer would, with reservations, support. At the same time, Walzer points out the inadequacy of the new American norm as it emerged from challenges to the New Deal welfare state, from both left and right. In particular, he regrets the lack of a fully socialized medical system and more radical conception of politics. In the introduction to *Radical Principles*, he writes:

> The welfare state, though it represents (as I shall argue again and again in these essays) an enormous political achievement and generates its own workaday politics, does not by itself produce either a community of workers or a community of citizens. It carries us beyond the class structures of bourgeois societies but not yet into a socialist society.[10]

During the 1960s Walzer was energized by the sense of possibility embodied in new social movements, in particular the democratizing tendencies inherent in the claims for women's liberation, black equality, and respect for gays and lesbians. Nor were these tendencies limited to these movements: local, participatory democracy seemed realizable within a lifetime.

Walzer himself expressed the stakes in terms of what he called 'insurgency'. Insurgency, he said, was a form of political action sparked by the looming contradictions in late-capitalist welfare societies. As Iris Marion Young puts it: 'Since the polity retains formal ideals of democracy, the more social spheres come under the purview of state policy, the more likely it is that people will demand meaningful public discussion of such policy.'[11] In this context, Walzer says, insurgency

> is the demand that bureaucratic services make possible, instead of replacing, local decision-making. Or rather it is the acting out of a new dialectic, which . . . seeks to make the 'helpfulness' of the welfare bureaucracy into the starting point of a new politics of resistance and self-determination.[12]

Insurgent political action has of course only been fitfully realized in American society since the 1960s, and the contradictions have become more protracted. Walzer has confessed that for these reasons and others – a decline in the idea of participation, disaffection with the political process, the dangers of unaccountable power – reconciling the tension between participatory democracy and representative democracy is going to prove extremely difficult, especially in the liberal-dominated United States:

> Somehow power must be distributed, as it is not today, to groups of active and interested citizens, but these citizens must themselves be made responsible to a larger electorate (the membership, that is, of the state, movement, union, or party). Nothing is more important than that responsibility; without it we will only get one or another sort of activist or *apparatchik* tyranny. And that we have already.[13]

With the growth of neo-conservatism in the 1980s, a movement spearheaded by disaffected former radicals, many of them New York Jews, Walzer's old-fashioned socialism fell out of favour. The new gospel of free-market competition, drastically limited government, and resulting cuts in the extensive social programmes of the New Deal, found approval both in Washington and in the political mainstream of the country.[14]

Concurrently, the 1980s saw an unprecedented growth of factional 'identity' politics in American culture. Racial, ethnic and community groups began staking out particularistic territory against the resurgent classical liberalism of the neo-conservatives. The result was a twin polarization of academic debate. The first divide took the form of a long-running debate, or rather impasse, between liberals and communitarians of various kinds.[15] The second and arguably more serious split occurred between the forces supporting some form of common political culture and those instead committed to retreat, even separatism, from the very idea of such a culture, which was understood by the particularistic forces to be a dominant (white, heterosexual, European, male) culture masquerading as a universal conception of humanity.

Although Walzer's work is radically particularistic, and decidedly left, it has not always found favour with the critics of liberal theories of justice. Young, for example, praises Walzer for joining her in refusing to accept the ruling paradigm of liberal justice, which favours static distribution over dynamic process, commodifying all social goods, and advancing its particular ends under allegedly neutral principles of just allocation. Nonetheless, she does not believe Walzer goes far enough in rejecting the language of distribution.[16] Others have criticized Walzer for not being sufficiently particularist. J. Peter Euben, for instance, reviewing Walzer's book *The Company of Critics*, chided him for ignoring lesbian, American Indian, and Chicano voices in his survey of great critical exemplars in the American political tradition.[17]

The objection that Walzer's particularism is idiosyncratic has also been voiced by the neutralist and universalist liberals. As Georgia Warnke notes, the objections can be grouped under three general headings.[18] The liberal critics object, first, to Walzer's idea of socially constructed meanings or values, and the related idea that such meanings are constitutive of a community. They suggest instead that members of a given political community may share no social understanding. They argue, second, that even if there are shared meanings in certain societies, or subsocial groupings, Walzer's interpretations of them are, in Joshua Cohen's words, 'arbitrary and tendentious'.[19] Finally, the liberals deny that social meanings, even if shared and correctly interpreted, can serve as the basis of the kind of 'critical principle' or point of entry demanded by Walzer's notions of social interpretation and criticism. Cohen goes so far as to suggest that Walzer's interpretive methods actually undermine his own commitment to the substantive political vision of democratic socialism. For these critics, who include Norman Daniels and Ronald Dworkin, Warnke concludes:

> any attempt to derive principles of justice from the way in which social agents understand the goods of their society is either empty or conservative, since it cannot go beyond the self-understanding of the society itself.[20]

I will return to these charges later when the outlines of Walzer's general theory and its place in democratic thought have been made clearer.

Just and Unjust Regimes

The guiding insight of the 'complex equality' defended in Walzer's *Spheres of Justice* is provided, he says, by two passages – one from Blaise Pascal and one from Karl Marx – about tyranny's true character. 'The nature of tyranny is to desire power over the whole world and outside its own sphere,' writes Pascal in the *Pensées*.

> There are different companies – the strong, the handsome, the intelligent, the devout – and each man reigns in his own, not elsewhere . . . Tyranny is the wish to obtain by one means what can only be had by another. We owe different duties to different qualities: love is the proper response to charm, fear to strength, and belief to learning.[21]

Marx's version of the same insight, from an early manuscript, begins as follows:

> Let us assume man to be man, and his relation to the world to be a human one. Then love can only be exchanged for love, trust for trust, etc.[22]

Having sounded these keynotes, Walzer says humbly that 'These are not easy arguments, and most of my book is simply an exposition of their meaning.'[23]

The first important insight in this exposition is what we might call the social construction of value: the things that citizens desire. Walzer rejects, without much argument, all theories of the metaphysical or pre-social good, insisting instead that things become desirable only to the extent that they take their place within a web of social relations in which they are thought to play some crucial role. 'Justice is relative to social meanings,' Walzer says. 'We cannot say what is due to this person or that one until we know how these people relate to one another through the things they make and distribute.'[24] Therefore, any adequate theory of social goods must be based on the following six propositions:

1   All the goods with which distributive justice is concerned are social goods. . . .

2 Men and women take on concrete identities because of the way they conceive and create, and then possess and employ social goods. . . .

3 There is no single set of primary or basic goods conceivable across all moral and material worlds – or, any such set would have to be conceived in terms so abstract that they would be of little use in thinking about particular distributions. . . .

4 [It] is the meaning of goods that determines their movement . . . All distributions are just or unjust relative to the social meanings of the goods at stake. . . .

5 Social meanings are historical in character; and so distributions, and just and unjust distributions, change over time. . . .

6 When meanings are distinct, distributions must be autonomous.[25]

Walzer adds the crucial point that social meanings, and the idea of relative autonomy that goes with them, are not inert properties but rather 'critical principles', indeed potentially radical ones, since they may provide a basis for challenging domination.

For Walzer it follows that, because these goods are the result of complex interplay among various social forces and desires, no single reference point or principle will suffice in coordinating their just distribution. This conclusion, as he notes, is at odds with the entire history of political theory in the West. Since Plato, philosophers have started from the assumption that there is only one philosophically correct system of distributive justice.[26] But Walzer's conclusion is consistent with the multi-vector nature of actual political life. Walzer's particularism therefore leads him, immediately, to pluralism:

I want to argue . . . that the principles of justice are themselves pluralistic in form; that different social goods ought to be distributed for different reasons, in accordance with different procedures, by different agents; and that all these differences derive from different understandings of the social goods themselves – the inevitable product of historical and cultural particularism.[27]

This is not, therefore, the pluralism of John Rawls, who conceives that individuals (or, sometimes, groups) with diverse 'conceptions of the good' can nevertheless reasonably and fairly band together in a moment of decision that generates conceptually quite simple but politically powerful principles of justice, and thus forge a political association that will, in turn, create a well-ordered society.[28] It is rather a pluralism of value within a single society already presumed to exist (and therefore available for critical social interpretation), where there is indeed divergence of value between people, but also between goods and between kinds of thinking with respect to their allocation.

On the basis of this notion of pluralism, Walzer advances his argument about the spheres of justice. He does so by contrasting monopoly with dominance, his word for what Pascal had called tyranny. Monopoly is the idea that a desired good is held in the hands of a certain class, often a minority of the population who desire the good. Monopoly may be just or unjust, but it is not, Walzer says, the most important social fact at issue in thinking about justice. Rather, what we need to see is that the *dominance* of several goods by a single one is at the root of injustice. Walzer explains: 'I call a good dominant if the individuals who have it, because they have it, can command a wide range of other goods.'[29] Sometimes there is a monopoly on the dominant goods, sometimes there is not. It is also possible to have monopolies on non-dominant goods, assuming that those who monopolize the dominant good do not set their sights there (as, say, when Catholics monopolize the good of Holy Communion without much interference from those who control the money markets). The problem is not monopoly; it is rather monopoly plus domination. The claim by a ruling class to monopolize a dominant good on the basis of their inherent superiority is what we call ideology.

Dominance and monopoly in social goods can be challenged. When the disenfranchised challenge patterns of distribution, or the allocation of goods, they make three kinds of claim. They are, writes Walzer:

1 The claim that the dominant good, whatever it is, should be redistributed so that it can be equally or at least more widely shared: this amounts to saying that *monopoly is unjust.*
2 The claim that the way should be opened for the autonomous distribution of all social goods: this amounts to saying that *dominance is unjust.*
3 The claim that some new good, monopolized by some new group, should replace the currently dominant good: this amounts to saying that *the existing pattern of dominance and monopoly is unjust.*[30]

Walzer says he is concerned with the first two kinds of claim, and in particular the second. It is this focus which leads him to reject what he calls 'simple equality' in favour of the 'complex' sort he wishes to defend.

The reason is rooted in what has been said so far. If goods are particular in their social construction, then they are plural. That means that the distribution of goods cannot reasonably proceed according to a single principle. Neither happiness nor goodness nor need nor market demand is an adequate single guideline for the allocation of all social goods. To refute the view that challenging monopoly over a dominant good like wealth can be solved by redistribution, Walzer imagines a 'regime of simple equality' which captures the idea of a social time-zero in which everyone has the same amount of currency and everything in society is up for sale. This will not in practice generate a just distribution. For one thing, market exchanges create new inequalities, often immediately, and the suppression of these would require the constant intervention of an overarching state: itself a form of tyranny.

These problems of the regime of simple equality derive, Walzer says, 'from treating monopoly, and not dominance, as the central issue in distributive justice'.[31] The aim of a just society should not be to even out social life in a fruitless attempt to realize simple equality, or to allow the purely formal and misleading equality of the dollar to masquerade as justice. It should be instead to separate out the autonomous spheres of social meaning so that their particular distributive principles can be interpreted back to citizens in a way that makes sense to them. This is a critical enterprise, for it may sanction all manner of social revision, especially where there are dominant relationships forming or in place, and it may lead to the need for sharp reallocation of goods when the inner logic of the sphere in question is properly read. 'Social goods have social meanings,' Walzer writes, 'and we find our way to distributive justice through an interpretation of those meanings. We search for principles internal to each distributive sphere.'[32] There may be several principles of distribution, and Walzer focuses on three: need, desert, and free exchange.

There can be no solution by ranking one of these above the others. Take, for example, the sphere of the market, for here we have the closest thing to a dominant good. 'Money,' Walzer claims, 'supposedly the neutral medium, is in practice a dominant good, and it is monopolized by people who possess a special talent for bargaining and trading – the green thumb of bourgeois society.'[33] The principle of free exchange can be just, indeed it is demanded, in the social allocation of certain goods. But free exchange may also be tyrannical if allowed to govern every aspect of social life. Hence the long list of 'blocked exchanges' that forms one of the most controversial sections of Walzer's book.[34] 'Dishonesty is always a useful guide to the existence of moral standards,' Walzer says there. 'When people sneak across the boundary of the sphere of money, they advertize the existence of the boundary.'[35] People are sneaky about buying and selling, for example, human beings, criminal justice, freedom of speech or political offices. What *can* money legitimately buy? What we might call consumer durables; but also services of various kinds. Although the market 'doesn't recognize desert,' according to Walzer, 'the exchange is in principle a relation of mutual benefit, and neither the money that the merchant makes, nor the accumulation of things by this or that consumer, poses any threat to complex equality – not if the sphere of money and commodities is properly bounded.'[36]

That bounding is, of course, rife with controversy. For example, are the services of a hired escort – companionship, conversation, possibly sex – justly open to exchange? What about the services of a lobbying consultant prepared to sell his insider's knowledge of Washington politics? Surrogate pregnancies are frequently condemned, but the donation of sperm is rarely subjected to either reaction. Why not?

Now, none of this is damaging to Walzer's general argument. That a line is hard to draw does not prove that we should not attempt the delineation. But it does suggest the depth of potential disagreement in the interpretive exercise that underlies Walzer's strong theory of complex equality. Some, for example, would react against any regulation of a free market. If people want to sell sex for money, or babies for money, or even married status for money, who is to object? On the other side, Walzer appears to underestimate the potential of the market to disseminate an ideology of money as the dominant good along with its dissemination of goods and services. He says that his theory requires 'not that the market be abolished, but that no one be cut off from its possibilities because of his low status or political powerlessness'.[37] Yet the problem in many modern consumer societies is not that people lack access to the market's possibilities, but rather that the market's subtle charms influence their behaviour and aspirations. The pathologies of market-based economies, not to mention the myriad messages of consumer conformity and over-spending that advertising and marketing encourage, seem missing from this reading of the market's inner logic. Given his socialist commitments, Walzer's acceptance of the market begins, even under his regulations, to seem excessively cheerful.

Nevertheless, the conclusion of this argument is powerfully critical of existing arrangements in American society, the society Walzer is purporting to interpret to its members. He writes:

> The appropriate arrangements in our own society are those, I think, of a decentralized democratic socialism; a strong welfare state run, in part at least, by local and amateur officials; a constrained market; an open and demystified civil service; independent public schools; the sharing of hard work and free time; the protection of religious and familial life; a system of public honoring and dishonoring free from all considerations of rank or

class; workers' control of companies and factories; a politics of parties, movements, meetings, and public debate.[38]

These, in short, are the social arrangements, the array of autonomous spheres, that would make for a just society.

Place of Democratic Theory in Walzer's Thought

So there is a strong critical thrust to Walzer's arguments, and one which has a crucial democratic component. Throughout the unfolding of the general theory of complex equality, there is a thread of an implicit defence of democratic decision-making and participatory politics, which, although largely unarticulated, is nevertheless crucial. This point is made clearer in Walzer's other works, and in his notion of social criticism in particular, than in the theory defended in *Spheres of Justice*.[39] Even there, however, some important insights about the relationship between justice and democracy are made explicit.

'Once we have located ownership, expertise, religious knowledge, and so on in their proper places and established their autonomy,' Walzer contends, 'there is no alternative to democracy in the political sphere.'[40] This is partly because political power is something that must be distributed free of domination by money, social position and other forms of autonomous goods. Indeed, basic political power is one place in which the ideal of simple equality has some meaning, in the form of universal franchise. '"One citizen/one vote",' Walzer writes, 'is the functional equivalent, in the sphere of politics, of the rule against exclusion and degradation in the sphere of welfare, of the principle of equal consideration in the sphere of office, and of the guarantee of a school place for every child in the sphere of education.'[41] It is, in other words, the guiding principle for the distribution of a crucial social good: 'This is what complex equality means in the sphere of politics: it is not power that is shared, but the opportunities and occasions of power. Every citizen is a potential participant, a potential politician.'[42]

This accords with an earlier discussion about the relationship between knowledge and political power, in which Walzer rejects Plato's idea in *The Republic* of the political leader as a kind of philosopher king, schooled in celestial navigation and therefore uniquely suited to steering the ship of state. On the contrary, Walzer says, the political leader may possess a certain kind of helmsman's knowledge – how to get past certain obstacles, how best to hold the tiller – but the real navigators of the ship, and at the same time its captain, are the citizens themselves. 'All arguments for exclusive rule, all anti-democratic arguments,' he claims, 'are arguments from special knowledge . . . the more deeply we consider the meaning of power, the more likely we are to reject Plato's analogy.'[43]

This suggests a strongly participatory and decentralized notion of political power, and indeed Walzer defends those ideals, but there is very little in the way of illustration concerning how such participation ought to take place. At one point, he gestures in the direction of deliberative democracy, the kind of theory defended by Habermas and those (including myself) influenced by the latter's notions of communicative action, the regulative ideal of agreement, and the guiding presuppositions of a political dialogue among free and equal citizens.[44] 'Democracy is a way of allocating power and legitimating its use,' Walzer writes, 'or better, it is *the political way* of allocating power. Every extrinsic reason is ruled out. What counts is argument among citizens. Democracy puts a premium on speech, persuasion, rhetorical skill.'[45]

At the same time, Walzer has been quite critical of Habermas's idea of unconstrained political discourse. Although this objection to Habermas's deliberative versions of democratic theory appears in various forms,[46] Walzer's brisk 'Critique of philosophical conversation' applies most clearly.[47] Habermas has argued that under ideal conditions discourse results in rational agreement, and so justifies the norms considered in conversation. Walzer is quick to point out the constraining features operating in Habermas's allegedly 'unconstrained conversation', features that in his view make it a *designed* conversation:

> Habermas argues for 'unconstrained communication', but he means only to exclude the constraints of force and fraud, of deference, fear, flattery, and ignorance. His speakers have equal rights to initiate the conversation and to resume it; to assert, recommend, and explain their own positions; and to challenge the positions of other speakers. . . . the universalization requirement is a powerful constraint.[48]

What such hidden constraints do, according to Walzer, is artificially narrow the field of possible locutions in practical discourse to those that produce the results desired in advance. Habermas's ideal speech is not recognizable as what we know as actual human conversation oriented to practical questions. Not enough account is taken of differences in rhetorical or argumentative ability. The complexity of human talk is narrowed into a limited discursive space in which only a certain kind of talk can carry on.[49]

Walzer suggests that no truly convincing results will be generated for justice theory unless and until theorists either (i) design conversations that are more like our actual ones, full of ambiguity, uncertainty, power plays, senseless repetition, rhetorical flourishes and wit, or (ii) give up the aspiration to design and instead investigate real talk about justice as a kind of descriptive/interpretive undertaking. Habermas believes that his rational reconstruction of communicative competence satisfies (ii), but the success of this undertaking has not been fully demonstrated. The conditions modelled in the ideal speech situation appear too strong and are not erected in the right place to allow actual normative results in practical discussion. A designed conversation of this kind, even though explicitly derived from the reconstruction of features evident in communicative competence, may prove too abstract to be effective in our real justifications. This is not because the presuppositions modelled there do not exist, but because they will not act as a real procedural grid through which we must pass our actually contested norms of justice.

The general objection is that rational reconstruction of communicative competence will not, in practical terms, generate the sort of justifications we require from a theory of justice. Walzer's objection captures the frequent criticism of Habermas that the ideal speech situation is too formal to provide norms, or even procedures, for real situations of social conflict. It also reprises the Hegelian criticisms of Kantian, and neo-Kantian, attempts to ground morality in procedural rules.[50] The universalization principle and the symmetric reciprocity among interlocutors are, like the categorical imperative and indeed political neutrality, notions not 'thick' enough, to use Walzer's language, to have critical bite in framing and applying principles of justice. They may prove so stringent that *no* norm or action can be justified on their basis, or, if justified, they would not make obvious how the norm ought to be applied.[51] Or, from a different critical perspective, they may prove so formal and ideal that *any* norm can be justified.[52]

Without a more concrete picture of political culture, therefore, one that pertains meaningfully to our actual political practices (and is not merely something to which our actual commitments ideally point), it is not clear to Walzer what role *this* kind of deliberative democratic theory can have for us. It may be, as Charles Larmore and Richard Bernstein have suggested, that in reforming Kantian ethics we need to rehabilitate a notion of 'practical judgement' to supplement these formal conditions of justification.[53] Without this concrete notion of judgement, we have no interpretive measure of success in our actual discursive encounters, and no standard by which we can judge the value of continuing the search for agreement on one level or, perhaps, moving to other spheres of discussion. Lacking such a standard, the commitments we share simply on the basis of our genuine willingness to argue will not be enough to generate political agreement, and will make any circumstantial agreement non-normative.

A successful democratic theory must therefore supplement an awareness of a commitment to the force of the better argument with an awareness of the value of practical judgement in discerning and feeling that force. Such a notion of practical judgement cannot, however, be recovered from the abstract structure of communicative rationality as Habermas understands it. Nor can it, therefore, be considered to have universal extension without further delay. Indeed, as Walzer's work demonstrates, a notion so concrete will not be universal in the strong sense. It is nevertheless necessary for the effective achievement of normative agreement by discursive means. Walzer's criticisms suggest that if we want justificatory talk to do any political work it has to be, crucially, both binding *and* real. And without those requirements, it could not be considered democratic.

Critical Assessment

In a sense, Walzer owes more to Gadamerian ideas of social interpretation than to the neo-Kantian tendencies evident in Habermas. Walzer does not believe that interpreting the text of a society's values will leave everything as it is, nor does he think that such interpretation is primarily an academic exercise.

Yet, as mentioned earlier, the critical worth of this view of interpretation as social criticism has been challenged. In some cases, Walzer's readings of the inner logic of spheres have seemed tendentious. In particular, criticis have argued that he seems willing to champion democratic decision-making and notions of political equality without there being either sufficient abstract argument, or sphere-internal interpretive sanction, for them. This suggests that democracy is a theoretical pre-commitment for Walzer, which would be unobjectionable except that he has set himself up as an interpreter of a political culture that may pull in other directions.

Indeed, Norman Daniels argues that Walzer's convictions about democracy quoted in the previous section – the rejection of Platonic expertise in politics, the idea that a properly constituted political sphere demands democracy, and the principle of one citizen/one vote – represent 'contradictions' in his theory, moments where he appears to leave the immanence of social criticism behind and move to more transcendental, universalistic political theorizing.[54] And this objection is simply a particular instance of what Joshua Cohen calls the 'simple communitarian dilemma'. This problem would afflict Walzer's social criticism even if it were not the case, as Cohen and Dworkin alike think it is, that Walzer's interpretations of American political culture are 'arbitrary and tendentious'. The *real* problem, says Cohen, is this:

> If the values of a community are identified through its current distributive practices, then the distributive norms subsequently 'derived' from those values will not serve as criticisms of existing practices. . . . On the other hand, if we identify values apart from practices, with a view to assessing the conformity of practices to those values, what evidence will there be that we have the values right?[55]

The result is that social criticism is either immanent (and therefore empty, or merely descriptively conservative), or it is incisive (but therefore must go beyond existing practices, and so shoulder precisely the usual burdens of abstract argumentative proof that the communitarian wants to avoid).

But perhaps, as Warnke suggests, these criticisms misrepresent the function of political criticism of this interpretive kind. First, the simple fact of disagreement is no argument against the validity of an interpretation, as Dworkin, for example, appears to believe. People may disagree about interpretations without finding themselves unable to share anything. More deeply, such disagreements may in fact depend on a high degree of prior agreement, for example, about the nature of the policy under discussion, or what the values in play might mean. When we, for instance, dispute the issue of socialized medicine, we do not articulate the depth of our agreement about the fact that health is important, that doctors in some sense are more than contractors, that the state has an interest in medical care, and so on. Nevertheless, it is there. Without it, there could be no discussion at all.

Nor is it the case that a controversial or partial interpretation will necessarily fail to find critical purchase in a political culture. Immanent critique, in the Gadamerian model, does not work by being the uniquely correct interpretation of a text or text analogue – the very idea of unique correctness being one of interpretation's first casualties. Nor does immanent critique aim at a 'full' or 'complete' reading of the 'text' in question. Something as complicated as a political culture cannot ever be fully articulated, and there is a sense in which only the political culture's dialogues themselves are the 'full' interpretation of that culture, and that is an ongoing process. A given interpretation is therefore understood to be merely one speech act, one conversational gambit, in this necessarily ongoing dialogue. Once an interpretation is made, a given critic can do nothing but await the reactions of his or her interlocutors.

As for the larger question of whether Walzer's form of social interpretation is ensnared in a contradiction, Warnke is right to point out that he is in fact nicely balanced on the issue of universalism versus particularism. In practice, social criticism carries on piecemeal, not wholesale, and there is no reason to suppose that social critics need to get conceptually 'outside' the political culture in some feat of transcendental elevation in order to bring critical insights to bear on some parts of the culture. Critics can assume a provisionally fixed background of political assumptions against which a given act, policy or judgement can be assessed for its validity. Such comparative critical assessment is never knock-down, to be sure, but it has the essential benefit of being conditioned by the 'thick' realities of the actual political culture. Warnke writes:

> [Walzer's] argument for complex equality is *neither* the Rortian one that it simply corresponds to our social self-understandings *nor* that of his critics, namely, that it conforms to the requirements of abstract justice. Instead, he thinks that complex equality resolves the age-old problem of both belonging to a community and yet retaining a sense of one's individuality.[56]

The result, in other words, is that the theory of complex equality resolves itself into a theory of democratic citizenship that is sensitive to the demands of both community and individuality. It does so, moreover, without surrendering to a false dichotomy between, on the one hand, an exclusive, and in principle indefensible, community-based relativism (that is, similar to Rorty);[57] and, on the other, a kind of thin, abstract, universalizing political theory, with its illusions of neutrality and potential for oppression. Walzer defends democracy not simply because it is part of our political culture as a matter of contingent fact, but rather because the critical ideal of democracy is deeply inscribed in the history, traditions, practices and deliberations of our political lives. 'This view of our heritage can be accepted or rejected but only, I think, on its merits,' Warnke concludes on this issue. 'In focusing on the alleged inadequacies of his method and its supposed tensions with his aims, [Walzer's] critics largely miss the point.'[58]

They do. They also, as even Walzer's supporters can, miss the illuminating democratic theory that lies within the explicit concern with justice. If at first these democratic commitments seem to cut against, or at least be in some tension with, the interpretive methods of the theory itself, there is, it seems, a kind of resolution of that tension in the idea of social criticism. Such criticism should no longer be an undertaking of experts, each wielding some transcendental telescope that allows him or her to see the world as it ought to be (and therefore see this benighted version of it as inadequate to that vision). Rather criticism should be the right, and responsibility, of each and every citizen involved in the daily realities of political life. All citizens are power-holders, in Walzer's view, even if their power lies in one sphere and not another. But they are also, by implication, all social critics. Or at least, they should be, and will be, when the radically democratic ideals buried within a political culture are, at long last, genuinely realized in a community of citizens.

Notes

1 My thanks to Rita Visconti for invaluable research assistance with this chapter, and to the students of my 1997 graduate seminar on justice at the University of Toronto for their many penetrating insights – and searching criticisms – of Walzer's work.

2 M. Walzer, *Spheres of Justice: A Defence of Pluralism and Equality* (New York, Basic Books, 1983).

3 See B. Barber, *Strong Democracy: Participatory Politics for a New Age* (Berkeley, CA, University of California Press, 1984); and W. Galston, *Liberal Purposes: Goods, Virtues and Diversity in the Liberal State* (Cambridge, Cambridge University Press, 1991).

4 See the adaptation of his PhD thesis, *The Revolution of the Saints: A Study in the Origins of Radical Politics* (Cambridge, MA, Harvard University Press, 1965) and, more recently, a controversial reading of biblical scripture as profound political document, *Exodus and Revolution* (New York, Basic Books, 1985). The latter book compared the movement of Mosaic liberation to social-justice politics everywhere, and in particular to the American Revolution.

5 See for example, M. Walzer, *Political Action: A Practical Guide to Movement Politics* (New York, Quadrangle, 1971).

6 The book is Walzer's version of the politico-intellectual manifesto, a series of linked essays, most of them first published in *Dissent* and the *New York Review of Books*, called *Radical Principles: Reflections of an Unreconstructed Democrat* (New York, Basic Books, 1980).

7 This language of thick and thin runs through several of Walzer's works. Walzer does not wish to dismiss the 'thin' idea of universal standards, or the important insights about justice that it generates, but he does want to put the 'thick' moral language of locally rooted conditions, events and history back into a central place in social theory. See M. Walzer, *Thick and Thin: Moral Argument at Home and Abroad* (Notre Dame, IN, Notre Dame University Press, 1994).

8 M. Walzer, *The Company of Critics: Social Criticism and Political Commitment in the Twentieth Century* (New York, Basic Books, 1989); quotation

from D. Donoghue's review in the *Times Literary Supplement* (3 March 1989), 217.

9   See M. Walzer, *Just and Unjust Wars: A Moral Argument with Historical Illustrations* (New York, Basic Books, 1977).

10 Walzer, *Radical Principles*, p. 9.

11 I. M. Young, *Justice and the Politics of Difference* (Princeton, NJ, Princeton University Press, 1990), p. 81.

12 M. Walzer, 'Politics in the welfare state: Concerning the role of American radicals', in Irving Howe (ed.), *Beyond the Welfare State* (New York, Schocken, 1982), p. 152.

13 M. Walzer, 'A day in the life of a socialist citizen', in his *Radical Principles*, p. 136.

14 The writings of the neo-conservatives are extensive. A good overview, though from a very particular point of view, is provided by I. Kristol in his *Neo-Conservatism: The Autobiography of an Idea* (New York, Free Press, 1995).

15 See S. Avineri and A. de-Shalit (eds), *Communitarianism and Individualism* (Oxford, Oxford University Press, 1992) and S. Mulhall and A. Swift (eds), *Liberals and Communitarians* (Oxford, Blackwell, 1992).

16 Young, *Justice and the Politics of Difference*, pp. 17–18.

17 J. P. Euben, 'Review of Walzer's *The Company of Critics*', *The New York Times Book Review* (18 January 1989), 18.

18 G. Warnke, 'Social interpretation and political theory: Walzer and his critics', *Philosophical Forum*, 21:1–2 (1989–90), 204–26.

19 See J. Cohen, 'Review of *Spheres of Justice*', *Journal of Philosophy*, 83:8 (August 1986), 457–68.

20 Warnke, 'Social interpretation', p. 205. See also R. Dworkin, 'To each his own' (review of Walzer's *Spheres of Justice*), *New York Review of Books* (14 April 1983), 4–6; and N. Daniels, 'The roots of Walzer's relativism', APA Western Division Meeting, Chicago, 26 April 1985.

21 B. Pascal, *The Pensées*, tr. J. M. Cohen (Harmondsworth, Penguin, 1971), p. 96 (no. 244).

22 K. Marx, *Early Writings: Economic and Philosophic Manuscripts*, tr. T. B. Bottomore (London, Watts, 1963), pp. 193–4.

23 Walzer, *Spheres of Justice*, p. 18.

24 Walzer, *Spheres of Justice*, pp. 312–13.

25 Walzer, *Spheres of Justice*, pp. 7–10.

26 Walzer, *Spheres of Justice*, p. 5.

27 Walzer, *Spheres of Justice*, p. 6.

28 That is of course a rather potted summary of the thrust of Rawls's theory. For the (extensive) details see J. Rawls, *A Theory of Justice* (Harvard, MA, Belknap Press, 1971) and the revised version of the theory in J. Rawls, *Political Liberalism* (New York, Columbia University Press, 1990).

29 Walzer, *Spheres of Justice*, p. 10.

30 Walzer, *Spheres of Justice*, p. 13, my emphasis.

31 Walzer, *Spheres of Justice*, p. 16.
32 Walzer, *Spheres of Justice*, p. 19.
33 Walzer, *Spheres of Justice*, p. 22.
34 Walzer, *Spheres of Justice*, pp. 98–106.
35 Walzer, *Spheres of Justice*, p. 98.
36 Walzer, *Spheres of Justice*, pp. 109–10.
37 Walzer, *Spheres of Justice*, p. 118.
38 Walzer, *Spheres of Justice*, p. 318.
39 See, for example, the essays in part IV of Walzer's *Radical Principles*, especially 'In defense of equality', pp. 237–56.
40 Walzer, *Spheres of Justice*, p. 303.
41 Walzer, *Spheres of Justice*, pp. 305–6.
42 Walzer, *Spheres of Justice*, p. 310.
43 Walzer, *Spheres of Justice*, pp. 285, 286.
44 See J. Habermas, *The Theory of Communicative Action, Volume Two: Lifeworld and System, A Critique of Functionalist Reason*, tr. T. McCarthy (Boston, Beacon, 1987). See also M. Kingwell, *A Civil Tongue: Justice, Dialogue and the Politics of Pluralism* (University Park, PA, Pennsylvania University State Press, 1995), ch. 5. I have followed the outlines of my earlier discussion in the remainder of this section.
45 Walzer, *Spheres of Justice*, p. 304.
46 See, for example, D. Ingram, 'The possibility of a communication ethic reconsidered: Habermas, Gadamer and Bourdieu on discourse', *Man and World*, 15 (1982), 149–61, where he criticizes Habermas for a conception of language that leaves out rhetoric, authority, preverbal play and other 'real' elements. As a result, Ingram considers that the theory fails as a justificatory procedure or ethical theory, succeeding only as a limiting force on ideological manipulation.
47 M. Walzer, 'A critique of philosophical conversation', *Philosophical Forum*, 21:1–2 (1989–90), 182–96. See also, in the same volume, G. Warnke, 'Rawls, Habermas and real talk: A reply to Walzer', *Philosophical Forum*, 21:1–2 (1989–90), 197–203.
48 Walzer, 'A critique', p. 186.
49 A cogent version of this point is made by J. B. Thompson in 'Universal pragmatics', in J. B. Thompson and D. Held (eds), *Habermas: Critical Debates* (London, Macmillan, 1982), pp. 120ff.
50 Habermas thinks that the strategy of rational reconstruction gives him good reason for thinking that Hegelian criticisms such as those against universalism and formalism do not hit the mark with discourse ethics. See his 'Morality and ethical life: Does Hegel's critique of Kant apply to discourse ethics?', in his *Moral Consciousness and Communicative Action*, and 'On the employments of practical reason', in *Justification and Application*.
51 Georgia Warnke makes this point effectively by emphasizing that Habermas's principle of conversational universalism depends centrally on consequences and interests. 'Once we focus on consequences, circumstances

and interests, however,' she says, 'it is not clear that we can ever agree on which interests are generalizable in this way unless we already share interests and circumstances.' See G. Warnke, *Justice and Interpretation* (Cambridge, MA, MIT Press, 1992), pp. 96–7.

52 D. Ingram, 'The possibility of a communication ethic reconsidered', p. 159.

53 C. Larmore, *Patterns of Moral Complexity* (Cambridge, Cambridge University Press, 1987), esp. ch. 1. R. J. Bernstein, 'From hermeneutics to praxis', in B. R. Wachterhauser (ed.), *Hermeneutics and Modern Philosophy* (Albany, NY, SUNY Press, 1986), p. 95. S. B. Smith also makes this point in a short but extremely lucid critical passage on Habermas found in his *Hegel's Critique of Liberalism: Rights in Context* (Chicago, University of Chicago Press, 1989), pp. 244–6.

54 Daniels, 'The roots of Walzer's relativism'.

55 Cohen, 'Review of *Spheres of Justice*', pp. 463–4.

56 Warnke, 'Social interpretation and political theory', p. 223.

57 See, for a representative example of his position, R. Rorty, 'Postmodernist bourgeois liberalism', *Journal of Philosophy*, 80:10 (1983), 583–9.

58 Warnke, 'Social interpretation and political theory', p. 224.

8

Charles Taylor: Selfhood, Community and Democracy

John Horton

Charles Taylor is one of the most ambitious and wide-ranging of contemporary political theorists.[1] He has written extensively on ethics, the philosophy of language, epistemology, the philosophy of the social sciences, the history of philosophy and Canadian politics, in addition to political theory more narrowly construed.[2] What links all these writings is Taylor's attempt to understand the experience of modernity – its achievements, challenges and perplexities – and to diagnose, combat and correct the misunderstandings prevalent in modern philosophy and in the broader culture of our age. Democracy enters as an issue in his writings in a variety of contexts, often only obliquely or indirectly. While he nowhere attempts to set out a systematic or comprehensive theory of democracy, Taylor does develop an interesting and distinctive perspective on it. His concern with problems of political identity, allegiance and cohesion focus on issues which lie at the heart of democracy but which a narrower concentration on democratic procedures and institutions is liable to neglect.

Taylor is critical of both instrumental views of democracy and views which invoke the ideal of a general will. The former presupposes an implausible individualistic ontology – what Taylor calls 'atomism' – while the latter requires a degree of uniformity which is neither desirable nor possible under modern conditions of individual and cultural diversity. Taylor's critique of these conceptions is informed by his philosophical work on the nature of selfhood and of community, which also leads him to sympathize with arguments for the recognition of cultural diversity and national difference within a democratic polity. The model of democracy which Taylor favours, therefore, seeks to combine the political expression of cultural diversity, through decentralization and a politically active citizenry, with a sense of belonging to one polity. This polity needs to be informed by a conception of a common good, sufficient to generate allegiance to it on the part of its citizens. These issues are illustrated most clearly in his treatment of the problem of Quebec nationalism within the Canadian Federation. While I argue that there are tensions in Taylor's position which he does not succeed in resolving, his primary contribution to democratic theory lies in his analysis of the philosophical presuppositions and social conditions of democracy, and in his diagnosis of the difficulties for modern democracies to which these give rise.

Background: Life and Intellectual Context

Charles Taylor is a Canadian from Quebec, with a French mother and an English father. He was a doctoral student at Oxford, and was later Chichele Professor of Political Theory there between 1976 and 1981. However, most of his life has been spent in Quebec and, to an extent unusual for a political theorist, Taylor has been actively involved in Canadian politics. He was one of the founders of the New Democratic Party, ran against Pierre Trudeau in the 1965 elections, and contested federal elections three other times without success. The intensity of his political involvement lessened considerably after 1971, but he has remained passionately interested in the status of Quebec within the Canadian Federation.[3]

Taylor's political theory, including his reflections on democracy, are shaped both by his philosophical concerns and by his practical political involvement. In some of his recent writings on multiculturalism and the politics of recognition, we see the attempt to think through his theoretical concerns, in the context of a pressing political issue which has absorbed his interest for most of his life. It is his ability to move between the philosophical and the concrete which is one of the most distinctive and rewarding features of Taylor's thought.

Taylor's approach to democracy has to be situated not merely within his political theory but as part of his much wider concern with the nature and intellectual genesis of modernity. This has led Taylor to undertake a number of historical investigations in philosophy in which a seminal place is occupied by his magisterial work on Hegel.[4] While there is no very illuminating sense in which Taylor can be aptly described as a Hegelian – indeed he says explicitly that Hegel's 'conclusions are dead'[5] – he clearly has considerable sympathy with some features of Hegel's philosophy. These include Hegel's anti-naturalism, his rejection of any empiricist epistemology, and the ineliminable historical dimension to his philosophy. Above all, however, Hegel's continuing importance lies in the claim that the 'contemporary attempt . . . to situate subjectivity by relating it to our life as embodied and social beings, without reducing it to a function of objectified nature, constantly refers us back to Hegel.'[6]

Specifically with respect to modern democracy, Taylor believes that the dilemma which Hegel identifies is one which must lie at the centre of any adequate understanding of it.

> The modern ideology of equality and of total participation leads to a homogenization of society. This shakes men loose from their traditional communities, but cannot replace them as a focus of identity. Or rather, it can only replace them as such a focus under the impetus of militant nationalism or some totalitarian ideology which would depreciate or even crush diversity and individuality.[7]

Hegel's own solution cannot now be accepted but 'the dilemma it was meant to solve remains.'[8] For, according to Taylor, the modern democratic polity needs 'to recover a sense of significant differentiation, so that its partial communities, be they geographical, or cultural, or occupational, can become again important centres of concern and activity for their members in a way which connects them to the whole'.[9] This is a problem which Taylor grapples with throughout his writings and while, or so it will be argued, he is ultimately no more successful than Hegel in solving it, he nonetheless contributes much to our understanding of it.

Taylor's situating of democracy within a much broader historical and philosophical context than is common has led him into a wide range of philosophical inquiries. While this work has been influenced by a number of important figures in the history of philosophy – most notably, in addition to Hegel, Herder and some of the German Romantics, Heidegger and Wittgenstein – I shall be concerned primarily with an analytical examination of Taylor's philosophical ideas rather than with a historical account of their development. To this end, I shall begin with a general account of his views of selfhood and community. These provide the essential underpinning of the discussion of democracy which follows.

Selfhood

From the very earliest of his philosophical writings, Taylor has been insistent that human beings cannot be understood in entirely scientific terms or on the basis of a naturalist or empiricist epistemology. Indeed, so strong is this theme in his work that Taylor has described himself as a 'monomaniac' perpetually polemicizing against 'the ambition to model the study of man on the natural sciences'.[10] Human beings are 'self-interpreting animals' whose self-interpretations have an essential role in understanding them.[11] Taylor's first book was a thoroughgoing critique of behavioural psychology and in an important early article he was similarly critical of the behaviouralist approach in political science.[12] The latter includes a brief critique of the attempt to develop a value-free, purely scientific theory of democracy.[13] More generally, however, the behaviouralist approach cannot deal adequately with the way in which human actions are constituted by their meaning and the ineliminable role of values in human action. Human actions are not reducible to brute data. Meaning is not straightforwardly observable but has to be interpreted. Voting, for example, can be manifested in many different physical forms, such as marking a cross on a piece of paper, raising a hand at a meeting, nodding one's head and so on. Furthermore, any one of these physical movements can have multiple meanings. In addition to being a vote, marking a cross on a piece of paper can be part of a game of noughts and crosses, a representation of a kiss, or a substitute for a signature and so on. In short, we cannot understand what people do without understanding its meaning. And the meaning of an action is typically characterized by reference to the purposes of agents and the social practices available to them. Voting cannot be understood apart from understanding what a person's purposes are and the practice of deciding matters through elections and suchlike.

Self-understanding is inextricably bound up with our understanding of the meaning of the world and our place within it. Our sense of who we are cannot be determined without reference to our commitments and identifications, our roles and circumstances. For instance, we are somebody's daughter, mother, sister or wife; we are committed to this or that cause, religion or political creed; we are members of this club, this neighbourhood and this nation; we are teachers, lawyers, or miners. The meaning these things have for us is largely constitutive of who we are. Moreover, they are inseparable from the evaluative frameworks we employ in judging and assessing them. We endorse them or reject them, love them or hate them, try to live up to the standards they require of us and much else.

The conception of human beings as self-interpreting animals, therefore, includes within it the idea that they are also evaluators. We take up attitudes to, judge, assess and respond to situations in which we find ourselves. These evaluations cannot be reduced to a mere stimulus–response model; they require interpretation and judgement. Furthermore, we not only evaluate situations or events external to us, but also evaluate our own desires, motivations and intentions. At any given time we may have numerous desires but we have to decide which of these we should or should not act on. This kind of evaluation requires us going beyond our preferences and subjective feelings. Taylor contrasts what he calls 'simple weighers' and 'strong evaluators'.[14] The choices of the former are flat and inarticulate in that little can be given by way of explanation for such choices beyond reference to the desire or feeling of the agent. By contrast, strong evaluation appeals to something beyond the state of the agent; strong evaluators explain their choices or judgements in terms of reasons which invoke features external to the agent. Taylor argues that strong evaluation in this sense is essential to any life which is recognizably human and that, in particular, our conception of morality is unintelligible without it.[15] Moral judgements are not reducible to expressions of taste or inclination, and moral decisions require us to choose in the light of our judgements about what is right or valuable, not merely to respond to whichever desire is the most powerful.

This conception of strong evaluation is integral to selfhood. For our identity is partly constituted through the process of strong evaluation. We think of ourselves as this or that sort of person, connected in specific ways to other people and the society around us. It is this sense of who we are which provides the criteria for identifying with or prioritizing some desires rather than others, and for acknowledging an obligation to this or that person, group or institution. Strong evaluation is a crucial part of what makes us the moral agents we are.

As the notion of strong evaluation implies, our sense of identity is not something which we construct entirely for ourselves; it has an essentially social dimension. The concepts and categories that we use in this process are given to us in our language. And our language is something which we cannot create individually; it is necessarily social and intersubjective.[16] Our identity is a dialogical product of our interactions with other people. Our sense of who we are is in part a function of what others take us to be – the image of ourselves which is reflected back to us, both by those individuals, such as parents, to whom we are especially close, and by the wider society. This, as we shall see later, has important political implications in Taylor's discussion of the politics of recognition. Moreover, the relationships, practices and institutions in terms of which we define ourselves are to some significant degree pre-given. This does not entail simply endorsing whatever confronts us in society but it does mean that we must locate ourselves in relation to what is already around us: even the rejection of a socially allotted role, for example, is unintelligible without understanding that role and the significance its rejection has for us and those around us. We are social beings and there is no self entirely apart from society.

Community and Common Goods

Taylor's emphasis on the interconnectedness of the self and society has led
to him being located firmly within what has become known as the
'communitarian' strand in modern political theory.[17] As with most labels,
however, this one is useful only if treated with considerable caution. He
does indeed share similarities with other so-called communitarians such as
Alasdair MacIntyre, Michael Sandel and Michael Walzer, but, while acknowledging these similarities, Taylor has been keen to distinguish two
different sets of issues around which the debate between liberals and
communitarians has been conducted. These he calls 'ontological' and
'advocacy' issues, and it is specifically in relation to the former that he sees
the sharpest distinction between himself and most contemporary liberals.

Ontological questions, for Taylor, 'concern what you recognize as the
factors you will invoke to account for social life. Or, put in the formal
mode, they concern the terms you accept as ultimate in the order of
explanation.'[18] In short, ontological issues relate to the sort of questions we
have been discussing in the previous section. On these questions Taylor is
a holist and an implacable opponent of atomism. He believes, as we have
seen, that society is not reducible to the properties of individuals. By
contrast 'advocacy issues concern the moral stand or policy one adopts.'[19]
Here there is a less sharp polarity of opinions (except at the extremes) and
more of a continuum between individualists and collectivists. At the
former end of the spectrum are views in which negative liberty and
individual rights have primacy, while at the latter end priority is given to
the community or collective good. Taylor is very far from being hostile to
traditional liberal freedoms but he does think that the way in which these
are typically defended by modern liberals is unsatisfactory.

One of the points Taylor is most concerned to make is that the
relationship between these two sets of issues is complex.

> They are distinct in the sense that taking a position on one doesn't force
> your hand on the other. Yet they are not completely independent in that
> the stand you take on the ontological level can be part of the essential
> background of the view you advocate.[20]

In Taylor's view, the standard discussions of the liberal–communitarian
debate have simplistically linked up atomism and individualism on the
one side, and holism and collectivism on the other. Nonetheless, other
combinations are possible. There can be atomist collectivists – Taylor cites
B. F. Skinner as an example – although he agrees that this 'category may

be of interest only for the student of the bizarre or the monstrous'.[21] Much more important, though, is the category of holist individualists which is a position with which Taylor himself largely identifies. Thinkers in this category, he says, 'represent a trend of thought that is fully aware of the (ontological) social embedding of human agents but, at the same time, prizes liberty and individual differences very highly'.[22] Defending liberal principles against the background of a holistic ontology, however, produces a rather different picture of the conditions of those liberties than that presented by atomist individualists.

Taylor argues that unless the importance of a holistic ontology is appreciated, moral or political individualism is likely to be unviable. This, he thinks, is especially true of the kind of procedural liberal theories associated with the works of Rawls, Dworkin and others.[23] In particular, a society which embodies no conception of the good and is unified only by subscription to a set of procedures is unlikely to be able to secure the allegiance of its citizens. The trouble with procedural liberalism is that it does not understand that citizens' willingness to make necessary sacrifices depends on identification with the polity. In so far as people are attached to the normative force of liberal principles and rules, this attachment does not bind them specifically to their political community or fellow citizens.

As an alternative to procedural liberalism, Taylor seeks to recover a tradition of republican political thought which more effectively combines freedom with a substantial sense of political community. This tradition of thinking has been obscured by the liberal-communitarian debate.[24] What this tradition has, which procedural liberalism so significantly lacks, is a vivid sense of the importance of the patriotic identification of citizens with their polity. This is made possible because the civic republican understanding of freedom is not merely as a property of the private life of independent individuals – the liberal sense of 'negative liberty' – but as a common good of a particular political community.[25] Freedom is associated with a self-governing polity, one in which citizens are politically active in shaping the public life of their community. The republican ideal is one of the self-government of a free people.

Before proceeding further with the discussion of democracy, however, it is necessary to explain what Taylor means by a common good. For a common good is not a good which just happens to be shared, in the sense that a number of individuals converge in their separate judgements about what is good. Nor is it a public good in the sense familiar in welfare economics. In this latter case a particular good is common because it can only be provided effectively on a collective basis. For example, it is not practically possible to make the streets safe for some people without making them safe for everyone. But, even in this sense, the *value* of the good of security in no way depends upon its being collective or common. If security could be provided on a non-collective basis its value to people would not be any the less. The sense of common goods, as Taylor conceives them, however, is one where their *value* is inseparable from what makes them common. That is, he claims that 'their being for us enters into and constitutes their value for us.'[26] The classic example of such a good is friendship. It is not the fact that friendship necessarily involves more than one person that is important – many non-common goods in this sense require more than one person for their enjoyment – but that the good of friendship is constituted by its commonality.

It is in this sense of a common good that Taylor thinks that the relationship between citizens in a civic republic is to be characterized. Self-government is a common good in that its value is inseparable from the relationship between people which is constituted by citizenship within a single polity. For Taylor, 'the identification of the citizen with the republic as a common enterprise is essentially the recognition of a common good.'[27] When people act together as citizens they constitute a 'we-identity' and engage in common action. They are not merely convergent but distinct 'I-identities', manifesting a collective instrumentality directed towards an end on which they just happen to agree and find it useful or essential to act collectively to achieve. This conception of a common good is simply unintelligible on atomistic assumptions and has no place in procedural liberalism.[28] Liberals who neglect the need to recognize a common good risk losing a viable political community capable of generating sufficient attachment on the part of its citizens to support and defend it. An adequate democratic liberalism, therefore, must jettison any lingering atomistic ontology. To explore what this involves we must look more closely at Taylor's ideas about democracy.

Democracy

According to Taylor the essential aspirations of the democratic ideal are that

> rules and decisions ought to be determined by the people. This means that (1) the mass of the people should have some say in what they are going to be, and not just told what they are; that (2) this say should be genuinely theirs, and not manipulated by propaganda, misinformation, irrational fears; and that (3) it should to some extent reflect their considered opinions and aspirations, as against ill-informed and knee-jerk prejudices.[29]

To many modern thinkers, however, these aspirations have appeared as either utopian or dangerous or both. This is because all three conditions are difficult to meet in mass societies: there can be no general assembly of the people; public opinion is prey to manipulation by media controlled by powerful interests; and in any case most people are simply too ill-informed, uninterested or incompetent to formulate reasoned opinions on complex issues. In consequence, there is a temptation to refashion our conception of democracy to try to avoid these difficulties. Taylor considers two such attempts and contrasts his own conception of democracy with each of these alternative models.

According to the first model, democracy is primarily an instrumental process. It is conceived as a means by which a large number of individual preferences or interests are aggregated into a collective decision. It is, in short, a kind of mechanism for transforming diverse individual interests and desires into legislative or policy outcomes. On this view, Taylor writes:

> People have interests that can be identified prior to decisions; and the decisions favour some interests and frustrate others. Is the majority fa-voured? Then democracy is served. If not then there has been illegitimate elitist control.[30]

This conception of democracy is, however, inadequate because what underlies it is the atomism which, as we have seen, is the fallacy at the heart of so much of modern, especially liberal, thought. It fails to explain how people come to be – what it is that makes them – an appropriate unit for collective decision-making. Without some understanding of that it is hard to see what authority a majority decision will have over those people who dissent from it. The idea of democracy presupposes that there exists a community with which its members, to some extent at least, identify themselves. People must 'understand themselves as belonging to a com-munity that shares some common purpose and recognizes its members as sharing in these purposes'.[31] This is something that the atomistic assump-tions of the instrumental view cannot satisfactorily explain.

The mention of shared purposes brings out the second related weakness of the instrumental view of democracy. This is its failure to find a place for the transformative possibilities inherent in democratic decision-making.[32] The instrumental view of democratic decision-making cannot 'take ac-count of the fact that people's views can be altered by the interchange, that consensus sometimes emerges, that citizens frequently understand them-selves as part of a community and don't vote out of individual interest alone'.[33] So the existence of a community is not only a condition of the authority of democratic decision-making, it is also something which informs, and enters into, political deliberation itself. In saying this, though, we must be careful to avoid a different kind of error, namely, that associated with a second model of democracy which Taylor also rejects.

If the problem with the first model of democracy is that it neglects democracy's communal underpinning, the problem with the second model is that it neglects the diversity which is an ineliminable feature of any free society under modern conditions. Proponents of this second model 'follow Rousseau and see genuine democratic decision as the effect of a general will, that is, some unanimous purpose'.[34] While there are very occasionally times and places where there is something close to a general will, it is not something which can reasonably be expected in modern societies.[35] To require it is to set the demands of democracy too high. It is to postulate a degree of uniformity which does not exist and can only be brought about by means which are themselves highly undemocratic. It is this model which has informed the 'people's democracies' and encouraged the view that democracy is antithetic to personal freedom. Any adequate model of democracy must take account of the diversity which is both an unavoidable and a desirable feature of modern societies.

A democratic society, if it is to function effectively, needs both a reasonable level of political participation, to reflect social diversity, and a genuine sense of community. Neither the 'instrumental' nor the 'general will' models of democracy accommodate both these requirements. These requirements are difficult to meet, however, especially under modern conditions, where they are subject to decline and decay. One of the most corrosive features of modern societies is their large, centralized and bureaucratic nature which results in a sense of powerlessness and political alienation on the part of the average citizen. The government is seen as beyond our (perhaps anybody's) control, and the institutions of the state are experienced as remote and external to our everyday lives, a process further reinforced by the growth of global markets. Taylor does not think this trend can simply be reversed but he does believe it can be offset, at least partially, through 'a double decentralization, toward regional societies and nested public spheres'.[36]

While the idea of geographical decentralization is familiar enough, Taylor's conception of 'nested public spheres' is more novel. These are substate arenas of public argument which can eventually contribute to shaping national political debates. Taylor has in mind in particular the 'new social movements' such as feminist and ecological groups. What is different about these movements is the way in which they combine shared concerns with often intense and sophisticated internal debate and disagreement. They are unlike both traditional pressure groups, which seek to mobilize political support exclusively behind a particular interest or opinion, and political parties, whose main concern is to capture control of political power and form a government. 'Nested public spheres' are forums of political argument which can feed into public debate at the national level.

The process of bureaucratization and centralization issuing in a kind of administrative despotism is only one of the threats to democracy. Another, related but distinct threat, and one perhaps of even greater seriousness, is fragmentation. This occurs where

> a people [is] less and less capable of forming a common purpose and carrying it out. Fragmentation arises when people come to see themselves more and more atomistically, as less and less bound to their fellow citizens in common projects and allegiances.[37]

Fragmentation sets up a potentially self-destructive dynamic within a democracy. Members find it hard to identify with the political community. This lack of identification reinforces an atomistic attitude 'because the absence of effective common action throws people back on themselves'.[38] This, in turn, further erodes the sense of community and buttresses atomism.

A significant contributory cause of fragmentation is the experience of political powerlessness, and an increased sense of empowerment is one way to strengthen identification with the political community. Taylor is, however, rather short on suggestions about how this may be achieved beyond reiterating the importance of decentralization. Moreover, as we shall see, the problem of reconciling at least some forms of decentralization with a strong feeling of belonging to a larger political community united by a robust sense of a common good is one which threatens the very coherence of Taylor's conception of democracy.

A third way in which the conditions necessary for effective democratic decision-making can be eroded is as a result of rifts within the political community. One form in which such a rift may occur is when a particular cultural community feels excluded from the political process because its values and aspirations are unrecognized by the wider society. This problem is likely to be most acute in multicultural societies where there is at least one minority group with a culture in some respects significantly different from that of the dominant group. Even in mild forms this can create tensions and hostilities which seriously undermine social cohesion, and in extreme forms, for example where it issues in demands for secession, it threatens the very existence of the political community.

Multiculturalism, Recognition and Democracy

The issue of how political community can be maintained in the face of potential rifts is worth close attention for two reasons. The first reason is that the issue is one which has long attracted Taylor's interest. He has been deeply engaged, politically as well as theoretically, with the challenge posed to the Canadian Federation by the threat of Quebec separatism. In this conflict Taylor has tried to occupy a position which seems to have become steadily more precarious, a position which combines a very real sympathy for the aspirations of the French majority of Quebec with a passionate desire to hold together the Federation.[39] But the issue is also worth exploring for a second reason: because it reveals some of the tensions inherent in Taylor's views.

The general importance which Taylor attaches to self-understanding and communal membership have made him sympathetic to recent developments emphasizing the importance of cultural membership in constructing people's identities. These developments are to be found for example in that strand of feminist theorizing in which 'difference' plays a prominent role; in the claims of aboriginal and immigrant peoples for greater respect for their distinctive cultural practices and heritage; in the impetus of many nationalist movements; and in the explosion of so-called 'identity politics' in the USA. Taylor is by no means equally sympathetic to all these developments but he does think that there is here an important question which needs to be addressed to do with what he calls 'the politics of recognition'.[40]

As was explained earlier, identity, for Taylor, is largely constituted dialogically through our interaction with others and through the meanings we derive from our culture.

> The thesis is that our identity is partly shaped by recognition or its absence, often by the *mis*recognition of others, and so a person or group of people can suffer real damage, real distortion, if the people or society around them mirror back to them a confining or demeaning or contemptible picture of themselves.[41]

Recognition operates at two levels: the intimate, in which selfhood is constituted through exchanges with those with whom we have close personal bonds, and in the public or political sphere.[42] It is the latter which is of primary interest here.

The explanation of the modern preoccupation with identity and recognition is to be found in two social tendencies and the corresponding responses to them. The first is the collapse of traditional social hierarchies in which identity was, to a significant degree, a function of a person's place in the hierarchy. This has been replaced by a universalist and egalitarian conception of the 'dignity of human beings' that has gone hand in hand with the growth of a democratic culture, to which the equalization of rights and entitlements has been integral. The second tendency, which becomes especially marked towards the end of the eighteenth century, is an increasingly individualized conception of identity, one in which individual uniqueness and a sense of authenticity lie at the centre.[43] There is a potential tension between these tendencies, however, which has been obscured by the rhetoric of the universal recognition of everyone as a unique individual. For the 'uniqueness' which universalist and egalitarian principles have acknowledged lies typically in sameness, in what individuals share – dignity, autonomy, a similar capacity for pleasure and pain or whatever – rather than in their particularity or distinctiveness.

In Taylor's view, the emergence of identity politics is to be understood in terms of this conflict and the tension between the two politics which these tendencies generate.

> These two modes of politics, then, both based on the notion of equal respect, come into conflict. For one, the principle of equal respect requires that we treat people in a difference-blind fashion. The fundamental intuition that humans command this respect focuses on what is the same in all. For the other, we have to recognize and even foster particularity.[44]

But how does this conflict bear specifically on the issue of minority groups and cultures? The problem appears to identify an issue which is of equal significance for everyone, namely the tension between the common and the particular. The answer is that this appearance is deceptive. For

> the supposedly neutral set of difference-blind principles of the politics of equal dignity is in fact a reflection of one hegemonic culture. As it turns out, then, only the minority or suppressed cultures are being forced to take alien form.[45]

The problem, then, is one of how, if at all, these two divergent understandings of equal respect and the politics that flow from them can be reconciled in a way which does justice to the insights and legitimate concerns of both. This is at least in part a problem for democratic theory. How can democratic political institutions provide the kind of recognition demanded by minority cultures, while at the same time preserving a structure of equal rights which seems integral to the democratic ideal? Rather than pursue this question in entirely general terms, it is more illuminating to explore it through a particular example: the conflict between English and French Canadians, more particularly the people of Quebec, over the proper terms of the Canadian Federation.

Multiculturalism and Democracy in Canada

A good way to focus on the dispute about the Canadian Federation is to look at the 1982 Canadian Charter of Rights around which the different positions of Quebeckers and English Canadians crystallized. In essence the Canadian Charter legally enshrines a number of individual rights in a manner similar to the US Constitution. These rights provide protection for individuals against encroachment by government (and other organizations) and establish provision for judicial review of legislation at all levels of government. The problem for Quebeckers (and indigenous peoples) is that these individual rights sometimes conflict with measures deemed necessary for their survival as a distinct cultural group. For example, Quebec has passed many laws with the object of seeking to ensure the preservation of the French language which is seen as essential to the distinctive culture of French Canadians. These include restrictions on who can be educated at English-language schools; the requirement that businesses of a certain size must use French; and a prohibition on commercial signage in any language other than French. These restrictions are justified in terms of the collective good of the survival of the French language. But all potentially conflict with the 1982 Charter.[46]

The attempt to accommodate the demands of Quebeckers led to the formulation of the Meech Lake Accord, which sought to recognize Quebec as a 'distinct society' within Canada. This would have allowed that the interpretation of the Charter could vary in Quebec from other parts of the country. But this was fundamentally unacceptable to many English Canadians, because it undermined the whole *raison d'être* of the Charter which was to ensure equal rights for all Canadians. Taylor's sympathy lies with the Quebeckers and their aspiration to protect the French language. He agrees with defenders of the Charter that it is important to protect fundamental rights, but he also maintains that something has gone badly wrong 'in speaking of fundamental rights to such things as commercial signage in the language of one's choice'.[47] A wide conception of individual rights which are always deemed to have primacy over collective goals will necessarily preclude a solution to the Canadian problem. In Taylor's view, the attempt to make procedural liberalism the basis of Canadian unity is both illegitimate and doomed to failure. For it represents the imposition of one society's model on another, and in the circumstances of late-twentieth-century Canadian democracy this cannot succeed.[48]

Some other basis for reconciling the two communities, therefore, needs to be found.

Taylor believes that the Canadian Federation's survival depends upon acknowledging the deep diversity at its heart; a diversity which goes beyond the first-level diversity of individual differences.

> For Quebeckers, and for most French Canadians, the way of being a Canadian (for those who still want to be) is by their belonging to a constituent element of Canada, *la nation québecoise*, or *canadienne-française*. Something analogous holds for aboriginal communities in this country; their way of being Canadian is not accommodated by first-level diversity. . . . To build a country for everyone, Canada would have to allow for second-level or 'deep' diversity, in which a plurality of ways of belonging would also be acknowledged and accepted.[49]

Canada would have to be a mosaic identity, combining deep diversity – the legal recognition of cultural differences – with a sense of belonging to the same community. Unless it does, genuinely democratic decision-making is impossible since one part of the country will continue to feel itself excluded from what holds the rest together. Nonetheless, this vision of a Canadian Federation as a genuine community which acknowledges the deep diversity at its heart and in which Quebec is recognized as a 'distinct society' is, even at a theoretical level, more problematic than Taylor allows. The question which becomes insistent is: what remains as a possible basis for any Canadian unity? Taylor himself, as we saw earlier, has emphasized the need for individuals to see themselves as members of a people if democratic decisions are to be experienced as binding. He has also rejected procedural liberalism as an adequate basis for such unity. What is it then that will bind the Federation together?

Taylor acknowledges that this is 'a very pertinent question'.[50] His attempt to answer it, however, is unsatisfactory. He invokes a common history and a shared national identity.

> For an indeterminate but large number of Canadians of both language groups, the history of their association with people of the other language

has become part of their sense of their own national identity. . . . For these people, this will be one strand of a many-stranded sense of a Canadian unity. But it is an essential one. If this were to fray to the point of rupture – as it certainly has for many Canadians – none of the others would suffice to keep the country together.[51]

The last sentence, however, clearly undermines the general drift of Taylor's claims. He may be right to argue that the 'demand for common traits, goals or purposes'[52] effectively weakens Canadian unity but he has given no real indication of what could be put in their place. Furthermore, it is as a result of Taylor's own arguments that we see that there needs to be *something* – some common good – which makes them a people if Canada is to survive and prosper as a democratic polity.

Taylor offers two principal reasons for his refusal to be pessimistic. First, he claims that 'deep diversity is the only formula on which a united federal Canada can be rebuilt, once we recall the reasons why we all need Canada – namely, for law and order, collective provision, regional equality and mutual self-help.'[53] It is in fact unclear that all these would be impossible without a federal Canada, but there is a deeper, theoretical problem. If people's primary identity is, say, as Quebeckers then, even if they do need to join with other Canadians to achieve these goods, the basis of this relationship looks suspiciously instrumental. Taylor himself has lucidly argued that securing common goods in this sense is not sufficient to make them a single people rather than an alliance of convenience.

Secondly, Taylor points out that the Canadian situation is replicated, to a greater or lesser extent and with local variations, in a large number of societies. The model of a uniform citizenship, therefore, is widely inappropriate. Although the world may indeed need other models of citizenship, this itself is hardly sufficient to show that deep diversity is a workable alternative conception of democratic citizenship. Taylor's reference to the experience of the European Union, where he claims that greater 'breathing space' has been afforded to regional societies like the Bretons, Basques and Catalans, is less than reassuring.[54] Even the European Union's best friends would not pretend that the democratic accountability of its institutions is one of its strengths. If greater freedom for regional societies has been achieved within the European Union, and this claim is certainly open to doubt, it has been attained through bureaucratic decree and the bypassing of democratic processes and institutions.

Conclusion

Taylor's most significant contribution to democratic theory lies in his analysis of the essential presuppositions of a democratic polity in terms of a community with a genuine sense of a common good. In modern societies this common good has to accommodate individual diversity. It cannot be based on a substantive commitment to a narrow way of life which fails to allow for the pursuit of individual authenticity, an attractive and fundamental feature of the modern self. Furthermore, in some societies the common good will need to accommodate the diversity which arises from membership of distinct cultural groups which are an important source of meaning for people's lives. Cultural groups in this sense cannot be reduced to voluntary associations formed as the result of individual choices. But preserving such cultural groups also needs to be consistent both with protecting the fundamental rights of individuals and with a conception of the common good.

Taylor's remarks about how a democratic society might meet these desiderata are not well developed. At a general level we are encouraged to think about decentralization, greater participation and a more deliberative conception of the democratic process. These are all familiar features of contemporary discourse about democracy. His views come out most clearly, perhaps, in his discussion of the fissure in the Canadian polity between English and French Canadians. At both the general level and in the specific context of Canada, however, his political prescriptions do not sit altogether easily with his philosophical arguments about the conditions of community. For instance, his claim that 'Canada has been fortunate' in the democratic empowerment that its federal system has maintained seems to be seriously undercut by the immediate admission that this has been accompanied by a failure to 'create a common understanding that can hold these regional societies together'.[55] In seeking to accommodate fundamental rights and the recognition of cultural diversity within a polity marked by a genuine sense of a common good, Taylor has posed, rather than resolved, a fundamental problem for democratic theory.

If Taylor's account of the conditions of democracy is anything like correct, however, and it surely has considerable plausibility, then he may have made a significant contribution to understanding why democracy is difficult not only to make work effectively but also to articulate theoretically. Although it is not a conclusion with which he would agree, Taylor's analysis does much to explain why, in the words of John Dunn, 'Today in politics, democracy is the *name* for what we cannot have – yet cannot also cease to want.'[56]

Notes

1   I am very grateful to Margaret Canovan and to the editors for their helpful comments on this chapter.

2   The most important of Taylor's writings are: *The Explanation of Behaviour* (London, Routledge and Kegan Paul, 1964); *Hegel* (Cambridge, Cambridge University Press, 1975); *Human Agency and Language: Philosophical Papers I* (Cambridge, Cambridge University Press, 1985); *Philosophy and the Human Sciences: Philosophical Papers II* (Cambridge, Cambridge University Press, 1985); *Sources of the Self: The Making of the Modern Identity* (Cambridge, MA, Harvard University Press, 1989); *The Ethics of Authenticity* (Cambridge, MA, Harvard University Press, 1992); *Reconciling the Solitudes: Essays on Canadian Federalism and Nationalism* (Montreal, McGill–Queens University Press, 1993); 'The politics of recognition', in A. Gutmann (ed.), *Multiculturalism: Examining the Politics of Recognition* (Princeton, NJ, Princeton University Press, 1994); and *Philosophical Arguments* (Cambridge, MA, Harvard University Press, 1995).

3   The information in this paragraph draws heavily on Guy Laforest's 'Introduction' to Taylor, *Reconciling the Solitudes.*

4   Taylor, *Hegel.* For an abbreviated account, focusing specifically on Hegel's contemporary significance, see C. Taylor, *Hegel and Modern Society* (Cambridge, Cambridge University Press, 1979).

5   Taylor, *Hegel,* p. 570 and *Hegel and Modern Society,* p. 167.

6   Taylor, *Hegel,* p. 570 and *Hegel and Modern Society,* p. 167.

7   Taylor, *Hegel,* p. 414 and *Hegel and Modern Society,* p. 116.

8   Taylor, *Hegel,* p. 415 and *Hegel and Modern Society,* p. 118.

9   Taylor, *Hegel,* p. 416 and *Hegel and Modern Society,* p. 118.

10 Taylor, *Human Agency and Language,* p. 1.

11 See particularly 'Self-interpreting animals', in Taylor, *Human Agency and Language.*

12 Taylor, *The Explanation of Behaviour,* and also 'Neutrality in political science', in *Philosophy and Human Sciences.*

13 Taylor, *Philosophy and Human Sciences,* pp. 66–70.

14 Taylor, 'What is human agency?', in his *Human Agency and Language,* pp. 16–27.

15 See particularly 'The concept of a person', in Taylor, *Human Agency and Language.*

16 This claim is part of Taylor's rejection of the broader Cartesian epistemological project which seeks to ground knowledge in the experience of the individual subject. See Taylor, *Sources of the Self,* ch. 8, and 'Overcoming epistemology', in Taylor, *Philosophical Arguments.* For a critique of Taylor's treatment of Descartes see S. James, 'Internal and external in the work of Descartes', in J. Tully (ed.), *Philosophy in an Age of Pluralism: The Philosophy of Charles Taylor in Question* (Cambridge, Cambridge University Press, 1994).

17   See, for example, S. Mulhall and A. Swift, *Liberals and Communitarians*, 2nd edn (Oxford, Blackwell, 1996), ch. 3, and W. Kymlicka, *Contemporary Political Philosophy: An Introduction* (Oxford, Oxford University Press, 1990), ch. 6.

18   Taylor, 'Cross-purposes: The liberal–communitarian debate', in his *Philosophical Arguments*, p. 181.

19   Taylor, *Philosophical Arguments*, p. 182.

20   Taylor, *Philosophical Arguments*, p. 182.

21   Taylor, *Philosophical Arguments*, p. 185.

22   Taylor, *Philosophical Arguments*, p. 185.

23   Probably the best defence of procedural liberalism against Taylor's charge that it presupposes an atomistic ontology is W. Kymlicka, *Liberalism, Community and Culture* (Oxford, Oxford University Press, 1989), ch. 5.

24   For a similar claim see P. Pettit, 'Liberal/communitarian: MacIntyre's mesmeric dichotomy', in J. Horton and S. Mendus (eds), *After MacIntyre: Critical Perspectives on the Work of Alasdair MacIntyre* (Cambridge, Polity, 1994).

25   For Taylor's criticism of negative liberty and its philosophical underpinning see his 'Atomism' and 'What's wrong with negative liberty', in *Philosophy and the Human Sciences*.

26   Taylor, *Philosophical Arguments*, p. 190.

27   Taylor, *Philosophical Arguments*, p. 192.

28   See Taylor, 'Irreducibly social goods', in *Philosophical Arguments*.

29   Taylor, 'Liberal politics and the public sphere', in *Philosophical Arguments*, p. 273.

30   Taylor, *Philosophical Arguments*, p. 275.

31   Taylor, *Philosophical Arguments*, p. 275.

32   This is an important element in deliberative conceptions of democracy. See, for example, J. Fishkin, *Democracy and Deliberation: New Directions for Democratic Reform* (New Haven, CT, Yale University Press, 1991).

33   Taylor, *Philosophical Arguments*, p. 276.

34   Taylor, *Philosophical Arguments*, p. 275.

35   In fairness to Rousseau it should be pointed out that he was well aware that the social conditions in which a general will could emerge would have to be very different from those of the modern state.

36   Taylor, *Philosophical Arguments*, p. 280.

37   Taylor, *Philosophical Arguments*, p. 282, and Taylor, *The Ethics of Authenticity*, p. 112.

38   Taylor, *The Ethics of Authenticity*, p. 117.

39   Although, as we shall see later, there are more specific reasons why Taylor wishes to keep the Canadian Federation together, it is clear that part of the motivation lies in his 'gut emotional identification with Canada'. Taylor, 'Reply and rearticulation', in Tully (ed.), *Philosophy in an Age of Pluralism*, p. 254.

40   One source of such claims to which Taylor has been markedly unsympa-

thetic is the 'subjectivist, half-baked neo-Nietzschean theories' of post-modernism and deconstruction. Taylor, 'The politics of recognition', p. 70.

41 Taylor, 'The politics of recognition', p. 25.
42 See Taylor, *The Ethics of Authenticity*, ch. 5.
43 See Taylor, *Sources of the Self*, part IV.
44 Taylor, 'The politics of recognition', p. 43. Taylor's account of the relationship between the politics of difference and the ideal of authenticity is subject to some acute criticism in M. Cooke, 'Authenticity and autonomy: Taylor, Habermas and the politics of recognition', *Political Theory*, 25 (1997), 258–88, esp. pp. 59–70.
45 Taylor, 'The politics of recognition', p. 43.
46 Potentially, because only the commercial signage provision has been tested in the Canadian Supreme Court. Moreover, while that was struck down, the judgement appeared to permit the possibility of insisting on French as one of the languages in which a commercial sign must be displayed.
47 Taylor, *Reconciling the Solitudes*, p. 176.
48 Taylor, *Reconciling the Solitudes*, pp. 178–9.
49 Taylor, *Reconciling the Solitudes*, pp. 182–3.
50 Taylor, 'Reply and rearticulation', p. 255.
51 Taylor, 'Reply and rearticulation', p. 255.
52 Taylor, 'Reply and rearticulation', p. 255.
53 Taylor, *Reconciling the Solitudes*, p. 183.
54 Taylor, *Reconciling the Solitudes*, p. 184. Taylor's views on 'European identity' seem extraordinarily naive, at least in a British context: I suspect that in most of Europe only the political and cosmopolitan elites would endorse them. See the interview 'Charles Taylor. Nations and federations: living amongst others', in R. Kearney (ed.), *Visions of Europe: Conversations on the Legacy and Future of Europe* (Dublin, Wolfhound, 1992).
55 Taylor, *The Ethics of Authenticity*, p. 119.
56 J. Dunn, *Western Political Theory in the Face of the Future* (Cambridge, Cambridge University Press, 1979), p. 27.

9

Carole Pateman: Participatory Democracy and Feminism

Barbara Sullivan

Carole Pateman is best known among feminists as the author of *The Sexual Contract* (1988), a text which delivers a powerful critique of social contract theory and of the role of contract in marriage, employment, prostitution and surrogacy. Pateman's argument here is both historical and contemporary. She claims that contract leads to the subordination of women to men in both public and private spheres, civil and political life. Pateman's feminist critique of contract has significant implications for democratic theory and practice, some of which are explored in her book of essays, *The Disorder of Women: Democracy, Feminism and Political Theory* (1989).

Pateman's feminist concerns with contract should, however, be seen as part of her longer-term engagement with the problems and concerns of democracy. Her first monograph, *Participation and Democratic Theory* (1970), presented a critical analysis of empirical (or realist) accounts of liberal democracy and made a strong case both for a more participatory society and for industrial democracy. The critique of liberal democracy was developed and the call for more participation was sustained in her next book, *The Problem of Political Obligation: A Critical Analysis of Liberal Theory* (1979).[1]

The terms of Pateman's engagement with democratic theory and practice underwent significant change between 1970 and the late 1980s, particularly as her writing became focused on the position of women in liberal democracies. Pateman's feminist analysis is, however, also committed both to a fundamental critique of liberal democracy and to increasing women's participation. Throughout her career Pateman has argued strongly for greater economic, political and sexual equality. She has drawn attention to the advantages of a participatory society, and pointed out the problems associated with the public/private distinction and narrow con-

ceptions of the political within liberal democracy. Pateman has also analysed the theoretical inadequacy of liberal individualism and exposed male
domination in the theory and practice of democracy.

In this chapter I focus on the evolution of Pateman's analysis of democracy. I examine her early arguments in favour of participatory democracy
and then consider her later feminist critiques of liberal democracy. Next,
I explore some of the changes and continuities in Pateman's work on
democracy between her pre-feminist and feminist periods. It is my argument here that Pateman's feminist writings should be seen not as a
separate development but as an extension of her pre-feminist studies on
democracy. The overall conclusion is that Pateman's work, both feminist
and pre-feminist, represents an important contribution to contemporary
debates about democracy.

Background: Life and Context

Pateman is currently Professor of Political Science at the University of
California, Los Angeles. She was born and educated in Britain and spent
more than a decade teaching at the University of Sydney in Australia
before moving to the United States. Her arguments about democracy have
been influenced by her different geographic and cultural milieux.

Pateman was born in rural England in 1940. Despite coming from 'the
wrong end of the class system', she obtained a good state education.[2] She
left school after taking O levels, however, worked as a clerk and married a
politically aware man who was very supportive of her later academic
career. They lived for a few years in Kenya before returning to Britain and
joining the Campaign for Nuclear Disarmament. In the early 1960s
Pateman was very active in the non-violent, direct action wing of the
peace movement. She also regularly attended evening classes run by the
Workers' Educational Association. In 1963 she became a mature student
at Ruskin College and then completed a degree and doctorate at Lady
Margaret Hall, Oxford University. Her *Participation and Democratic
Theory* (1970) focused on the place of popular participation in a democracy. Pateman's experience of the inequalities of the British class
system, and her association with the new left, were important influences
upon her arguments in support of equality, participation and industrial
democracy.

Pateman's turn to feminism began in the 1970s under the influence of
a world-wide revival of organized feminism. In 1973 Pateman took up a
teaching post in the Department of Government at the University of
Sydney. At this stage, she says, she was 'excited' by feminist ideas but had

not yet made the connections between feminist arguments and her own life and work.[3] The catalyst for her rethinking these issues occurred during her first few years at Sydney University which she says were 'politically eventful'.[4] Significant disputes took place in the Philosophy and Economics Departments of the university, about the teaching of feminism and political economy and about broadening the basis of participation in academic decision-making. Pateman's own department was not untouched by these developments; she and some of her colleagues joined the strike. Pateman also became involved in setting up women's studies courses and taught a course entitled 'The Political Economy of Women'. This experience led her to recognize the importance of feminism, to ask new questions of her own discipline of political theory and to re-evaluate her earlier arguments about both participatory and liberal democracy.

Pateman as a Participatory Democrat

In *Participation and Democratic Theory* Pateman presents a substantive critique of what she calls 'the contemporary theory of democracy'.[5] This theory, she says, is exemplified in the influential work, during the 1950s and 1960s, of authors like Berelson, Dahl, Sartori and Eckstein, who argued for an empirical or realist view of democracy grounded in the actual conditions of existing democracies. From this perspective, democracy is not a normative ideal but a political method or set of institutional arrangements characterized by competition between elites.[6] As Pateman suggests, this view of democracy implies a narrow approach to equality and political participation. For the 'realist' theorists of democracy 'political equality' refers primarily to universal suffrage and 'participation' to the activity of voting. The theorists that Pateman criticizes consider participation of the majority beyond this limited role as a danger to the stability of a liberal democracy. Widescale participation could threaten the system by bringing fundamental disagreements on policy to the fore. Moreover, if the normally apathetic majority, who tend to hold liberal and undemocratic views, are mobilized they may undermine the necessary consensus on values.

Pateman notes that empirical theorists of democracy have been strongly influenced by Schumpeter's formulation of democratic elitism. Schumpeter argued that the classical doctrine of democracy was problematic because the participatory and decision-making role of the people rested on an empirically unrealistic foundation. He claimed, therefore, that a more modern and realistic theory was needed in which democracy should be regarded simply as a method, not as a normative ideal or inherent good. The central feature of this approach to democracy was, therefore, competition for leadership in free elections.[7]

The dominant empiricist interpretation of democracy in the 1960s had been challenged by a number of critics, such as Bachrach, Bay, Davis and Duncan and Lukes. They disputed the empiricist claim to have provided a value-free descriptive theory of democracy, and argued that democratic realism was itself a normative theory implicitly endorsing existing Anglo-American institutions as the democratic ideal, thereby excluding the possibility of greater political participation.[8]

Pateman suggested that the critics of empirical democracy had not, however, provided a fully convincing refutation of democratic realism.[9] To achieve this it was necessary to do two things. The first was to demonstrate the inadequacy of 'the classical theory of democracy' which Schumpeter had constructed and to review why participation was central to democracy by drawing on participatory theorists within the democratic tradition. The second was to show that the empiricists were wrong in claiming that the participatory ideal was impossible to achieve in practice. Pateman attacked Schumpeter's misleading composite of 'the classical theory of democracy', arguing that he had amalgamated diverse philosophical and political interpretations with contradictory implications. She then went on to examine the work of three theorists who provide the foundations for her own argument in favour of more participation: Rousseau, John Stuart Mill and G. D. H. Cole.[10]

Pateman was not opposed to representative political institutions. But, following J. S. Mill, she argued that for these to operate effectively and democratically, 'social training' for democracy must take place in other spheres of society. Pateman argued that a participatory society, and direct participation in non-government spheres, enables individuals to develop political skills, and has an important psychological impact, encouraging individuals to develop a sense of political efficacy which can then be translated to other representative political institutions. Participation also promotes the development of responsible individuals who are not wholly focused on their private interests.

Pateman referred briefly to families and universities as spheres where participation should be encouraged, but she argued that participation in decision-making was most important in industry.[11] Industrial participation was crucial because 'most individuals spend a great deal of their lifetime at work and the business of the workplace provides an education in the management of collective affairs that is difficult to parallel elsewhere.'[12] She examined whether low-level participation in industry in Western countries, for example workers having some control over the organization of their work, promoted a greater sense of political efficacy and found positive evidence to support this hypothesis.[13] She also considered whether opportunities for worker participation in high-level policy-making for a company had proved politically educational and had been effective in encouraging participation, and found that evidence drawn from three companies in Britain was inconclusive.[14]

Pateman then formulated her central argument, that non-governmental spheres were political systems in their own right and should be democratized. Industry was particularly important, because of the authoritarian relationships characterizing it and because of the impact of decisions taken there on citizens' lives.[15]

Pateman supports her argument with a case study of workers' self-management in Yugoslavia in the 1960s. This system, she claims, provides the only contemporary example of an attempt to introduce industrial democracy on a large scale, 'covering enterprises of many sizes and types over a whole economy'.[16] Therefore, the Yugoslav system offers 'some ideas' about how far it would be possible to replicate the direct participatory model of democracy in the context of modern, large-scale industrial society. While 'few firm conclusions can be drawn', she concludes there is no empirical evidence to suggest that industrial democracy is impossible.[17] Although this is hardly a decisive argument in favour of industrial democracy, it is enough to call into question the assumption that industrial democracy, or more participation generally, is unrealistic in the modern world.

In *Participation and Democratic Theory* Pateman establishes a convincing case against empirical or realist theories of democracy and, therefore, against elitist accounts of liberal democracy. She also establishes both theoretically and (to a lesser extent) empirically a more detailed, systematic and persuasive case in favour of a participatory society as the grounds of a truly democratic polity.

This latter argument, in favour of participatory democracy, is also sustained in *The Problem of Political Obligation*, in which Pateman develops her critique of the abstract individualism underpinning liberal democratic theory, and in particular the social contract. She contends that political obligation in the liberal state is an 'insoluble problem', because it rests on the concept of individual consent. The liberal emphasis on free individual choice poses, she argues, a constant threat to the requirement of obedience to government, and she suggests that the concept of political obligation provides a voluntarist façade for the necessity of political obedience.[18] She also claims that contemporary attempts to interpret the act of voting in liberal democracies as a form of consent ignore the extent to which voting may be manipulated, or be understood as pursuit of purely individual self-interest. In addition it takes no account of the fact that voters may not use their votes, and fails to investigate the implications of the empirical findings that non-voters 'tend to be drawn from lower socio-economic backgrounds and to be disproportionately female'.[19] Even if the liberal theory of political obligation in general could be sustained, it emerges that political obligation 'is differentially distributed'.[20] A democratic, as opposed to a liberal, concept of political obligation requires a community of citizens. It also requires, Pateman argues, an understanding that the 'political' is not separate from day-to-day life: 'The political sphere is one dimension, the collective dimension, of social life as a whole.'[21] Pateman's solution to the problems of political obligation therefore is 'the development of the theory and practice of participatory or self-managing democracy'.[22]

Pateman as a Feminist

Pateman's turn to feminism is clearly evident in her work by the late 1970s. Important feminist questions about the gendered nature of democratic theory and practice are raised in both *The Problem of Political Obligation* (and her 'Afterword' to the revised edition), and in the three essays with the earliest original publication dates in *The Disorder of Women*.[23] These publications can be regarded as a bridge between Pateman's pre-feminist and feminist periods. The most explicit and sustained elaboration of her views on feminism and democracy are, however, to be found in *The Sexual Contract*, and in the later essays in *The Disorder of Women*.[24] Several key themes and arguments about democracy appear in this context. For example in her essay 'Feminism and democracy', Pateman makes the following claim:

> For feminists, democracy has never existed; women have never been and still are not admitted as full and equal members and citizens in any country known as a 'democracy'.[25]

Her supporting arguments are both empirical and theoretical, as well as historical and contemporary. Women have been and continue to be excluded from democratic polities and this exclusion has been facilitated by the masculinist assumptions of democratic theorists.

Pateman frequently reiterates the argument that the widespread belief in women's 'natural' attributes militates against their full and equal inclusion in democratic polities. In an essay titled ' "The disorder of women": women, love and the sense of justice' Pateman looks at the unexamined tension inherent in liberal democracy between ideas about women's nature and those about individual equality. She demonstrates, through a reading of J. S. Mill, Mary Wollstonecraft and John Rawls, that liberals have been unable to resolve this tension when discussing the position of women in democratic theory and practice, because they assume explicitly or (in the case of Rawls) implicitly that women's primary role will be in the home.[26] She also examines how Rousseau, a critic of liberal individualism, identifies women as a permanently subversive force within the political order because they lack, or are unable to develop, the capacities required for participation in civil life. In particular, Rousseau claims that women lack the sense of justice which underlies civil association.[27] In Pateman's view, Rousseau's arguments are not simply of historical interest. They are, she suggests, illuminating about the position of women in society today. Although women have been granted voting and other rights in contemporary liberal democracies, many people still believe they are unsuited for political life and that it would be dangerous if the state was led and directed by women.[28]

Pateman argues, then, that widespread social beliefs about women's 'natural' role in the private sphere and 'natural' subjection to men fundamentally undermine any progress they might make towards equality within liberal democracies.[29] 'At the heart of democratic theory and practice,' according to Pateman, there is a practical contradiction 'between the premise of individual freedom and equality . . . and the assumption that women (wives) are naturally subject' to their husbands.[30] Because women are seen in this way they fundamentally lack status as individuals in democratic polities.

In another essay entitled 'Women and consent' Pateman examines one important consequence of this problem with women's status.[31] Because women's standing as individuals is compromised by social beliefs about women's natural subjection to men, there are also significant problems with women's capacity to consent, both in private or domestic associations, such as marriage, and in public associations such as liberal democratic polities. Through her reading of Locke and Rousseau, she argues that women 'exemplify the individuals whom consent theorists have declared to be incapable of consenting'. At the same time, however, women are also represented as 'always consenting' to men's sexual domination.[32]

Pateman demonstrates this latter point, and its implications for women in liberal democracies, via an examination of rape and rape law. Here, as she suggests, women's submission, or even explicit non-consent to sexual intercourse, is consistently interpreted as consent. This specific problem with women's consent has not, however, been 'noticed' by contemporary consent theorists. Even those theorists who identify a general problem with the voluntaristic assumptions of liberal democracy, where the consent of male citizens is assumed to be present in political and everyday life, do not usually see the problem associated with women's consent which proceeds from their lack of status as individuals.[33]

Because women lack standing as individuals they also, according to Pateman, lack equal standing as citizens and workers in democratic polities. In her essay on 'The patriarchal welfare state', Pateman argues that the category of 'citizen' is premised on phallocentric notions of (paid) work and 'independence'.[34] Consequently, the welfare state tends to privilege male breadwinner/workers and to protect patriarchal rights. Women are perceived as dependants and, unlike men, they are not incorporated into the welfare state as citizens. Women are seen primarily as members of the family, a sphere which is regarded as separate from civil society and the state.[35] Pateman castigates democratic theorists for failing to recognize the implications of this. She comments that 'the very different ways that women and men have been incorporated as citizens is rarely seen to be of significance for democracy.'[36]

This critique of liberal democratic practice and of liberal democratic theorists is continued in Pateman's work on the sexual or fraternal contract. In *The Sexual Contract* and in an essay on 'The fraternal social contract', Pateman argues that the classic social contract theories of the seventeenth and eighteenth centuries contained a repressed (patriarchal) dimension.[37] While social contract approaches offered new rights and freedoms to men, they created new forms of patriarchal subordination for women. Drawing on Freud, she argues that when men as brothers overthrew patriarchal rule they not only established their political equality but staked a claim to equal rights in access to women. Only men as 'free and equal masters of "families" could take part in the social contract'.[38] The original contract contains therefore a sexual contract which establishes men's sex right over women and men's political right to rule women. This masculine right over women was embodied in the marriage contract, which simultaneously assumed women's capacity to give their free consent and assumed their social subordination, because women only became part of the political order through marriage.[39] Contracts in both theory and practice have therefore reinforced women's subordination to men. Consequently, contemporary deployments of contract, for example in marriage, employment, surrogacy and prostitution, will tend to uphold men's freedom and women's subordination. For Pateman, the contracting, civil individual has been conceived in opposition to women and all that women's bodies symbolize. Because of this she argues that 'the categories and practices of civil society cannot simply be universalized to women.'[40] Pateman sees, therefore, fundamental obstacles to the full and equal inclusion of women in democratic polities.

Similarly, Pateman argues that the public/private dichotomy, inherent in the liberal foundations of liberal democracy, fundamentally militates against the full and equal inclusion of women in democratic polities. In the essay on 'Feminist critiques of the public/private dichotomy', Pateman reviews the work of liberal theorists, such as J. S. Mill and Locke, and contemporary commentators like Benn and Gaus.[41] Like other feminist theorists she is critical of the way in which liberalism maintains a separation between the public and private spheres and presupposes that relationships in the private sphere are irrelevant to politics. One important consequence of this strategy is an exclusion or marginalization of women in civil and political life. Through her examination of the feminist slogan 'the personal is political', Pateman concludes 'that although the personal is not the political, the two spheres are interrelated, necessary dimensions of a future, democratic feminist social order'.[42] Because of this stance she is also critical of participatory democratic theorists who conceptualize the private wholly in terms of the industrial realm and who, like liberal democrats, ignore the impact of the domestic sphere and of 'normal' relations between the sexes. Thus, both liberal and participatory democrats disregard the consequences of sexual inequality. Pateman is emphatic about the necessary foundations for democratic reform:

> Neither the equal opportunity of liberalism nor the active, participatory democratic citizenship of *all* the people can be achieved without radical changes in personal and domestic life.[43]

This insight signals the core of Pateman's feminist approach to democracy, which is to create a more thoroughgoing participatory society. In her view, democratic values and practices need to be instituted 'in the kitchen, the nursery and the bedroom'.[44] If women are to become truly equal citizens, then 'democratic theory and practice has to undergo a radical transformation.'[45] The aim for feminists is 'to transform personal and public relations between the sexes into genuinely consensual and mutual interaction'.[46] Although she has no illusions about the enormity of the task, it is one she says 'has to be attempted if "democracy" is not to remain the preserve of men' and if mainstream democratic theory is going to become 'genuinely democratic'.[47] Without these changes no real democracy is possible.

Continuity and Change

Despite Pateman's turn to feminism there are clearly significant continuities in her work on democracy. She remains convinced that a true democracy is a participatory one and that democracy should not focus solely on the activity of elites. The main goal of Pateman's analysis is still to identify and address barriers to participation. In 1970 she saw these barriers mainly in terms of class. Although Pateman still thinks that class is important, by the 1980s she was more concerned with sexual and domestic relations. Pateman also remains committed to equality as the basis of democracy although, once again, her focus has largely shifted from class to sex.

In addition, Pateman retains her belief that it is necessary to expand definitions of 'the political'. In 1970 she argued that the industrial realm is a political realm, not a 'private' realm which lies outside the political concerns of the public sphere. In her feminist writings Pateman argues that domestic relations and, in particular, the relations between husbands and wives, are an important part of the political realm. Throughout her work, therefore, she has engaged in critiques of the public/private distinction present in most (historical and contemporary) accounts of liberal democracy.

There have also been significant changes in Pateman's approach to democratic theory and practice since 1970. The most obvious one is the shift to an almost exclusive concern with feminist issues and with the exclusion and/or marginalization of women in civil and political life. In 1970, Pateman's main theoretical objective was to criticize dominant conceptions of liberal democracy and to establish the participatory foundations of a truly democratic theory. Her main practical concern was to identify the conditions necessary for establishing a participatory democracy in the present day. In her view, the most important precondition was a democratization of the industrial realm because this would provide training in democratic participation for the majority, that is, workers.

At this time Pateman did not think that her overall approach was problematic for women. In the conclusion of *Participation and Democratic Theory* she does briefly raise the problem of the full-time housewife who is not in the paid workforce and, therefore, misses out on training for democracy in the industrial realm. Pateman suggests that housewives might instead find opportunities to participate 'at the local government level', particularly in the field of housing.[48] This was hardly an adequate solution to the exclusion of women from the main avenues of training for democracy. But Pateman's class-based focus on industrial democracy as the basis of a participatory polity excluded proposals which would fully address women's subordination. In 1970, Pateman did not consider domestic and family relations to be a problem for democracy. In *Participation and Democratic Theory* she briefly addresses 'the family' and suggested that 'modern theories of child rearing, notably those of Dr Spock, had helped to influence family life, especially among middle class families, in a more democratic direction than ever before.'[49]

By the 1980s, Pateman had significantly shifted her position on many of these issues. Most obviously, she adopts a much more critical stance on domestic and family relations, seeing these as a major factor in the oppression of women and the failure of democracy for women. In particular, the private servicing of men and families which women undertake in the domestic sphere and the (assumed/enforced) subordination of wives to husbands within marriage are seen to contradict women's status as citizens and workers in the public sphere.

Another significant change in Pateman's theory relates to her concept of citizenship. In *Participation and Democratic Theory* Pateman saw class differences as a significant obstacle to democratic participation. The whole point of increasing participation was to increase political equality and, therefore, minimize the effects of class and economic difference. In *The Disorder of Women*, however, she looks to the formulation of a sexually differentiated citizenship where women can be 'citizens as *women*, as autonomous, equal, yet sexually different beings from men'.[50]

The argument is not fully elaborated in this text. In an essay published in 1992, however, Pateman develops her analysis of the sexually differentiated nature of citizenship, and suggests a slightly different emphasis. Historically, women have been excluded from citizenship because of their bodily difference from men and, in particular, because of their roles as mothers. While this exclusion is no longer so complete, women are still incorporated into modern polities as subordinates and their 'political duty' is still motherhood.[51] The central issue for Pateman here, however, is not so much the sexual differentiation of citizenship as women's subordination and lack of freedom. In a 'genuinely democratic citizenship' sexual difference would not have the same political meaning. Men and women would have citizenship of equal worth.[52] But the substance of this citizenship 'must differ according to the diverse circumstances and capacities of citizens, men and women'.[53]

In her feminist writings, Pateman also identifies important problems for women when the focus is on 'workers'. She notes: 'Women and men stand in a different relation to the work which is undertaken in workplaces. Women do not have the same status as workers as men.'[54] Discussions of industrial democracy need to take into account this sexual differential. Pateman is now critical of theoretical arguments about the public world and workplace which 'proceed independently of any consideration of the connection between the public and the private'.[55]

In 1970, Pateman's text delivered a critique of empirical theorists of liberal democracy and made a strong case in favour of a radical, participatory democracy. By 1989 she is critical of all democratic theorists, including participatory democrats, for failing to pay attention to the implications of women's situation for the theory and practice of democracy. In referring to the 'vigorous' debate between liberal democrats and radical participatory democrats, she says that from her 1989 perspective she can now identify 'assumptions and premises that unite the antagonists as strongly as those that divide them'.[56] While liberal democrats and radical democrats argue about whether the economy and the workplace are private or public and whether democracy in the workplace is feasible or desirable, neither side sees anything of significance in categorizing the domestic, conjugal and intimate life as both 'private' *and* opposed to the public. As Pateman argues, this is an opposition which is both 'presupposed and repressed' by democratic theorists, including participatory democrats.[57]

In a rare moment of empathy for liberal democrats, Pateman comments that it is perhaps understandable that liberal democrats have ignored questions about the impact that 'private' sexual inequalities have on 'public' life. After all, she notes, the separation of public and private is an explicit foundation of liberal democracy.[58] But she suggests that radical, participatory, democrats might have been expected to do better because of their recognition of class and the way that class inequality undermines political equality. According to Pateman, however, radical or participatory democrats have rarely examined sexual inequality and have generally resisted feminist arguments.[59] This is because feminists and radical/participatory democrats see the division between public and private very differently. For radical democrats, 'private' generally refers to the economy rather than to private/domestic life. Pateman's critique of the radical/participatory tradition in democratic theory is that it fails to take into account a more sophisticated and critical understanding of 'private' life. Thus, by ignoring the family and the structure of relations between the sexes, 'participatory democratic arguments for the democratization of economic life have neglected a crucial dimension of democratic social transformation.'[60] Generously, Pateman includes her 1970 text in this critique of participatory democratic theory.[61] When she wrote *Participation and Democratic Theory* she, like other radical democrats, was not interested in the particular situation of women. The way forward now, in her view, for all types of democrats, is to bring the feminist critique of democracy 'into the centre of reflection, debate and political action'. Otherwise, she argues, women will remain 'as peripheral in a future participatory "democracy" as they are at present in liberal democracies'.[62]

Given her critique of participatory theory it is perhaps not surprising that Pateman has also taken a more critical attitude to the work of both Rousseau and J. S. Mill who (together with G. D. H. Cole) provided the theoretical foundation of *Participation and Democratic Theory*. She says that her earlier reading of Rousseau as 'the exemplar of a participatory democratic theorist' was incorrect because she 'overlooked the fact that Rousseau declares that political order depends on the exclusion of women from citizenship'.[63] Consequently, Rousseau's democracy:

> is a masculine preserve in which the political right of self-government is exercised only by men. Nor can his theory simply be revised to include women. The meaning of 'political' and 'democracy' in Rousseau's theory depends upon the meaning he gives to manhood and womanhood.[64]

Pateman does not, however, want to completely discard Rousseau's democratic theory. She claims, for example, that Rousseau 'presents us with many insights into the problem of the disorder of women'.[65] That is, a feminist reading of Rousseau will make visible many of the ideas and practices which presently obstruct women's full and equal inclusion in democratic polities.

Pateman is critical of J. S. Mill, despite his combination of liberal feminism and advocacy of a participatory society, because he failed to question the apparently natural division of labour within the home. If women remain sequestered in their private roles and confined to the domestic sphere, they will also lack the opportunities to learn what it means to be a democratic citizen. Consequently, Pateman concludes that this means Mill's 'arguments for democratic citizenship apply only to men'.[66] She does, however, suggest that an examination of the work of feminist liberals like J. S. Mill and Mary Wollstonecraft gives some insight into why liberal accounts of democracy do not work for women. Pateman regards Mill's feminist prescriptions for equal legal treatment in the public sphere as insufficient to deal with the exclusion of women from democracies. She levels a similar charge against Wollstonecraft.[67]

Unlike some other feminists (see, for example, Drucilla Cornell[68]), Pateman does not regard the work of the contemporary liberal theorist, John Rawls, to be useful for feminism. Rawls, in her view, like Mill and Wollstonecraft, fails to deal with the implications of both the sexual division of labour and the privatization of women in the domestic sphere.[69] Moreover, Rawls also supports a 'natural', hierarchical view of society.[70] His account of the obligation which citizens owe to 'just' political societies does not take into account the differential position of women, in particular the 'normal' lack of equality of protection from rape and domestic violence that women experience.[71]

In her feminist work, Pateman has also adopted a much more critical approach to liberal democracy than in her earlier work. Originally, Pateman wanted to expand participation, because participation was a

Barbara Sullivan

virtue in itself and because it would make liberal democratic institutions function better. The thrust of her feminist critique, however, indicates that liberal democracy has little to offer women. It is not simply that the liberalism of liberal democracy fails to address the situation of women; it was and is instrumental in producing the oppression of women. In the introduction of *Disorder of Women* she notes that she has amended her earlier argument about the lack of any common bond uniting '"individuals" participating in the economy and the practice of contract'.[72] In her feminist mode, then, Pateman is suggesting that men have a common (patriarchal) interest in the oppression of women. This interest is partly pursued through liberal and liberal democratic discourse. It is reasonable to assume, therefore, that Pateman is much less optimistic than she was in 1970 about the possibilities of combining a genuinely participatory democracy with liberal democratic institutions. She does not, however, completely exclude the possibility of radical transformation of democratic theory and practice:

> The possibility of such a change is more open at the end of the twentieth century than ever before. Patriarchal institutions are less solid than they once were, familiar political arguments look increasingly inadequate in the face of current economic and political changes and feminists have turned the patriarchal separation of private and public into a political problem. But there are anti-democratic trends too.[73]

Critiques of Pateman

A critique of Pateman's arguments about democracy can proceed from two different starting points. In the first place, from a 'postmodern' feminist perspective, there are problems with, and important political implications which proceed from, Pateman's construction of a narrative about the role of the sexual contract in the oppression of women in liberal democracies. In the second place, from a perspective inside 'modernist' approaches to democracy, there are significant problems with Pateman's characterization of democratic participation and critique of the public/private distinction.

Recently, several influential 'postmodern' feminists, Nancy Fraser, Wendy Brown and Moira Gatens, have pointed to fundamental problems in the method of argument adopted by Pateman in *The Sexual Contract*.[74] 'Postmodern' feminists are critical of feminist theorists, like Pateman, who utilize 'modernist' (universal and totalizing) notions of truth, power, rights and the subject.[75] What is at issue here is the foundation of a feminist politics. Fraser, for example, criticizes Pateman's utilization of the notion of a sexual contract for analysing contemporary gender relations.[76] According to Fraser, the sexual contract assumes a master/subject model of gender relations which is unitary, essentialist and unable to deal with notions of resistance and change. She claims that there has been a historical shift in contemporary society 'from dyadic relations of mastery and subjection to more impersonal structural mechanisms that are lived through more fluid cultural forms'.[77] In Fraser's view, the complexity of contemporary gender relations and of important contestations around the position of women cannot be dealt with by Pateman's account of the sexual contract.

Both Gatens and Brown utilize an approach based on Nietzschean genealogical method to arrive at a similar conclusion about *The Sexual Contract.*[78] For Gatens, the problem is that Pateman adopts a 'strategic essentialism' which, she says, has significant political costs for women.[79] According to Gatens, Pateman's history of the sexual contract presents the body of woman as always appropriable by men and struggles between the sexes as always already lost by women. For these reasons, Pateman's approach closes off any appreciation of the diversity (and perhaps new possibilities) of contemporary political struggles over the bodies of women and sexual relations more generally. Brown's main quarrel with Pateman is also about how her historical account of the sexual contract bears on the conduct of politics in the present. She claims that Pateman's account of the legacy of the sexual contract in contemporary liberalism, and in contemporary configurations of male dominance, is unconvincing.[80]

This postmodern feminist critique calls into question both Pateman's feminist strategy and the specific link between a historical sexual contract and manifestations of this in the contemporary arrangements governing marriage, women's employment, prostitution and surrogacy. These critiques have important implications for Pateman's feminist arguments about democracy. The 'postmodern' feminist critique of Pateman suggests that existing configurations of gender relations, and sexual oppression, are more fluid and contingent than Pateman's approach indicates. It is therefore arguable that the possibilities for changing democratic practice are more multiple and open-ended than Pateman implies. While there remain significant battles to be waged, perhaps there are no fundamental reasons to suggest that women will always be excluded or marginalized in democratic polities. Interestingly, the 'postmodern' feminist critique of Pateman does *not* call into question the thrust of her arguments about the inherent value of participation. Indeed, greater participation is probably

an important aspect of 'postmodern' contestations around both gender
relations and democracy.

Pateman's work does not engage with the postmodern/modern divide
in contemporary feminism. Even within 'modernist' feminism, however,
there are problems with aspects of Pateman's work on democracy. Anne
Phillips, for example, uses empirical arguments against those who, like
Pateman, call for more direct democratic participation.[81] Phillips
examined the nature and impact of participatory democracy in the wom-
en's movement in Britain during the 1970s. She found that the emphasis
on direct participatory democracy in women's groups had 'contradictory
effects'. The emphasis on meeting and talking, for example, enabled
women to rethink and develop their ideas. But the push to consensus
decision-making, rather than just taking a vote, also made conflicts more
difficult to acknowledge and resolve. Similarly, while the desire to change
formal meeting and organizational structures did foster participation and
counter the tendency to divide into leaders and led, it also made accountability almost impossible.[82] In Phillips's view, therefore, to put undue
emphasis on participation may produce unforeseen undemocratic consequences.[83] This finding has important implications for Pateman.

Phillips also offers a careful and qualified criticism of calls, by Pateman
and other feminists, for a democratization of personal and everyday life.[84]
She has no difficulty with the view that private, domestic relations influence the public sphere and constrain women's participation in public
politics. Like Pateman, she argues that an equalization of domestic duties
and responsibilities is essential for the development of a true democracy.[85]
Unlike Pateman, however, Phillips wants to emphasize the importance of
maintaining a clear distinction between the public and private spheres.
Although she does not directly refer to Pateman, Phillips is critical of
feminists who act as if public and private are 'an amorphous continuum in
which there are no distinctions beyond those of size'.[86]

Pateman in fact argues that the personal is *not* the same as the political,
but she does tend to stress that the two are interrelated.[87] Phillips, on the
other hand, tends to emphasize the substantial differences between public
and private and the need to ensure that these differences are maintained.
Phillips contends there are some decisions that should properly remain a
private concern, for example, the decision to terminate a pregnancy. In her
view, we are entitled to exclude others (and the state) from these decisions.
Following the lead of Iris Marion Young, however, Phillips argues there
should be no aspect of our lives which we are compelled to keep private.[88]

For Phillips, there remain important distinctions between the public
and private spheres, between the realms where democracy can be imposed
and those where it should only be 'enabled'. Phillips cites Pateman in

support of this view although Pateman's arguments about the distinctions, as opposed to the interrelationship, between public and private are only rudimentary.[89] Phillips argues that equality between the sexes can and should be regulated in the public sphere which is why she advocates measures – such as parliamentary quotas – to increase women's participation in public institutions. In the private sphere, however, explicit regulation is inappropriate.[90] It is notable that Pateman's feminist writings on democracy do not include any specific recommendations, akin to her earlier calls for workers' control and industrial democracy, for increasing participation by women in the public sphere (apart, that is, from a democratization of the domestic realm). In her feminist theory, Pateman is a lot less certain about what, if anything, can be done to improve or reform existing democratic processes.

Conclusion

In her 1994 Presidential Address to the International Political Science Association, Pateman returns to the subject of democracy. While the main focus of her speech is on the emergence of a global language of democracy, many themes present in her earlier, pre-feminist and feminist, work are still evident. Pateman argues that political events in the late 1980s and 1990s have led to a new appreciation of 'people power' and of the importance of active, democratic participation.[91] She also calls attention to the relationship between social conditions and the operation of democratic institutions, arguing that issues like North/South economic inequalities, child labour and the world-wide persistence of sexual oppression are important obstacles to democratization. In response to postmodern criticism of Western democratic theory, however, Pateman argues against a rejection of universalism, so that democracy and 'the practice of rights can be developed in a variety of cultural contexts'.[92]

From 1970 through to the present day Pateman offers a compelling critique of democratic theory and practice and she engages with some of the central problems of our time. In particular she addresses the role of popular participation in democratic polities and canvasses the dilemmas posed for democratic government by economic and sexual inequality. Critics are correct, however, to call attention to the political effects of both the latent and the explicit essentialism adopted by Pateman in her work on the sexual/fraternal contract. It is important that feminist critiques of democratic theory and practice are not limited by totalizing and rigid accounts of sexual relations. Moreover, it is evident that Pateman's advocacy of more participation and a democratization of public and private/

domestic life are, in many ways, insufficiently detailed to address some of the specific issues facing women (and men) in the 1990s. But this is simply to call attention to a few, inevitable problems and inadequacies. Pateman's work presents us with a rich and diverse critique of democratic theory and practice. It reminds us that democracy is not simply a set of procedures and institutions. Pateman's contribution is to demonstrate that definitions of the political raise important issues of power in democratic polities and that equality is a central requirement of democratic governance.

Notes

1 Pateman's important works are: C. Pateman, *Participation and Democratic Theory* (Cambridge, Cambridge University Press, 1970); *The Problem of Political Obligation: A Critical Analysis of Liberal Theory* (Chichester and New York, Wiley, 1979), republished in paperback in 1985 by Polity Press with an 'Afterword'; *The Sexual Contract* (Cambridge, Polity, 1988); and *The Disorder of Women: Democracy, Feminism and Political Theory* (Cambridge, Polity, 1989).

2 C. Pateman, 'An unfinished political education', in M. Dawson and H. Radi (eds), *Against the Odds: Fifteen Professional Women Reflect on Their Lives and Careers* (Sydney, Hale and Iremonger, 1984), pp. 39–55, esp. p. 42.

3 Pateman, 'An unfinished political education', p. 51.

4 Pateman, 'An unfinished political education', p. 50.

5 Pateman, *Participation and Democratic Theory*, p. 13.

6 Pateman, *Participation and Democratic Theory*, p. 14.

7 J. A. Schumpeter, *Capitalism, Socialism and Democracy* (London, Allen and Unwin, 1943).

8 See H. S. Kariel (ed.), *Frontiers of Democratic Theory* (New York, Random House, 1970).

9 Pateman, *Participation and Democratic Theory*, pp. 16–17.

10 Cole, a twentieth-century theorist of 'guild socialism', has been included by Pateman because he developed a theory of participatory democracy suitable for contemporary, large scale, industrialized society. For Pateman, then, Cole translates the insights of J. S. Mill and Rousseau to a modern setting.

11 Pateman, *Participation and Democratic Theory*, pp. 108–9.

12 Pateman, *Participation and Democratic Theory*, p. 43.

13 Pateman, *Paticipation and Democratic Theory*, p. 66.

14 Pateman, *Participation and Democratic Theory*, pp. 82–3.

15 Pateman, *Participation and Democratic Theory*, pp. 83–4.

16 Pateman, *Participation and Democratic Theory*, p. 88.

17 Pateman, *Participation and Democratic Theory*, p. 106.

18 Pateman, *Problem of Political Obligation* (1985), p. 168.

19   Pateman, *Problem of Political Obligation*, p. 68.
20   Pateman, *Problem of Political Obligation*, p. 8.
21   Pateman, *Problem of Political Obligation*, p. 174.
22   Pateman, *Problem of Political Obligation*, p. 1.
23   These are 'Sublimation and reification: Locke, Wolin and the liberal-democratic conception of the political' (1975); 'Justifying political obligation' (1979); and '*The Civic Culture*: A philosophic critique' (1980).
24   The later essays include ' "The disorder of women": Women, love, and the sense of justice' (1980); 'Women and consent' (1980); 'Feminist critiques of the public/private dichotomy' (1983); 'Feminism and democracy' (1983); 'The patriarchal welfare state' (1988); and 'The fraternal social contract' (1988).
25   Pateman, *Disorder of Women*, p. 210.
26   Pateman, *Disorder of Women*, pp. 26–8.
27   Pateman, *Disorder of Women*, pp. 17–32.
28   Pateman, *Disorder of Women*, p. 17.
29   Pateman, *Disorder of Women*, pp. 210–11.
30   Pateman, *Disorder of Women*, p. 213.
31   Pateman, *Disorder of Women*, pp. 71–89.
32   Pateman, *Disorder of Women*, p. 72.
33   Pateman, *Disorder of Women*, p. 84.
34   Pateman, *Disorder of Women*, pp. 179–209.
35   Pateman, *Disorder of Women*, p. 182.
36   Pateman, *Disorder of Women*, p. 179.
37   See Pateman, *The Sexual Contract*, and also Pateman, *Disorder of Women*, pp. 33–57.
38   Pateman, *The Sexual Contract*, p. 49.
39   See Pateman's reply to criticisms of her interpretation of the marriage contract: 'Reply to reviews on *The Sexual Contract*', *Political Theory Newsletter*, 2 (1990), 78–82, esp. pp. 79–80.
40   Pateman, *Disorder of Women*, p. 52.
41   Pateman, *Disorder of Women*, pp. 118–40.
42   Pateman, *Disorder of Women*, p. 134.
43   Pateman, *Disorder of Women*, p. 222.
44   Pateman, *Disorder of Women*, p. 222.
45   Pateman, *Disorder of Women*, p. 14.
46   Pateman, *Disorder of Women*, p. 15.
47   Pateman, *Disorder of Women*, p. 15.
48   Pateman, *Participation and Democratic Theory*, p. 109.
49   Pateman, *Participation and Democratic Theory*, p. 108.
50   Pateman, *Disorder of Women*, p. 14.
51   C. Pateman, 'Equality, difference, subordination: the politics of motherhood and women's citizenship', in G. Bock and S. James (eds), *Beyond Equality and Difference: Citizenship, Feminist Politics and Female Subjectivity* (London, Routledge, 1992), p. 19.

52 Pateman, 'Equality, difference, subordination', p. 28.
53 Pateman, 'Equality, difference, subordination', p. 29.
54 Pateman, *Disorder of Women*, p. 8.
55 Pateman, *Disorder of Women*, p. 9.
56 Pateman, *Disorder of Women*, p. 5.
57 Pateman, *Disorder of Women*, p. 5.
58 Pateman, *Disorder of Women*, p. 211.
59 Pateman, *Disorder of Women*, pp. 220–1.
60 Pateman, *Disorder of Women*, p. 220.
61 Pateman, *Disorder of Women*, pp. 220–1.
62 Pateman, *Disorder of Women*, p. 221.
63 Pateman, *Disorder of Women*, p. 6.
64 Pateman, *Disorder of Women*, p. 6.
65 Pateman, *Disorder of Women*, p. 24.
66 Pateman, *Disorder of Women*, p. 217.
67 Pateman, *Disorder of Women*, p. 27.
68 D. Cornell, *The Imaginary Domain: Abortion, Pornography and Sexual Harassment* (New York, Routledge, 1995).
69 Pateman, *Disorder of Women*, p. 28.
70 Pateman, *Disorder of Women*, p. 28.
71 Pateman, *Problem of Political Obligation*, pp. 122–3.
72 Pateman, *Disorder of Women*, p. 7.
73 Pateman, *Disorder of Women*, p. 14.
74 See N. Fraser, 'Beyond the master/subject model: On Carole Pateman's *The Sexual Contract*', in Fraser's *Justice Interruptus: Critical Reflections on the 'Postsocialist' Condition* (New York and London, Routledge, 1997); W. Brown, *States of Injury: Power and Freedom in Late Modernity* (Princeton, NJ, Princeton University Press, 1995); and M. Gatens, *Imaginary Bodies: Ethics, Power and Corporeality* (London and New York, Routledge, 1996).
75 Brown, *States of Injury*, pp. 30–51.
76 Fraser, 'Beyond the master/subject model', pp. 225–35.
77 Fraser, 'Beyond the master/subject model', p. 234.
78 See Gatens, *Imaginary Bodies*, pp. 76–91, and Brown, *States of Injury*, pp. 136–9.
79 Gatens, *Imaginary Bodies*, p. 86.
80 Brown, *States of Injury*, pp. 137–8.
81 See A. Phillips, *Engendering Democracy* (Cambridge, Polity, 1991) and A. Phillips, *Democracy and Difference* (Cambridge, Polity, 1993).
82 Phillips, *Engendering Democracy*, p. 145.
83 Phillips, *Engendering Democracy*, p. 145.
84 Phillips, *Democracy and Difference*, pp. 80–7.
85 Phillips, *Engendering Democracy*, pp. 100–1.
86 Phillips, *Engendering Democracy*, p. 119.
87 Pateman, *Disorder of Women*, pp. 135–6.
88 Phillips, *Engendering Democracy*, p. 109.

89   Phillips, *Engendering Democracy*, p. 104.
90   Phillips, *Engendering Democracy*, p. 119.
91   C. Pateman, 'Democracy and democratization. Presidential Address: XVth
     World Congress of the International Political Science Association', *Interna-
     tional Political Science Review*, 17 (1996), 5–12, esp. p. 6.
92   Pateman, 'Democracy and democratization', p. 10.

10

Iris Marion Young: The Politics of Difference, Justice and Democracy

Don Fletcher

Iris Marion Young's major work, *Justice and the Politics of Difference*, addresses primarily the issue of what constitutes justice and how it might be enhanced in practice. Yet, given her claim that democracy is 'both an element and a condition of justice', questions about appropriate forms of democracy figure prominently in her analysis. Young goes beyond previous feminist critiques of Rawls and other theorists who emphasize impartiality and universality to provide a substantive prescription of her own. Young aims to provide an emancipatory notion of difference to replace exclusionary ones. Central to that effort are her arguments for participatory democracy and for direct political representation for oppressed social groups. Her proposals include specific suggestions for institutional reform. Part of Young's project is to extend the concept of deliberative democracy to take account of aspects of communication that do not involve formal, 'rational' argument and discussion.

In this chapter I will focus particularly on Young's arguments in *Justice and the Politics of Difference*. My organizational strategy will be as follows. I will briefly place Young as a contemporary theorist and indicate the themes she addresses in articles published before *Justice*. Then will follow a detailed account of her arguments in that book, supplemented where relevant from recent articles. Finally, I will examine major criticisms of Young's analysis and proposals and discuss the logic of her responses to those criticisms both in *Justice* and in her more recent publications.

Background

Iris Marion Young was born in 1949 and completed her doctorate at Pennsylvania State University in 1974. Her interests span political philosophy, critical social theory and feminist theory, and she is now a Professor in the Graduate School of Public and International Affairs at the University of Pittsburg, where she also teaches in the Department of Philosophy. In addition to her academic activities she has been engaged in the social movements which have inspired her writing. Her participation in the women's movement and in rainbow coalitions seem particularly consistent with the direction of her proposals. Young has engaged in debates over concrete political issues of the day such as abortion and over the appropriateness of single motherhood. She has also offered concrete proposals for rehabilitating pregnant drug addicts.[1]

Young has been influenced by the emphasis on democratic practice characteristic of the US new left in the 1960s and women's movements of the 1970s. In these ways she falls into what Held calls the 'new left' stream of democratic theorizing.[2] Her work also reflects the turn to the political and questions of citizenship of the 1980s, with participatory notions of Arendtian civic republicanism supplementing her socialist feminist concern with material distribution. Finally, she has also been influenced by existential phenomenology and the poststructuralism of French feminism, and by Habermas's 'account of advanced capitalism and his general notion of communicative ethics'.[3] While she rejects what she sees as Habermas's unfortunate commitment to universality, she generally adopts his 'communicative ethics' and his critical theory orientation, by which she means starting with actual social life and specifying groups that are oppressed rather than starting with abstract notions of justice.[4] Young's ability to harness these diverse strains to a critique of contemporary assumptions about justice is a major strength of her work.

Early Essays

Justice and the Politics of Difference was published in 1990. That same year a collection of essays indicative of Young's approaches to feminist theory was published as *Throwing Like a Girl and Other Essays in Feminist Philosophy and Social Theory*.[5] Those essays were organized under three headings: 'socialist feminism', 'the politics of difference', and 'female body experience'. Central to Young's contribution to debates within and about socialist feminism was her argument that while sex should not be considered secondary to class, neither is a 'dual systems' theory positing patriarchy as separate from capitalism appropriate. In Young's view, contemporary patriarchy and contemporary capitalist appropriation are interrelated. She emphasizes not only the importance to capitalism of women as a secondary labour force but also the theoretical need to

elevate the concept of a gender division of labour to analytical centrality.[6]
In *Justice*, Young assumes that social categories, such as women, have had
time to consolidate as groups and are now ready for rainbow coalitions,
and her analysis focuses more generally on the politics of difference.
Nonetheless, the question of whether women can be categorized as a single
group without resort to reification and essentialist implications remains
relevant.

The second theme in *Throwing* is the politics of difference, which is
Young's central project and which, as articulated in *Justice*, is the focus
of my essay. Two of the contributions to that section of *Throwing* constitute significant portions of *Justice*.[7] The third essay in that section is
'Humanism, gynocentrism and feminist politics', which indicates the
strengths and weaknesses of humanistic feminism (advocating full participation in humanity by women) and of gynocentric feminism (deploring
the devaluation of specifically feminine virtues and characteristics).[8] This
essay is important to note here because of Young's shift within this debate.
By 1990 she expresses a strong preference for gynocentric feminism[9] that
incorporates her rejection of the justice of claims to gender blindness, or
other forms of alleged neutrality or impartiality, that are central to her
analysis.

Under the third heading, 'female body experience', Young combines
existential phenomenology (especially Maurice Merleau-Ponty and Erwin
Straus), French feminist theory (especially Luce Irigaray but also Julia
Kristeva), and feminist film theories of the gaze (Maureen Turim, Laura
Mulvey, Annette Kuhn) to explore the experiences of living in the socially
constructed female body, particularly bodily motility, pregnancy, breasts,
and clothes. How and to what social purposes are girls taught the particu-
larities of 'feminine bodily comportment' as part of the manner in which
women are 'physically inhibited, confined, positioned, and objectified'?[10]
How does pregnancy challenge a woman's sense of bodily integrity, and
why is pregnancy assumed to be a disease and treated in an alienating
manner?[11] How is the cultural centrality of breasts manifested, and how
might nipples be deployed to disrupt the patriarchal dichotomy between
motherhood and sexuality?[12] Women's clothes are to be worn for men,
possessors of the subjective gaze, but women may appropriate clothes by
taking their own pleasure from them, enjoying the touch of fabric, bond-
ing with other women over clothes sharing, and fantasizing about possible
identities in other times and places.[13] In *Justice*, this theme feeds into
Young's analysis of cultural imperialism as a form of oppression, especially
as that relates to Foucault's notion of the normalizing gaze and Kristeva's
concept of the abject.[14]

Justice and the Politics of Difference

Justice and Difference

The key to Young's analysis in *Justice* is her perception of existing structural injustice, defined in terms of domination and oppression. In her view, welfare capitalism may be more humane than its predecessors, but injustice continues to be structural, and participatory decision-making has even decreased. Young defines domination as institutional constraint on self-determination, and therefore directly opposed to democracy, understood as participation. She defines oppression as institutional constraint on self-development. Oppression has a variety of 'faces' which are both directly and indirectly related to her arguments for democracy as participation. To combat injustice requires not only democracy but particular kinds of democracy. Young advocates, for example, a form of participatory democracy whose goal is to increase individual control over economic and social institutions. She also proposes a form of democracy that recognizes and sustains group differences while providing additional resources for the presently disadvantaged or oppressed. In explicating Young's arguments I will not completely follow the sequence of argument in *Justice*. I will start with her comments about injustice and how they lead to her two major conclusions, namely the need for strong democracy (including her arguments against alternatives) and the need for a democracy of difference based on group participation. I then examine her more specifically institutional suggestions.

It is best to indicate Young's overt assumptions at the outset. She assumes, she says, 'that basic equality in life situation for all persons is a moral value; that there are deep injustices in our society that can be rectified only by basic institutional changes; that the groups I have named are oppressed; that the structures of domination wrongfully pervade our society'.[15] Young's first move is to challenge the emphasis on distribution that she attributes to Rawls and to many other theorists. In raising this issue, Young states that it is important to consider justice from the perspective of what people do rather than what they have, that is, in terms of people's relationship to the means of production rather than simply in terms of distribution.[16] Young offers two criticisms of theories that focus on distribution: they tend to a focus on the individual or family in a way that obscures institutional context, and the logic of distribution does not work when extended to non-material goods.[17] She disagrees with Nozick that outcomes are not important – people need minimum outcomes to survive and to participate – but nonetheless she considers process most important.[18] Young recognizes the need for a general and significant redistribution of resources for participatory democracy to work effectively, but argues that it would be counterproductive to wait for that redistribution as a prerequisite to other changes.

In Young's view, to focus simply on distribution is to miss much about how people are oppressed, and she provides a number of examples to illustrate her concerns. One of her examples involves a state decision to site a hazardous waste dump in a town without consultation, while another involves a large enterprise deciding unilaterally to move, decimating a local economy.[19] In both of these cases there are distributional consequences, but an even deeper concern is exclusion from decision-making participation relating to issues that greatly affect one's own life. Similarly, television depiction of blacks, Arab Americans, and others is something those depicted have no control over, which nevertheless has significant cultural importance.[20] In addition, distributional approaches often simply assume as given existing class and family relationships and political decision-making structures.[21] The point is, then, that not only do some have more wealth than others but some have decision-making power over the economy and others do not.[22] The second problem with distributional approaches is that the attempt to extend 'distribution' to include non-material goods fails, because rights, power and so on are relations, not possessions.[23]

The key for Young, then, is justice, and while justice is not identical to 'the good life', it requires access to it.[24] The good life, in turn, involves two values: '(1) developing and exercising one's capacities and expressing one's experience, and (2) participating in determining one's action and the conditions of one's action'.[25] There are systemic reasons why everyone does not enjoy justice in this sense. Welfare capitalism is an improvement, because it does involve inclusion of welfare provisions within partially planned economies. There is a recognized conception of social citizenship and procedures are less arbitrary.[26] At the same time, Young argues that the New Deal and post-war bargain in the USA were based on the assumption that only distribution issues were central, with unions and workers settling for higher incomes in exchange for not contesting other issues.[27] In addition, acceptance of rule by experts as 'non-political' has increased bureaucratic control at the expense of general participation in decision-making,[28] and there has recently been a 'dialectic of re-containment' triggered by participation gains initiated by the left-wing politics of the 1960s.[29]

For Young, injustice consists of domination and oppression. Oppression, in particular, is structural even in contemporary welfare democracies, and can be characterized as having five faces: exploitation, marginalization, powerlessness, cultural imperialism, and violence. Citing Marx via

Macpherson, Young explains exploitation as a process in which not only are some people richer than others but also there is 'a steady process of the transfer of the results of the labour of one social group to benefit another'.[30] The rules and conditions of work are central here, including the ways in which women systematically provide unpaid services for men, and non-whites tend to be confined to menial jobs.[31]

Young's second face of oppression is marginalization, which entails the identification and expulsion from useful life of a non-employed underclass, usually but not always 'racially marked'.[32] The third face is powerlessness, referring to the fact that the working class does not even have the superficial kinds of control over conditions of work accorded professionals.[33] Fourth is cultural imperialism, by which Young means essentially hegemonic control over meanings or definitions.[34] The fifth face of power is violence as perpetrated in a systematic way against members of particular social groups by police and others, in a manner virtually condoned by the society.[35] These faces of oppression, in Young's view, are objective. That is, the theorist inside the society can see the pain and the violation of principles that characterize oppression and differentiate it from simply paranoia on the part of some groups.[36]

To emphasize the cultural aspects of oppression, Young devotes chapter 5, 'The scaling of bodies and the politics of identity', to exploring some aspects of oppression, particularly cultural imperialism and the kind of fear and hatred of others that leads to violence against some groups. In this chapter Young argues that the unconscious reactions that people have to others of different races, sex, abilities, and sexuality must also be changed. People should not be blamed for what they do unconsciously, but nonetheless they must be held responsible because these actions have real consequences. The answer might lie in using consciousness raising groups to supplement school workshops, and other activities.

This chapter extends the concept of cultural imperialism, using especially Foucault's notion of the 'normalizing gaze' to indicate how all models but that of white males are judged inferior. Because dominant groups project their own norms as universal, others are both invisible and stereotyped.[37] This need not but usually does involve 'imprisoning others in their bodies', which are constructed as 'ugly, dirty, defiled, impure, contaminated, or sick'.[38] The 'normal' seek to avoid 'others' because they become anxious with them, and this anxiety also is a major cause of violence against marginalized groups.[39]

Again following Foucault, Young argues that the normalizing process coincident with modern science has led to an association of maleness and whiteness with reason,[40] excluding others from that association so rendering them 'degenerate'[41] and subject to stereotype:

As a group women [for example] are physically delicate and weak due to the
specific constitution of their bodies, the operation of their reproductive and
sexual parts. Because of their ovaries and uterus women are subject to
madness, irrationality, and childlike stupidity, and they have greater tendencies toward sexual licentiousness than men.[42]

Kristeva's concept of the abject is called upon to explain conscious
and unconscious aversion to some types of bodies and bodily attributes,
turning differentiation into hierarchization and even active rejection
and hatred. 'Abjection is expressed in reactions of disgust to body
excretions. . . . I react to the expelled with disgust because the border of
myself must be kept in place.'[43] Challenges to that border maintenance are
unsettling and provoke aversive reactions to the presence of members of
groups perceived as other: 'Racism, sexism, homophobia, ageism, and
ableism, are partly structured by abjection, an involuntary, unconscious
judgement of ugliness and loathing.'[44] Young also indicates special explanations in some cases, such as rejection of the old because in them we
confront our own deaths (now that only the aged die in significant
proportions), and rejection of those with different sexual preferences
because 'we are all ambivalent about our own sexuality.'[45]

Democracy and Justice: Deliberation and Communication

Justice entails the concept of social equality, which may need to be set
against equality of opportunity and even equality of treatment, involving
equality of participation for all in a manner that affirms differences among
groups. Also, because justice is the goal, and because justice means lack of
domination and oppression rather than everyone being treated alike,
discrimination may be justified. Discrimination against members of disadvantaged groups is bad, but positive discrimination leading to greater
justice is morally dictated.[46]

Young's objection to 'authoritarian contract theory', delegating authority to government officials controlled by impartial laws, also rests on her
view that impartiality is impossible. Detachment is not possible,[47] reduction to a single universal is not desirable, and since all people are not alike
they should not be treated alike. This line of criticism overtly includes
Rawls. Young argues that 'the reasoning of [Rawls's] original position is
monological' because differences among subjects or even communication
between them is ruled out by Rawls's conditions,[48] and the impartiality that
Rawls seeks is unattainable because difference is real and total empathy is
impossible.[49] Moreover, an ideology of impartiality is dangerous because it

'both allows the hegemonic to claim universality, and appears to justify or legitimate bureaucratic hierarchies acting with "impartiality"'.[50]

The merit principle, as an instance of impartiality in relation to who has what job, must also be rejected. The assumption that there are objective criteria for merit is false. Thus, Young challenges two basic assumptions of modern working life: that a hierarchical division of labour is functional, and that the more desirable positions in that hierarchy should be distributed by merit.[51] In her view there is no way to objectively measure merit, so all such decisions are 'political', and the question of who decides on appropriate qualifications is central to the entire issue of justice.

At times, Young's argument seems to be that although there are differences in the degree of technical competence required for different jobs, neutral criteria cannot be established. Citing Offe's notion of 'discontinuous hierarchies',[52] she argues that jobs are too complex, a variety of workers make indistinguishable contributions, jobs involve discretion, and bosses cannot judge because they do different tasks.[53] At other times, Young seems to suggest that all jobs could be done by anyone and are equally prized by everyone, with only 'politics' deciding who gets the plums: 'But does it really take more intelligence to be a doctor than a librarian? To be a sales representative than a plumber?'[54]

For Young domination is involved here, and perhaps also exploitation, as the work of professionals rests on that of menials, and it is at least questionable that professionals add new value to the economy.[55] In addition, the positing of some work as inherently more important than other kinds of work is a form of cultural imperialism.[56] Division of labour is acceptable, but the division of jobs into those involving task design and those involving task execution is not acceptable because being limited to the latter inhibits self-development and involves 'powerlessness'.[57] Because the question of who has which job is crucial, this is clearly an area where democratic decision-making is important.[58]

A major part of Young's proposed solution to the problem of contemporary injustice involves changing to a system of democracy that includes direct representation for and participation by disadvantaged social groups. Participatory democracy is part of Young's solution by definition. A pluralist democracy based upon competition between interest groups is inadequate because it involves a numbers game in which the strong win, often unjustly, without engaging the ideas of others. Participation in decision-making has both instrumental and intrinsic value in challenging oppression and domination.[59] Participation which includes oppressed groups is instrumentally valuable because it means that all interests will be voiced. Intrinsically, it develops the capacities of participants. More specifically, it encourages people to think about their own needs in relation to the needs of others, to take an interest, to become articulate and persuasive, and so on. It also provides people with an awareness that social relations are humanly constructed, not natural or simply given, and therefore susceptible to change.[60]

Participation leads to just outcomes, provided all take part, because in the absence of philosopher kings justness depends on a process in which decisions are arrived at via free expression of differing needs and perspectives.[61] It also leads to best outcomes because all relevant information and considerations will be tapped in the process. A process of democratic deliberation has the additional advantage that participants are forced to formulate their arguments in a principled way.[62] In Young's view, this is a way in which people learn about each other and learn to respect different positions.

Young's goal is not, however, communitarian harmony. While she agrees with some of the arguments that communitarians such as Sandel and Barber make against liberalism, Young denies their basic premise that people can understand each other in community as shared subjectivity.[63] In her view, such harmony would rely on a homogeneity involving the repression of difference.[64] She finds the communitarian assumption that unmediated social relations are possible and desirable to be 'wildly utopian'.[65]

There are three particular characteristics of Young's notion of participatory democracy. One is the standard 'new left' proposal that democracy should extend to the workplace. People ought to have a say in their own chores and in the decisions relating to their own work.[66] In addition, decision-making procedures in the workplace and in bureaucracies should be democratic so that people holding hierarchical positions in such institutions do not have that leverage available to use in the more 'democratic' legislative arena. Thus, Young redefines 'private' away from the liberal distinction that categorizes economic activity as private in the sense of private enterprise.

Young's second particular proposal concerning democracy is that participation ought to be by social groups in addition to, or eventually even instead of, by individuals. Since the Enlightenment, Western theories of justice (and Western political thinking generally) have focused on individuals rather than groups, and Young argues that now it may be more appropriate to think in terms of group identities.[67] Groups do in a sense precede individuals,[68] and the self-assertion of groups such as the Black Panthers has contributed to liberation.[69] Nor is it desirable to deny the real differences between social groups, as assimilation would 'allow the dominant group to ignore its own specificity' and impose its own norms as universal.[70]

For Young, differences between social groups should be maintained, and the positive aspects of differences should be emphasized in policy. For example, pregnancy leave should be designed to recognize not only an inability to carry on work as usual but also the positive and unique social contribution of childbearing. Other examples include giving Chicanos support for retaining their own culture as well as for learning English, or providing American Indians with controlling rights over reservations as well as full national citizenship rights.[71]

The upshot of this is that mechanisms should be created by which social groups can organize, analyse policy and exercise a veto over policy areas that directly affect them. For example, she suggests that women should be able to veto legislation on contraception or abortion which denies them the right to control their own reproduction.[72] She includes only 'social' groups which have some sense of shared identity, not all groups or aggregates, and only disadvantaged social groups,[73] acknowledging also that there may be a need for special representation for some groups within others (e.g. women within blacks). The advantages of group participation would be 'procedural fairness', an assured voice for the disadvantaged, the necessity that appeals would have to be presented in terms of 'just' outcomes rather than simply the will of majorities, and the achievement of more just outcomes because wide participation means tapping broad social knowledge.[74] Thus, the reasons for social group representation involve compensation for the ways in which institutional structures restrict those groups and overlap with the justifications for participatory democracy generally.

The third particularity of Young's approach is her argument for 'communicative' democracy. She accepts the superiority of a model of deliberative democracy (which derives from Habermas, and conceives democracy as rational debate about the public good) over interest group democracy, because deliberative democracy requires decisions based on strength of argument rather than simply numbers. But she also notes that persuasiveness is not an equally distributed resource and that many people, especially the disadvantaged, are intimidated by the formal rules of deliberative institutions.[75] Therefore, deliberative democracy needs to incorporate a broader range of modes of communication. Her idea of communicative democracy differs in form and in purpose from other types of deliberative democracy. In form it would include all kinds of communication, from hugging to story-telling to humour to biography and philosophy, rather than being confined to 'rational' arguments.[76] Its purpose would be less to contest and to persuade than to provide a basis for mutual understanding and the acceptance of differences held in good faith.

In Young's view, there are three advantages to this approach. One is that although this approach would not focus on changing others, it would, nevertheless, change preferences. Involvement would lead people to recognize their own positions as 'perspectival', and people would have to speak to justice rather than 'interests' to communicate across differences. Because of this everyone's social knowledge would be enhanced. The second advantage is that the major drawback of deliberative democracy – those with skills and resources always win – would be avoided. The third advantage is that broader integration *would* be achieved. Without the atmosphere of cold rationality and of politics being treated as a numbers game, and with the need to understand and respect people across differences, the social group focus could be transcended.

Young also proposes provisions to protect against the so-called paradox of democracy, the problem that democratic procedures may produce undemocratic or oppressive results. In addition to proposing the extension of democracy to such non-government organizations as workplaces, she advocates that essentials should be protected constitutionally against the whims of changing majorities and that local control should be avoided because it often leads to discrimination against minorities.[77]

Young's specific institutional suggestions are based on identifying some of the potential characteristics of cities without their present bases of injustice. From Young's perspective, there are many potential advantages of cities despite present inequalities. One is the existence of a great variety of overlapping social groups where group affinity is still important. Similarly, there is a great variety of activities and interests available in cities, plus what Young calls the eroticism of city life, 'the pleasure and excitement of . . . the novel, strange and surprising'. Finally, public places and forums are available where people may meet and discuss their differences as well as their commonalities.[78]

As Young uses an idealized view of cities as the inspiration for positive proposals, it is appropriate to note that she sees cities as presently sites of injustice, despite their potential.[79] They are dominated by centralized bureaucracies and highly mobile capital, as well as being dependent on national and state governments.[80] City decisions about zoning and land use are not open but are made semi-privately by city officials, bureaucrats and developers.[81] The fact that neighbouring municipalities are legally separate inhibits planning and leaves them each at the mercy of corporate and bureaucratic domination.[82] In addition, space use increasingly involves segregation of different types of function that may serve top-down planning for cost minimization but is dysfunctional for people, especially women with children.[83]

Young's relatively specific proposals are designed to overcome those shortcomings. Her preferred democracy would be best achieved by regional governments cutting across municipalities (with suburban communities denied their present ability to reap the benefits of proximity to cities without sharing the costs)[84] and state boundaries, including one or more cities plus suburban and rural areas.[85] This would allow decision-making without inhibition by divisions between municipalities or differences in state laws. Governments should be more broadly involved, and/but promote more participation.[86] In particular, regional investment decisions should be made by accountable representative bodies.[87] At the same time, zoning against multi-dwelling development should not be allowed, and 'speechmaking, sign-carrying, and other modes of expression' should not be prohibited or controlled.[88] Local groups and organizations would participate in neighbourhood assemblies, which in turn would elect representatives to oversee the decision-making of regional governments and implement their policies at the local level. At the regional level, 'group representation would be guaranteed by right'.[89] Young argues that, with a sensible geographical base – the region – and democratic decision-making and planning, many current problems would be overcome.

Young concludes with a short epilogue on 'international justice', which she characterizes as an introduction to the topic, in which she claims that her approach to systemic injustice in the United States could be effectively applied in other social settings.

Criticisms and Responses

While Young's work has been highly praised, it also has attracted criticism. The discussion here focuses on differences of emphasis and issues of continuing debate, and thus problems that are not easily resolved. Young acknowledges these issues as dilemmas and has made a choice. They revolve around her critique of impartiality and universality, her emphasis on social groups and group differences, and on her democratic prescriptions.

For Young the central question is, if we desire justice how might we achieve it, and what is the role of democracy in that effort? As indicated above, her first target is the concept of impartiality and its implications. Her response is to provide bases for effective participation by the disadvantaged via an emphasis on difference and on defining a role for social groups. Nevertheless, her emphasis on groups raises a number of questions. One is whether all women, for example, can be said to have shared interests or to be part of a single social group, without resort to the difficulties inherent in essentialism. While Young recognizes that social groups may need provisions for subgroups and despite her attempt to move away from 'interests' to 'justice' as the criterion for decisions, her argument seems to rely on the assumption that these social groups have consistent interests. To the extent that Young's view of groups is ultimately essentialist, her politics is similar to interest group politics in that already existing entities compete.[90] In addition, providing a special voice for designated social groups does not guarantee equal benefits for all group members unless one assumes that participation skills are equally distributed within each group. As we have seen, Young rejects this kind of assumption in relation to deliberative democracy generally.

As an additional point here, the dangers of universalization that Young assigns to theories advocating impartiality may result from the very demands for group solidarity that she would support. As Benhabib argues, when attempting to identify which groups are oppressed or to adjudicate between competing claims from different groups, one may be confronted with conflicting accounts rather than clear cases.[91] Furthermore, without transcendental values, why should we, morally, respect everyone? Young has argued that, because Maori and Pakeha in New Zealand realize that they have through interaction defined themselves as both similar and different, they therefore should mutually respect each other's rights.[92] As Flynn notes, however, that imperative follows only if one acknowledges a conditioning assumption of moral commitment to the principle of mutual toleration.[93] Young does list assumptions of this type in *Justice*, including the assumption 'that basic equality in life situation for all persons is a moral value'.[94] But these are clearly general political values, and they may be seen as cutting against her arguments against universality.

These are issues of continuing concern and major debates within feminist theorizing. It is important to Young's argument that oppression is 'structural', that is, group based, and she has recently attempted to retheorize this issue. Using Sartre's notion of seriality she proposes that people constitute a series when they exhibit a passive unity through being positioned around structures and material objects, and they constitute a group when they actively acknowledge common purposes.[95] It is not at all clear, however, that this adaptation solves the problem.

Young's emphasis on difference raises additional problems. Anne Phillips, for example, has argued that abandoning universality and impartiality, or the right to equal treatment, will increase discrimination against disadvantaged groups rather than assisting them.[96] Others have claimed that this focus on group difference may intensify group conflict.[97] Jean Bethke Elshtain, for example, has recently criticized the generic condition of enhanced group exclusivity without discussing Young specifically.[98] Elshtain laments the decline of civility in American politics, a development which she attributes to an emphasis on group homogeneity and solidarity with the consequence of increased hostility toward and a refusal to work with others. While she shares with Young an emphasis on the importance of discussion and interaction, her vision is of an older period of cross-cutting organizations and social networks.

Young also, of course, argues against general exclusivity while advocating formal recognition and granting of compensatory rights to social groups as she defines them. Young is challenging such basics of liberal democracy as the assumption that everyone should be treated equally. She argues that treating each person as an abstract, equal individual is not desirable because there *are* social groups and the differences between them do matter. In Young's view, the state cannot be impartial anyway because it is implicated in reproducing inequalities. In addition, to pretend that everyone is the same allows the dominant not only to win but to appear universal. Young's solution is a politics of difference including participatory democracy leading to mutual respect.

Nancy Fraser clarifies these disagreements by making her criticism of Young very specific on this point.[99] While Young indicates that the cultural aspects of oppression are additional to distributional ones rather than replacing them entirely, nonetheless, she emphasizes the problems of distributional strategies and advocates a politics of difference to overcome cultural oppression. Fraser recognizes Young's attempt to bring together those two types of oppression as a strength of her work, but also sees Young's failure to perceive fully the differences and their implications as a weakness. As Fraser argues, some of Young's five faces of oppression are based primarily on culture (cultural imperialism and violence), but the others are based primarily on distribution (exploitation, marginalization and powerlessness). Similarly, while the position of some collectivities might be enhanced by a politics of difference, that would be the case for those collectivities differentiated by characteristics that represent desirable diversity (such as ethnic groups) but not those characterized by distributional deprivation (such as class) or by both distributional and cultural differences (such as, possibly, women). In Fraser's view, therefore, not only will a politics of difference not work universally, but it may be counterproductive in some cases, and a differentiated response to different types of oppression and to different types of collectivities is the most appropriate approach.

A third problem with Young's argument is that while deliberative forms of democracy meet some of her objections to interest group democracy, they may introduce new problems. Young is particularly sensitive to the manner in which 'neutral' procedures favour the strong. In addition, while she acknowledges her debt to Habermas she also recognizes that it may be impossible to have effective dialogue when oppression inherently includes a biased perspective on the part of the oppressors. Young's answer to that problem is adopting communicative rather than deliberative democracy, but it is not entirely clear why this blindness will not also be carried over into communicative democracy.

Finally, Young pays little attention to the question of why the powerful would agree to changes that would eliminate their advantages in the present system without some promise of future benefit. One basis for defining justice is mutual advantage, but in practice that brings into play relative bargaining positions, clearly something that Young wants to avoid except in reverse, by organizing for extra input from those with fewest resources. Presumably the powerful might gain in terms other than those that constitute central preferences in contemporary society. That is, everyone might benefit both from an appreciation of diverse cultures and by enjoying an ability to be open through communicative democracy that is not available in present interest-oriented systems. At the same time, there is little evidence of receptivity to such potential advantages in today's political climate, as one would expect from Young's argument about the ills of the present system.[100]

Conclusion

Iris Marion Young has certainly succeeded in providing 'inspiration for imagining alternatives'.[101] She has done so by going beyond critique to think positively about justice and democracy, to provide an emancipatory notion of difference in place of an exclusionary one. She has done so in specific detail, and she continues to illuminate central issues in feminist and democratic theory by bringing together disparate ways of thinking and frames of reference. In particular, she has demonstrated the ways in which oppression is structural and detailed its 'faces' in a convincing manner. Young has alerted us to the subtlety of how we respond to difference, and proposed ways in which particular forms of democracy might help. Liberalism does tend to assume that political equality without social or economic equality is possible, and Young puts a strong case for the need to change types of political participation to compensate for that circumstance. Further, she has attempted to recognize practical difficulties by differentiating her analysis from those of communitarians and other advocates of participatory democracy. She prompts us to think more seriously about major and difficult problems of current concern. Nevertheless, each of the points raised in the previous section poses significant difficulties for Young's analysis. Despite her alertness to the issue of essentialism and her general stance against universalism, her emphasis on groups does implicate her in a form of essentialism, and her preferences seem to be accorded absolute value. In addition, emphasizing difference may intensify conflict rather than mutual respect. Finally, Young's cogent critique of present power relations and biases opens up questions of why existing blindness would not be carried over into communicative democracy and why those who are presently advantaged would accept systemic change.

Notes

1 I. M. Young, 'The Supreme Court and abortion', *Dissent* (Fall, 1992), 425–7; I. M. Young, 'Making single motherhood normal', *Dissent* (Winter 1994), 88–93; I. M. Young, 'Punishment, treatment, empowerment: Three approaches to policy for pregnant addicts', *Feminist Studies*, 20:1 (1994), 33–57.
2 D. Held, *Models of Democracy* (Cambridge, Polity, 1987), pp. 253–64.
3 I. M. Young, *Justice and the Politics of Difference* (Princeton, NJ, Princeton University Press, 1990), pp. 7, 106.
4 Young, *Justice*, p. 5.
5 I. M. Young, *Throwing Like a Girl and Other Essays in Feminist Philosophy and Social Theory* (Bloomington, IN, Indiana University Press, 1990).
6 See especially I. M. Young, 'Socialist feminism and the limits of dual systems theory', *Socialist Review*, 50/51 (1980), 169–88, reprinted in *Throwing Like a Girl*, pp. 21–35; I. M. Young, 'Beyond the unhappy marriage: A critique of the dual systems theory', in Lydia Sargent (ed.), *Women and Revolution: A Discussion of the Unhappy Marriage of Marxism and Feminism* (Boston, South End Press, 1980), and in Lydia Sargent (ed.), *The Unhappy Marriage of Marxism and Feminism: A Debate of Class and Patriarchy* (London, Pluto, 1991), pp. 43–69.
7 Young acknowledges inclusion of five previously published articles in *Justice*. The two referred to here are I. M. Young, 'Impartiality and the civic public', *Praxis International*, 5:4 (1986), 381–401, reprinted in Seyla Benhabib and Drucilla Cornell (eds), *Feminism and Critique: On the Politics of Gender* (Oxford/Minneapolis, Polity/University of Minnesota Press, 1987), pp. 56–76, reprinted in Young, *Throwing Like a Girl*, pp. 93–113; and I. M. Young, 'Polity and group difference: A critique of the ideal of universal citizenship', *Ethics*, 99:2 (1989), 250–74, reprinted in Young, *Throwing Like a Girl*, pp. 114–37.
8 I. M. Young, 'Humanism, gynocentrism and feminist politics', *Women's Studies International Forum*, 8:3 (1985), 173–83, reprinted in Young, *Throwing Like a Girl*, pp. 73–81.
9 This shift is indicated by Young in 'Introduction', *Throwing Like a Girl*, p. 7.

10   I. M. Young, 'Throwing like a girl: A phenomenology of feminine body comportment, motility, and spatiality', *Human Studies*, 3 (1980), 137–56, reprinted in Young, *Throwing Like a Girl*, pp. 141–59, quotes at pp. 154, 153.

11   I. M. Young, 'Pregnant embodiment: Subjectivity and alienation', *Journal of Medicine and Philosophy*, 9:1 (1984), 45–62, reprinted in Young, *Throwing Like a Girl*, pp. 160–76.

12   I. M. Young, 'Breasted experience: The look and the feeling', in Young, *Throwing Like a Girl*, pp. 189–209.

13   I. M. Young, 'Women recovering our clothes, perhaps', in Hugh Silverman and Donn Welton (eds), *Postmodernism and Continental Philosophy* (Albany, NY, SUNY Press, 1988), pp. 13–16, reprinted in Young, *Throwing Like a Girl*, pp. 177–88.

14   The normalizing gaze involves the dominant perspective rendering alternatives abnormal and unacceptable. Abjection involves rejection of the non-self (body excretions) that 'arises from the primal repression in which the infant struggles to separate from the mother's body': Young, *Justice*, p. 143. Both of these concepts are discussed further below.

15   Young, *Justice*, p. 14.

16   Young, *Justice*, p. 16.

17   Young, *Justice*, p. 18.

18   Young, *Justice*, p. 28.

19   Young, *Justice*, p. 19.

20   Young, *Justice*, p. 20.

21   Young, *Justice*, p. 21.

22   Young, *Justice*, p. 23.

23   Young, *Justice*, pp. 25, 31.

24   Young, *Justice*, p. 37.

25   Young, *Justice*, p. 37.

26   Young, *Justice*, p. 67.

27   Young, *Justice*, pp. 70–1.

28   Young, *Justice*, pp. 76, 80.

29   Young, *Justice*, p. 89.

30   Young, *Justice*, p. 49. C. B. Macpherson, *Democratic Theory: Essays in Retrieval* (Oxford, Clarendon Press, 1973), ch. 3.

31   Young, *Justice*, pp. 50–2.

32   Young, *Justice*, p. 53.

33   Young, *Justice*, p. 56.

34   Young, *Justice*, p. 60.

35   Young, *Justice*, pp. 61–2.

36   Young, *Justice*, pp. 5–6.

37   Young, *Justice*, p. 123.

38   Young, *Justice*, p. 123.

39   Young, *Justice*, p. 124.

40   Young, *Justice*, p. 127.

41 Young, *Justice*, pp. 127–9.
42 Young, *Justice*, p. 129.
43 Young, *Justice*, p. 144.
44 Young, *Justice*, p. 145.
45 Young, *Justice*, p. 155.
46 Young, *Justice*, pp. 195–7.
47 Young, *Justice*, pp. 102–3.
48 Young, *Justice*, p. 101.
49 Young, *Justice*, p. 104.
50 Young, *Justice*, p. 10; see also pp. 97, 112–16.
51 Young, *Justice*, p. 193.
52 C. Offe, *Industry and Inequality: The Achievement Principle in Work and Social Status* (New York, St Martin's, 1976), pp. 25–8.
53 Young, *Justice*, pp. 201–3.
54 Young, *Justice*, p. 221.
55 Young, *Justice*, p. 219.
56 Young, *Justice*, p. 221.
57 Young, *Justice*, p. 193.
58 Young, *Justice*, p. 212.
59 Young, *Justice*, pp. 91–3.
60 Young, *Justice*, p. 92.
61 Young, *Justice*, p. 92.
62 Young, *Justice*, p. 93.
63 Young, *Justice*, pp. 230–2. See Benjamin Barber, *Strong Democracy: Participatory Politics for a New Age* (Berkeley, CA, University of California Press, 1984); Michael Sandel, *Liberalism and the Limits of Justice* (Cambridge, Cambridge University Press, 1982).
64 Young, *Justice*, p. 234.
65 Young, *Justice*, pp. 233–4.
66 Young, *Justice*, p. 223.
67 Young, *Justice*, p. 156.
68 Young, *Justice*, p. 9.
69 Young, *Justice*, pp. 160–1.
70 Young, *Justice*, p. 165.
71 Young, *Justice*, pp. 173–83.
72 Young, *Justice*, p. 184.
73 Young, *Justice*, pp. 186–7.
74 Young, *Justice*, p. 185.
75 See, for example, I. M. Young, 'Justice and communicative democracy', in R. S. Gottlieb (ed.), *Radical Philosophy: Tradition, Counter-Tradition, Politics* (Philadelphia, PA, Temple University Press, 1993), pp. 123–43.
76 The following discussion of communicative democracy is based on I. M. Young, 'Communication and the other: Beyond deliberative democracy', in M. Wilson and A. Yeatman (eds), *Justice and Identity: Antipodean Practices* (Wellington, Bridget Williams, 1995), pp. 134–52, reprinted

virtually verbatim in S. Benhabib (ed.), *Democracy and Difference: Contesting the Boundaries of the Political* (Princeton, NJ, Princeton University Press, 1996), pp. 120–35.

77   In *Justice*, Young cites Mansbridge on the manner in which local school-board decision-making often increases the degree of discrimination; J. Mansbridge, *Beyond Adversary Democracy* (New York, Basic Books, 1980). This reflects US experience more generally of initiatives in civil rights coming from the national level rather than the local or state levels.

78   Young, *Justice*, pp. 238–40.

79   In an attack on utopian postmodern views of the city, from which he does not altogether exempt Young, Harvey asks 'can homelessness be understood as spontaneous self-diversification?'; D. Harvey, 'Social justice: Postmodernism and the city', *International Journal of Urban and Regional Research*, 16:4 (1992), 588–601.

80   Young, *Justice*, p. 243.

81   Young, *Justice*, p. 244.

82   Young, *Justice*, p. 247.

83   Young, *Justice*, p. 246.

84   Young, *Justice*, p. 248.

85   Young, *Justice*, p. 252.

86   Young, *Justice*, p. 251.

87   Young, *Justice*, p. 253.

88   Young, *Justice*, p. 255.

89   Young, *Justice*, p. 253.

90   See, for example, Chantel Mouffe, 'Feminism, citizenship and radical democratic politics', in J. Butler and J. W. Scott (eds), *Feminists Theorize the Political* (New York, Routledge, 1992), pp. 369–84, here p. 380.

91   S. Benhabib, 'In defense of universalism – yet again! A response to critics of *Situating the Self*', *New German Critique*, 62 (1994), 173–89.

92   I. M. Young, 'Together in difference: Transforming the logic of group political conflict', *Political Theory Newsletter*, 4:1 (1992), 11–26.

93   J. R. Flynn, 'Postmodernism and empiricism: No substitute for moral principles', *Political Theory Newsletter*, 4:2 (1992), 138–54.

94   Young, *Justice*, p. 14.

95   I. M. Young, 'Gender as seriality: Thinking about women as a social collective', *Signs*, 19:3 (1994), 713–28.

96   A. Phillips, *Democracy and Difference* (Cambridge, Polity, 1993), pp. 93–4.

97   See especially W. Kymlica and W. Norman, 'Return of the citizen: A survey of recent work on citizenship theory', *Ethics*, 104 (1994), 352–81, for a summary of arguments and references; many critics have noted the length of Young's list of oppressed groups, and Kymlica and Norman estimate that it might include 80 per cent of the US population.

98   J. B. Elshtain, *Democracy on Trial* (New York, Basic Books, 1995).

99   N. Fraser, 'Culture, political economy, and difference: On Iris Young's

Justice and the Politics of Difference, in N. Fraser, *Justice Interruptus* (New York, Routledge, 1997), pp. 189–205; revised from N. Fraser, 'Recognition or redistribution: A critical reading of Iris Young's *Justice and the Politics of Difference*', *Journal of Philosophy*, 3:2 (1995), 166–80.

100 At the same time there is some evidence that Young is correct that an appeal to equal treatment rather than a recognition of meaningful difference has missed its moment; see, for example, the attempted use of an excerpt from Martin Luther King's 'I have a dream' speech to promote the anti-affirmative action proposition in the 1996 California election.

101 Young, *Justice*, p. 256.

11

Michel Foucault and Agonistic Democracy

Lois McNay

Michel Foucault's work occupies an ambivalent position with regard to the democratic project. His devastating attacks on what he regards as the illusory nature of freedom in liberal democracies are well known. Yet, his work on power and the subject has been influential for those who seek to formulate a more radical understanding of democratic politics for late modernity. This ambivalence remains unresolved in Foucault's work and commentators have explained it in varying ways, for example, as a tension between his theoretical relativism and his practical political commitment or as a covert reliance on the liberal values he explicitly claims to reject.[1]

In this chapter I explore this ambivalence in relation to Foucault's work during the 1970s on disciplinary power and his final work on government and the self. Many commentators have noted that the earlier work on discipline has nihilistic implications in so far as it shows how practices assumed to exemplify democratic freedoms are in fact the mechanisms through which an insidious form of 'normalizing' social control is exerted. While this is undoubtedly an implication of Foucault's work, I show how his reconceptualization of power has had a significant influence upon thinkers such as Ernesto Laclau and Chantal Mouffe, who aim to revise classical democratic theory to take account of the pluralist and dynamic nature of late capitalist societies. Although Foucault's work provides a starting point for radical theories of democracy, it is hampered by his understanding of power primarily as a material force or 'positivity'. This approach tends to result in an understanding of democratic forms reduced to their *de facto* functions, namely the control of social organization. For Foucault, any radical challenge to democratic systems cannot emerge from within conventional democratic routes – such as appeals to rights or justice – because they will inevitably be reimplicated within the normalizing structures that are essential to control within democracies. The limitations of such a functionalist approach will be illustrated through comparison with the work of Claude Lefort on rights, who shows that their political efficacy lies in the extent to which they are symbolic forms rather than legally objectified categories.

I conclude by arguing that Foucault's late work on the self represents a significant alteration in his views on the possibilities for autonomous action and change within capitalist democracies. Furthermore, the idea of an 'ethics of the self' has been influential on the work of such thinkers as William Connolly on 'agonistic' democracy. Despite this alteration in Foucault's thought, I argue that he retains a materially reductive notion of power so that it is unclear how a practical and self-referential ethics of the self can extend beyond itself to the political domain.

Background

Michel Foucault was born in Poitiers in 1926 to a Catholic medical family. He gained a degree in philosophy from the École Normale Supérieure in 1948 and was influenced by the post-war intellectual climate of existentialism, phenomenology and Hegelian Marxism. A year later he obtained a second degree in psychology, during which he also worked as an intern in a mental hospital, an experience which was to influence heavily much of his work, especially his doctoral thesis on madness written during the 1950s. During this period, Foucault also took up positions as a cultural official in the French Institutes at Uppsala, Warsaw and Hamburg. He then became Professor of Philosophy at Clermont-Ferrand from 1960 to 1966, taught in Tunis from 1966 to 1968, returning finally to Paris to teach at Vincennes and, from 1970, at the Collège de France.[2]

Apart from a brief period at the beginning of the 1950s when, under the influence of his tutor Louis Althusser, Foucault was a rather inactive member of the PCF, he was, until the beginning of the 1970s, relatively indifferent to political activism. His lack of concern with direct political involvement during the 1950s and 1960s is reflected in his intellectual interests of this period which comprised philosophical and literary explorations of notions of transgression and the 'archaeological' analyses of the latent 'epistemic' structures constitutive of thought.[3] Nonetheless, this did not prevent much of Foucault's work from this period – most notably his doctoral thesis on madness published as *Histoire de la Folie* – being heralded, after 1968, as the embodiment of an 'anti-repressive sensibility'.[4]

Foucault's political activism dates from around the time of his inauguration at the end of 1970 as Professor of the History of Systems of

Thought at the prestigious Collège de France. Although not reducible to each other, Foucault's new involvement in militant political activity is paralleled in his intellectual concerns with the shift from a formal mode of analysis to the more explicitly partisan mode of 'genealogy'.[5] Foucault's political activities were by and large confined to *ad hoc* bodies whose orientation could be defined loosely as 'gauchiste'. He was involved in activism over prisons, the reform of psychiatric hospitals, ideas of popular justice, state racism and gay politics.[6] Perhaps his most well-known political involvement was with the campaigning group GIP (Groupe d'Information sur les Prisons) that he helped to found in February, 1971. GIP arose out of the aftermath of 1968 when the French government proscribed far left groups and imprisoned some political activists. Initially set up to draw attention to the conditions endured by these political prisoners, the focus of the group soon broadened to highlight the poor conditions and brutal regimes that existed in French prisons in general. GIP's aim was not to promote reforms but to gather and disseminate information about conditions within prison through the organization of demonstrations and so forth. GIP succeeded in organizing a series of high profile protests and enlisted the help of many intellectual luminaries including Sartre, Deleuze, Cixous, de Beauvoir, Faye and Clavel.[7]

Foucault ceased to be involved with GIP from the end of 1972 and turned his attention to a wider array of political issues, particularly those connected to racism and the status of immigrants in France. Much of the activity he participated in was quite militant and, on several occasions, it resulted in his arrest. In the early 1980s, along with Pierre Bourdieu, he orchestrated protests about the imposition of martial law in Poland and about the French government's inaction in this regard. He also began to speak more publicly about gay culture and politics. Until his death in June 1984, he remained a non-aligned radical, refusing to endorse Mitterrand's presidency. Indeed, it is believed that he was planning to write a book with the journalist Didier Eribon on the mistakes which had brought left-wing governments to grief, entitled *La Tête des Socialistes*.[8]

Foucault's reluctance to align himself with any established political line is echoed to some degree in his work by a refusal to ground his thought in any systematic set of norms. For his critics, this lack of normative foundations illustrates an irresponsible radicalism or even nihilism. If critique is to move past the negative moment of criticism it must be accompanied by a positive moment of reconstruction. For Foucault, however, it arises from his belief that the role of the intellectual consists not in legislating for others, but rather in 'problematizing' certain issues from which others may draw their own conclusions. We shall see how this ambivalent movement between criticism and commitment is played out in Foucault's thought on the nature of freedom and resistance in democratic systems.

Discipline and Democracy

Until the final phase of his work where he significantly modified his approach to the Enlightenment tradition, most of Foucault's thought can be understood as an unrelenting critique of the nature of freedom in Western democracies. Foucault's work during the 1970s on disciplinary power is the culminating point of this critique, although the thrust of these criticisms is already anticipated in his early work, notably *Madness and Civilization*. This book brings into question the assumption that with the spread of reason from the Enlightenment onwards, society's understanding and treatment of mental illness has become progressively more scientific, tolerant and humane. Foucault contends that, on the contrary, the claims of Enlightenment rationality to an objective universality can only be maintained at the cost of the exclusion and derogation of forms of thought, paradigmatically madness, that are not fully accessible to reason. He shows how various philosophical and institutional practices of confinement and exclusion of madness form a brutal underside to Enlightenment thought and are necessary to the maintenance of the illusion of a self-transparent and total rationality.

It is in *Discipline and Punish*, in the first volume of *The History of Sexuality*, and in a series of interviews that he gave around that time, that Foucault extends his critique of Enlightenment rationality to its political embodiment in democratic practices and institutions. Like *Madness and Civilization*, *Discipline and Punish* throws into doubt the meliorist view of history as progression with regard to the development of the modern penal system. Foucault claims that underlying Enlightenment reformers' attacks on the feudal system of justice was not a distaste for the excessive and brutal nature of its punishments, but rather a dislike of the irregularity and inefficiency of feudal punishments as a form of social control. Reforms to the penal system initiated by the Enlightenment were not motivated by a more humane understanding of crime, but instead served to institute a new economy of power based on the creation of a rationalized, calculable and efficiently organized social field. This emergent *disciplinary* power is as crucial to the development of modern societies as the accumulation of capital and it centres around the production of 'docile bodies': the organization, disciplining and subjection of the human body in such a way as to provide a submissive, productive and trained source of labour power.[9] The prison regimes of the eighteenth century were laboratories where methods for the 'political investment' of the body were developed and eventually generalized into other institutional regimes such as factories, schools, the army, hospitals and so forth, constituting a 'carceral network' of power/ knowledge. In these regimes, order is ensured through the strategic control of space, deploying tactics such as the enclosure and separation of individuals, the homogenization of physical being and activity and the installation of permanent and intense forms of surveillance.[10]

In the first volume of *The History of Sexuality* Foucault extends his genealogical analysis of the emergence of disciplinary power to the development during the nineteenth century of medical and psychiatric discourses on sexuality. He shows how in practices such as the 'confessional', disciplinary power is internalized by individuals so that they become 'self-policing subjects'. In educational, psychiatric, medical, legal and other practices, individuals are encouraged to divulge their innermost feelings in the presence or virtual presence of an authority who has power to 'judge, punish, forgive, console and reconcile'.[11] The urge to confess becomes so deeply embedded in the modern subject that it is no longer perceived as solicited or coerced but is regarded as a voluntary act of disencumberment or liberation from psychical repression. In Foucault's view, however, the disclosure of one's inner self and desires does not lead to greater self-knowledge, but instead implicates the subject further in a network of disciplinary power relations. Disciplinary control is so effective because it operates not through direct repression but through more invisible strategies of normalization. The 'judges of normality' in the figures of the social worker, the analyst, the teacher and the doctor typify modern practices and assess and diagnose each individual according to a normalizing set of assumptions. Individuals are controlled through the power of the norm and this power is effective because, embedded in a network of ostensibly beneficent and scientific practices, it is relatively imperceptible and insidious.

Foucault's claim that many of the emancipatory practices and beliefs of modern society in fact institute more insidious forms of disciplinary social control can be extended to central tenets of democratic theory and practice. Foucault's depiction of modern society as a 'carceral archipelago' has provoked much criticism in that it filters out the intricate nature of freedom in liberal democracies arising from the complex relations between different social fields. Some commentators have claimed, for example, that Foucault ignores the role played by democratic legal systems in the regulation of the unhindered growth of tutelary powers. Gillian Rose argues that by reducing democratic forms to a precipitate of power Foucault simplifies 'those paradoxes and antinomies of law and social control which have been identified as definitive of industrial or capitalist society by non-

Marxist and by Marxist sociology alike'.[12] In a similar fashion, Habermas claims that Foucault levels down the dilemmatic structure of legal regulation whereby 'the legal means for securing freedom . . . themselves endanger the freedom of their presumptive beneficiaries'.[13] For Foucault, however, this notion of the law as a mediatory structure between state and civil society rests on a fundamental misconception of how power operates in modern society. Foucault calls this misconception the 'juridical' or 'sovereign' notion of power based on the idea that power is inherently repressive or prohibitory in order to control the unruly forces that would otherwise throw civil society into chaos.[14]

Against such 'negative' conceptions of power as a legislative force applied *a posteriori* to pre-existent social relations, Foucault claims that power is 'positive' in that it is constitutive of all social relations. Power is not exterior to other social relations operating upon them in the form of prohibition, control or repression. Instead, power is only realized through other social relations (sexual, knowledge, medical, educational) and is productive in its effects. Sovereign conceptions of power are obfuscatory in that they act as a kind of smokescreen behind which the disciplinary process of normalization operates. Some of the basic categories central to democratic theory and practice, such as 'right and violence, law and illegality, freedom and will . . . the state and sovereignty', presuppose this sovereign conception of power and therefore misconstrue the nature of liberty in modern society.[15] For example, if, as Foucault claims, power is not the property of state institutions, classes or elite groups, it is not something that can be 'acquired, seized, or shared'. It is instead an 'intentional and non-subjective' relation which permeates all forms of social interaction like a net, so the classical dualisms of bourgeoisie–proletariat and state–individual in which political conflict is construed are thrown into question.[16] If power relations are both constitutive of and coextensive with the social realm then correspondingly the notion of the political is enlarged to include issues that are conventionally relegated to the private realm. In this regard, Foucault's work on sexuality as a construct of different regulatory regimes (*apparatuses*) has had a tremendous impact on feminist and other critiques of conventional notions of gender identity whose starting point is a deconstruction of the traditional public–private distinction.[17]

It follows from Foucault's reconceptualization of power relations as constitutive of social being that liberation from power relations is illusory. This throws into question the distinction between liberty and constraint that underpins much democratic political theory. As Anthony Giddens shows, both liberal and Marxist utopias are based on a 'flight from power' that presupposes that power is inextricably based in conflict and that liberty is possible without power relations.[18] In Foucault's view, power relations are the condition of the possibility of liberty which leads to a revised understanding of freedom as a practice operating within power relations rather than as a telos or end in itself. The multiform nature of power relations means not only that is there no single source, 'or pure law of the revolutionary', but also that resistance emerges at the very points at which power relations are most tightly bound together and is mobile and transitory in form.[19] Resistance is mobile in the sense that it emerges randomly throughout the social totality. It is also transitory in that it necessarily eludes systematic generalization into alternative institutions or codes of practice lest it result in the installation of new regimes of normalization. The unsettling implications of Foucault's belief in the necessarily sporadic and ephemeral nature of resistance is illustrated in a discussion he held in the early 1970s with Maoists on the topic of popular justice. Throughout the discussion, Foucault rejects repeatedly the possibility that the momentum unleashed in instances of popular justice could be used as the foundation for more radical judicial practices.[20]

One interpretation of Foucault's insistence upon the transient nature of political resistance is that such a stance undermines any form of sustained political action and instead naively celebrates marginal and spontaneous acts of non-conformity.[21] Another interpretation, the one which will be considered in the next section, is that the 'anti-essentialist' implications of Foucault's notion of resistance and of his reconceptualization of power – that is the idea that there is no fixed point or definitive social group from which opposition emerges – contest conventional conceptions of socio-political identity and present the challenge of rethinking the nature of political action in liberal democracies.

Radicalizing Democracy

A common criticism of Foucault's work on disciplinary power, particularly from feminist commentators, has been that the anti-essentialist critique of identity as a normalizing concept completely undermines any stable basis for political action. This has led to the claim that the dissolution of identity is a classic manoeuvre on the part of privileged male thinkers for whom a politics of identity has never been an issue.[22] In contrast, Ernesto Laclau and Chantal Mouffe have shown how an anti-essentialist perspective can be used as a powerful tool in redefining conceptions of democracy and citizenship along more radical lines. Although they do not often explicitly acknowledge Foucault's work, his influence can be seen in several key respects. First, Foucault's idea that power relations are neither uniform nor stable informs Laclau and Mouffe's idea of the 'impossibility of society'. Second, the idea that democratic alliances are contingent and in need of constant reformulation resembles Foucault's idea of resistance as heterogeneous and uneven and also his idea that liberty must be conceptualized as a practice rather than an end-state. Finally, the idea that individual identity does not pre-exist but rather is an effect of discursive formations is used by Mouffe in her redefinition of citizenship.

The starting point of Laclau and Mouffe's reformulation of democratic theory is a critique of conceptions of society as a totality united by necessary laws. This critique resembles that of Foucault, who understands power as a set of variable, productive relations or, in his terms, their 'tactical polyvalency'.[23] For Laclau and Mouffe, a unified conception of society is an 'impossibility', it does not exist, in the sense that it is an unstable and open-ended system of relationally constructed identities. Social identities are not fixed, they have no essence, but can only be asserted in relation to their other, to what they are not. For example, in a colonial situation, the various attributes of the colonizing power, such as colour of skin, way of dressing, customs, etc., are linked together in a relation of similitude that signifies their anti-colonized status. The overarching relation that establishes a connection between differential elements is one of negativity, because the identity of the colonizer cannot be stated positively but only indirectly through reference to what it is not.[24] Thus, all social identities are negatively constituted through 'relations of equivalence' – the establishment of similitude between diverse elements – and, in so far as they are historically variable, these relations are themselves neither essential nor necessary.[25] Although social forms are fundamentally indeterminate, they are not, however, in a constant state of flux. Social identities are partially stabilized around certain privileged symbolic or ideological points (what Lacan calls *points de capiton).* For example, stereotypical notions of masculinity and femininity are central to the construction of socio-sexual identities of men and women even if they are not directly reproduced in their day-to-day practices. Despite this process of overdetermination, there is always an infinitude of potential meaning from which new relations of equivalence can be constructed, thereby threatening any final closure of social identities.[26]

Just as Foucault's reformulation of power relations as heterogeneous and variable leads him to assert that there are no privileged sites of political conflict in capitalist society, so Laclau and Mouffe claim that the impossibility of closure of the social manifests itself in a multiplication of points of political struggle or antagonism. The pluralist democracies of the capitalist West are marked by a proliferation of social identities and, as a result,

an extension of potential sites of democratic struggle. The opposite side
of this process of pluralization is whether any form of collective action is
possible or whether democracies are threatened by the spectre of
ungovernability. It is the task of left politics to attempt to construct a
discourse of radical democracy through the articulation of 'hegemonic'
links – democratic equivalences – between diverse socio-political movements.[27] The construction of such hegemonic links should not undermine
the autonomy of movements by attempting to pull them back to a unified
political space. At the same time, the assertion of democratic alliance is not
sufficient in itself to establish links between autonomous and incompatible
groupings. For a radical democratic politics to become hegemonic it must
involve the articulation of a 'new common sense' (or democratic imaginary) which overcomes an individualistic approach to political demands
through promoting an openness to the other and a recognition of the
interdependence of group rights. Democratic equivalence is never fully
instituted and must be rearticulated constantly around the demand for
liberty which recognizes the 'irreducible moment of the plurality of [politi-
cal] spaces'.[28] In this respect, Laclau and Mouffe show how Foucault's idea
of the transience of resistance need not necessarily result in the undermining of political action, but rather points to the recognition that, in a plural
society, democratic closure is an impossibility. There always remain
groups exterior to a given community (a 'constitutive outside') and the
possibility of their inclusion creates the potential for change. This does not
place the democratic ideal in jeopardy but rather guarantees that the
dynamics of the democratic process will be kept alive in a permanent
process of contestation. It is a similar idea that lies behind Foucault's claim
that liberty is a practice rather than an end-state.[29]

The final respect in which Foucault's influence can be seen is in
Mouffe's work on democracy after *Hegemony and Socialist Strategy*.
Mouffe takes the Foucauldian idea that individual identity does not exist
prior to discourse, but rather is an effect of its operations, to develop a
notion of citizenship that runs counter to much other feminist work
on democracy. As we have seen, it is a common criticism that the
poststructuralist dissolution of the concept of identity deprives feminists
of a category through which the marginalized experiences of women can
be rediscovered and re-evaluated. It follows that much feminist work on
democracy insists that key concepts such as the public sphere and citizenship must be redefined in a more inclusive manner, recognizing the
experiences of women and other marginal groups.[30] Against this, Mouffe
claims that the problem with feminist reworkings of the notion of citizenship in terms of an emphasized gender differentiation (Pateman) or group
differentiation (Young) is that they presume fixed or essentialist notions of

identity. Gender differentiated conceptions often privilege a romantic notion of motherhood, while group differentiated conceptions tend to a rigid view of identity as pre-given in the social realm rather than open to reconstruction within the political.[31] Mouffe argues that a radical conception of citizenship would attempt to reshape and reform identities through the attempt to articulate a collective political identity based on a principle of democratic equivalence. Generalizing Oakeshott's notion of *societas*, Mouffe argues for a principle of civil–political association which is based not on a substantive idea of the common good or some other purposive goal but on a common bond. This bond is, in effect, a public concern (*res publica*) which links individuals through a shared recognition of the norms of conduct governing their common or 'public' concern. Individuals recognize a complex of rules which do not pertain to a particular end or goal but which are performative in that they delineate ethical standards governing civil intercourse. The shared recognition of the rules of conduct establishes a common political identity whilst allowing individuals space to pursue diverse ends. This leads to a notion of political community as 'a community without a definite shape or a definite identity and in continuous re-enactment'.[32] Citizenship then becomes a form of ethico-political articulating principle which attempts to construct democratically allied identities whilst allowing for individual freedom.

Foucault's thought has had a significant influence, albeit indirect, on Laclau and Mouffe's work. His view that power relations are essentially unstable allows them to understand democracy as a 'vanishing point', as a symbolic goal to which all citizens refer but which can never be fully realized. Nonetheless, while there is a submerged recognition of the symbolic indeterminacy of democratic forms in parts of Foucault's work, his conceptualization of power primarily in terms of its material effects results in a reduction of democracy to its *de facto* functions and in an overestimation of its disciplinary effects. It is this issue which will be considered in the next section through a comparison with the work of Claude Lefort on the concept of rights.

Rights and Symbolic Power

Foucault's notion of modern democratic regimes predicated on an increasingly effective form of corporeal control contrasts with Lefort's approach which configures democracy in the opposite terms as a process of 'disincorporation'. Lefort characterizes the shift from feudal to capitalist regimes as a process where the idea of power is disentangled from the image of the king's body and comes to reside in the 'empty place' of popular sovereignty. The legitimacy of democratic regimes derives from the notion of popular sovereignty, a place which it is impossible to occupy entirely in that it cannot be definitively equated with any particular individual or group of individuals.[33] Thus democracy is centred upon a contradiction: power emanates from the people and yet it is the power of nobody. Democracy thrives on this contradiction: its insolubility invests its political forms with dynamism in so far as their legitimacy is open to contestation.[34]

Lefort's idea of the symbolic indeterminacy of democratic forms contrasts with Foucault's reduction of these forms to their normalizing function. This contrast is evident in their differing views on the idea of rights. In Foucault's work on disciplinary power, the concepts of law, rights, the state, citizenship and so on are the 'terminal forms' that power assumes. As such, they are obfuscatory of the multiplicity of localized force relations that permeate any sphere of social action. Classical liberal theories view rights as 'protective capsules' for certain human and social attributes regarded as essential to the adequate functioning of human beings.[35] The problem for Foucault is that rights are not *a posteriori* constructions designed to protect pre-existing human qualities; rather rights and the discourse of rights are constitutive of the individual herself. The individual does not exist before the political discourse of rights; she is not a 'primitive atom' upon which 'power comes to fasten or against which it happens to strike' but is herself a vehicle of power.[36] Rights are disciplinary modes that serve to naturalize particular conceptions of human nature and thereby regulate available forms of identity. It is this logic that underlies Foucault's infamous position on rape where he argued that rape should be decriminalized and treated as an act of violence, like other acts of aggression, rather than as a sexual act. Feminists have objected that this line of argument fails to recognize that the category of rape signifies recognition, albeit imperfect, on the part of the legal system of the asymmetrical nature of relations between men and women of which the act of rape is an extreme expression. In Foucault's view, however, his argument is an attempt to liberate sexuality from the normalizing effects of legal intervention through severing connections between sexual behaviour and legal punishment.[37]

Foucault's belief that rights are normalizing in that they serve to naturalize certain hegemonic conceptions of human nature illustrates his tendency to overlook the symbolic role of democratic forms in his emphasis on their *de facto* function of social control. In contrast, Lefort claims that the notion of rights is indeterminate. Rights are grounded in a paradoxical notion of 'man' which, lacking reference to any fixed group, establishes a relation of externality with regard to systems of power. This inherent paradox derives from the simultaneously foundational and performative function of the declaration of rights in that rights are seen to be at once self-evident and in need of declaration.[38] There is a further paradox in that rights assume both an individual and a universal form: they are attributed to individuals but imply a formal universality and a recognition of duties towards other individuals. This synchronicity of the particular and the collective is constantly negotiable and means that rights can never be reduced to a question of the protection of individuals.

This indeterminable core at the heart of rights – the 'fiction of man without determination' – means that they retain a dynamic, symbolic element which cannot be reduced to the determinate effects of their institutional realization.[39] This is not to deny a connection between the symbolic and the institutional, but rather to assert that this relation is ambiguous and this ambiguity signals the 'irreducibility of the awareness of right to all legal objectification'.[40] The symbolic nature of rights initiates a new relation to political power – evident in 'new social movements' – that does not involve direct opposition to institutions but rather suggests a more tangential contestation of authoritative notions of legitimacy. Demonstrations and other forms of popular protest, for example, often challenge legality in a way that has deeper contestatory implications for established legitimacy. These counter-movements do not remain, as they do for Foucault, localized and relatively transient instances of resistance. They have a transverse symbolic significance in that they attest to 'a vague sense of justice and reciprocity, or of injustice and the breakdown of social obligation'.[41] The symbolic efficacy of the notion of rights lies in the paradoxical manner in which it enables movements to combine the representation of their own particularity with a more general idea of legitimacy. Foucault's failure to recognize the relatively enduring symbolic significance of rights-based claims is the result of his reduction of power to a concept of technology or, in Lefort's words, his confusion of the 'image of power' with the 'image of competence'.[42]

I now want to consider how Foucault's final work on government and the self presents a significant revision of the earlier work on discipline. By introducing a more complex notion of power as both normalizing and enabling, Foucault can explain how individuals may oppose the threat of disciplinary control through an 'ethics of the self'. I will show how these ideas have had an influence on certain theories of 'agonistic' democracy. I conclude, however, that the notion of power that Foucault works with is still materially reductionist and, therefore, cannot adequately explain how an individual's ethical behaviour can have a wider symbolic impact on the realm of the political.

Government and the Self

Foucault's later work on government and the self initiates some important conceptual and thematic shifts which, to a certain degree, indicate a revised understanding of the nature of democratic systems in contemporary society. Like the idea of discipline, the concept of government or governmentality is counterposed to conventional analyses in political theory which tend to regard power as the property of the state and, as a consequence, attribute to the latter a unity or 'rigorous functionality' that it does not have. Against these conceptions which result in the '*étatisation* of society', the notion of governmentality denotes a multifarious series of regulatory strategies which, though pertaining to the state, are not necessarily immanent to it or deployed in an intentional fashion.[43] In so far as it refers to a form of technical administration of social practices, or 'apparatuses of security', the idea of government simply elaborates on Foucault's earlier idea of discipline. Governmental techniques seek to augment the happiness of citizens in terms of the conditions and quality of life, the achievement of which simultaneously intensifies the regulatory controls of the state over civil society.[44] Central to these governmental techniques is the idea of a pastoral power as a form of regulation that is originally exogenous to the state domain but is eventually absorbed into it. Its mode of functioning is through strategies of totalization and individualization. It is a totalizing form of power in that it deploys 'techniques . . . intended to rule [individuals] in a continuous and permanent way'.[45] At the same time, power takes as its objects the individual and everyday life, drawing out peculiarities and idiosyncrasies in a way that links their identity to larger normalizing structures: 'This form of power applies itself to immediate everyday life which categorizes the individual, marks him by his own individuality, attaches him to his own identity, imposes a law of truth on him which he must recognize and which others have to recognize in him.'[46]

The notion of pastoral power extends Foucault's earlier work on the confessional as the central strategy of regimes of disciplinary control (medicine, psychiatry, education, social work, etc.) in the surveillance of individuals. In the work on discipline this dual strategy of totalization and individualization is understood in terms of an objectivizing, material power which marks the 'docile bodies' of those subject to it. As a somatic or positive force, disciplinary power need not pass through consciousness: 'If power takes hold on the body, this isn't through its having first been interiorized in people's consciousness.'[47] In the work on government, however, pastoral power is defined not only as a material, objectivizing form of power, but also as a subjectivizing force which yields a more dialectical understanding of the subject: the subject as both subjected and subjectified. The ways in which constraints are imposed upon individuals are simultaneously the means through which they are endowed with a capacity for autonomous action. Thus, as Foucault shows in the first volume of *The History of Sexuality*, the construction of the category of deviant homosexuality within the medical and psychiatric practices of the nineteenth century also had the paradoxical effect of providing a coherent and potentially enabling identity for previously dispersed and isolated individuals. In short, subjectification does not just involve the manipulation of consciousness, but simultaneously institutes the capacity for autonomous action.

The replacement of the notion of docile bodies with a more active understanding of the subject renders the idea of resistance more plausible. The folding back of power relations upon themselves endows individuals with the capacity for rational and purposive action, enabling them to resist the 'government of individualization':

> The political, ethical, social, philosophical problem of our days is not to try to liberate the individual from the state, and from the state's institutions, but to liberate us both from the state and from the type of individualization which is linked to the state. We have to promote new forms of subjectivity through the refusal of this kind of individuality which has been imposed on us for several centuries.[48]

The form the resistance of the government of individualization might take is sketched out by Foucault in his work on ethics of the self. In the essay 'What is Enlightenment?', Foucault draws upon the work of Kant to define the critical attitude that he sees as typifying an ethics of the self. The title 'What is Enlightenment?' is taken from an essay of Kant's where he defines modernity as a critical awareness of the present grounded in the 'mature use of reason', namely the moment when 'humanity is going to put its own reason to use, without subjecting itself to any authority'.[49] Foucault disengages this critical awareness from the transcendental imperative that governs Kant's thought, arguing that an ethics of the self should express a critical ethos which is primarily a historical and practical form of reasoning used to interrogate the limits of identity. The freedom of the individual from the government of individualization cannot be grounded in counter-narratives of justice or morality but must embody a principle of permanent self-critique and experimentation.[50] Critique is a necessary moment in the formation of autonomy which permits a practical form of transcendence or self-overcoming where it is possible to explore and go beyond the limits of identity that have been historically imposed. Foucault explains:

> the critical ontology of ourselves . . . has to be conceived as an attitude, an ethos, a philosophical life in which the critique of what we are is at one and the same time the historical analysis of the limits that are imposed on us and an experiment with the possibility of going beyond them.[51]

Agonistic Democracy

Foucault is fairly elusive about the relation of an ethics of the self to contemporary political practice. He illustrates the notion of ethics of the self with reference to ancient Greek practices and also through an idea of self-creation – an 'aesthetics of existence' – derived from Baudelaire's notion of *dandyisme*. This has led to charges of elitism and the elevation of a solipsistic aesthetic over other forms of political struggle.[52] There is no doubt, however, that Foucault's late work on the self represents a significant reappraisal of the potential for opposition and change provided by democratic forms, in particular the concept of rights. This is evident in an address he gave to a UN conference on the issue of piracy in 1981 where he speaks of a notion of 'international citizenship which has its rights, which has its duties and which implies a commitment to rise up against any abuse of power'.[53]

Some thinkers have recognized the significance of this shift in Foucault's thought and have used it to rethink the idea of democracy along the lines of an agonistic politics. Thinkers such as William Connolly, Judith Butler, Bonnie Honig and Chantal Mouffe have argued that the political dilemmas of identity and difference characteristic of a plural society cannot be solved so long as democracy is conceived as a form of government; rather it must be thought of as a 'mode of being'.[54] Theories of 'agonal' democracy reject procedural solutions to these dilemmas suggested in, for example, the liberal neutralism of Rawls and the communicative ethics of Habermas because each, albeit in differing ways, prioritizes a formal or rational model of democracy that filters out existential and potentially incompatible issues pertaining to the good life.[55] Rather than solving such dilemmas, agonal political practice must seek to occupy the paradoxical. Paradoxes crystallize discontinuities and conflicts in the social order and it is only by embracing them, in what Foucault would call a ceaseless process of problematization and experimentation, that the critical exploration of what is held to be natural or inevitable in identity can begin.

William Connolly is one of the theorists most explicitly influenced by Foucault. He argues that Foucault's genealogical approach to the question of identity provides a 'second-order ethicality' which exposes rather than suppresses the productive possibilities of the paradox of a pluralist politics and thereby gives rise to 'an ethic of agonistic care for identity and difference'.[56] The foundation of this ethical behaviour lies in the cultivation of an experience of contingency in identity along the lines suggested by Foucault's idea of an 'aesthetics of existence'. Connolly acknowledges that many aspects of the experience of the self are deeply entrenched but argues that it is only by questioning their seemingly natural status that 'antagonistic formations' both within the self and between selves can be broken down or converted into an 'agonism of difference'.[57] Critical genealogies of the self subvert the tendency of identity to fixation by aiming not to replace established norms with counter-truths but to problematize identity and thereby throw up new ethical possibilities or new ways of being.[58]

A difficulty that confronts theorists of agonistic democracy who draw on Foucault's notion of an ethics of the self is how it may be possible to establish connections between the interrogation of identity and a broader political dimension. It is necessary to establish such connections between the individual and the collective if the radical force of an ethics of the self is to have a wider political impact rather than resulting in an individualistic process of self-stylization.[59] Foucault clearly does not intend his idea of an ethics of the self to be a solipsistic form of aesthetic practice or an endorsement of a liberal pluralism. He emphasizes that the different 'practices of the self' that govern an aesthetics of existence are not unique to the individual but are 'proposed, suggested and imposed on him by his culture, his society and his social group'.[60] Furthermore, he claims that an aesthetics of existence should not become a 'cult of the self', for example, the Californian-style search for one's true self, but should aim to promote new 'conception[s] of the self' by shifting an awareness of seemingly ineluctable aspects of being from the level of practical to that of reflexive consciousness.[61]

The notion of aesthetics with its utopian implications clearly suggests the broader complications of Foucault's process of self-stylization. Yet, these claims for a wider radical impact remain at the level of assertion rather than being logically developed. There are many reasons for this gap in Foucault's logic: the one most relevant here is that the idea of an aesthetics of existence does not fully overcome the difficulty of a materially reductionist notion of power that hampers the earlier notion of discipline. Therefore, just as he understands democracy only in terms of its *de facto* functioning rather than as a set of socio-symbolic relations, so an aesthetics of the self is defined predominantly as a self-referential and self-evident practical activity rather than, in broader terms, as one that is always already symbolically mediated. Thus Foucault refers to an ethics of the self as primarily a form of practical rationality, a 'historico-practical test', a 'limited and determined' experience of our limits that 'put[s] itself to the test of reality'.[62] The category of aesthetics, however, is underdeveloped. Foucault uses it primarily to refer to a sensuous and immediate labour upon identity where the self is transformed like 'a work of art', rather than to a symbolic process of self-transfiguration which necessarily has broader implications.[63] While Foucault is right to suggest that self-knowledge is never 'complete and definitive', his fetishization of the practical and self-referential nature of an ethics of the self seems to foreclose how any self-knowledge, apart from the most concrete and immediate, can be acquired. Indeed, at points, Foucault seems to fall back into the erroneous assumption that there exists some level of pure, unmediated 'reality' or experience. Without a notion of symbolic mediation, we do not have any means of explaining how the general and particular are interrelated. It is not possible to explain the process of investment through which individuals both identify with and adapt dominant meaning systems in the construction of identity. By failing to elaborate more fully the dimensions of these circuitous processes of identification and reflexivity, Foucault institutes a rupture between the self and the determining environment. One consequence is that Foucault attributes individual action to a self-evident or apodictic radicality.[64]

The difficulty emerging from Foucault's emphasis on a localized and hermetic notion of practice is that it is unclear how it can form the basis for an agonistic democratic practice that must necessarily have broader implications if it is to have political effect. Connolly recognizes this shortcoming in Foucault's work and argues that ethicality must not stop at a genealogy of identity but must be linked to a wider notion of the democratic political space. Comparable with the ambiguities that haunt individual identity, democratic systems are also marked by a tension between 'political place' and 'global time'. Territorial definitions of the sovereign state increasingly clash with the globalization of economic and social structures. This clash places democratic accountability under increasing stress because the transposition of sovereignty from a national to a supranational level attenuates the lines of accountability between democratic institutions and the populace. In order to avert these threats, the survival of democracy depends upon a process of non-territorial democratization of global issues which would disrupt 'state-centred' definitions of political responsibility, public identity, normality etc., and suggest new forms of collective identity.[65] Thus an agonistic politics of individual identity sustains and is drawn out by an analogous process of contestation at the level of democratic forms.

The future of democracy depends on the extent to which it is possible to 'develop political strategies to fold agonistic generosity more deeply into the cultural ethos of a democratic society'.[66] The weakness in Connolly's argument is, on his own admission, that the precise connections between the micro and macro levels of political action remain underdeveloped and often seem to rest on little more than an analogy between an agonism of the self and the undecidability of democratic structures. In short, Connolly's failure to develop a fuller notion of symbolic mediation reproduces the weakness of Foucault's work, namely, that it leaves unexplained how an individualized agonistic politics of the self can refer beyond itself in order to have a properly political impact upon the democratic space.[67]

Conclusion

In this chapter, I have explored the ambivalent relation of Foucault's thought to democratic ideals. This ambivalence does not represent a 'retreat from politics', and it does not arise from any apathetic or nihilistic sentiments on Foucault's part as some of his more hostile critics have claimed. Rather the source of the ambivalence is conceptual. On the one hand, Foucault's reformulation of the concepts of power and the self have had a significant influence on attempts to reshape classical liberal conceptions of democracy and citizenship to accommodate the irreducible plurality of late-capitalist society. On the other hand, Foucault's understanding of power primarily in terms of its disciplinary effects obscures the symbolic dimension of democratic forms that exists over and above their institutional existence. The failure to recognize this symbolic dimension leads Foucault to underestimate the essential indeterminacy that endows democratic systems with a dynamism and perpetual contestability. Although Foucault's later work comes closer to such a recognition, it is not clear how the individualistic exploration of identity can have a wider political impact.

Notes

1   For example, P. Dews, *Logics of Disintegration: Post-Structuralist Thought and the Claims of Critical Theory* (London, Verso, 1987); N. Fraser, *Unruly Practices: Power, Discourse and Gender in Contemporary Social Theory*

(Cambridge, Polity, 1989); J. Habermas, *The Philosophical Discourse of Modernity*, tr. F. Lawrence (Cambridge, Polity, 1987).

2   The best biographical accounts of Foucault's activities are D. Eribon, *Michel Foucault*, tr. B. Wing (London, Faber, 1989) and D. Macey, *The Lives of Michel Foucault* (London, Vintage, 1993).

3   The collection of essays edited by Donald Bouchard provides an excellent introduction to Foucault's early work on transgression. See D. Bouchard (ed.), *Language, Counter-Memory, Practice: Selected Essays and Interviews*, tr. D. Bouchard and S. Simon (Ithaca, NY, Cornell University Press, 1977). For the principal works of Foucault's archaeological period see *The Birth of the Clinic: An Archaeology of Medical Perception*, tr. A. M. Sheridan Smith (London, Tavistock, 1973); *The Order of Things: An Archaeology of the Human Sciences*, tr. anon. (London, Tavistock, 1970); *The Archaeology of Knowledge*, tr. A. M. Sheridan Smith (London, Tavistock, 1972).

4   On the reception of Foucault's doctoral dissertation on madness in France see Macey, *The Lives of Michel Foucault*, pp. 115–19. An abridged version of *Histoire de la Folie* was published in English as *Madness and Civilization: A History of Insanity in the Age of Reason*, tr. R. Howard (London, Tavistock, 1967).

5   There is some concern that certain biographical accounts simplify the complexity of Foucault's work by reducing it to a more or less direct reflection of his life. This criticism has been voiced by David Halperin about James Miller's biography. See D. Halperin, *Saint Foucault: Towards a Gay Hagiography* (Oxford, Oxford University Press, 1995) and J. Miller, *The Passion of Michel Foucault* (London, Harper Collins, 1993). The essay 'Nietzsche, genealogy, history' in P. Rabinow (ed.), *The Foucault Reader* (Harmondsworth, Penguin, 1984), pp. 76–100, is Foucault's central statement about the genealogical method. Key works of this period are *Discipline and Punish: The Birth of the Prison*, tr. Alan Sheridan (Harmondsworth, Penguin, 1979) and *The History of Sexuality, Volume I: An Introduction*, tr. R. Hurley (Harmondsworth, Penguin, 1978).

6   David Macey explains how the term 'gauchiste' was originally pejorative and was used by the PCF to denounce what it saw as irresponsible leftist groupings. The term then came to designate the many radical groups that were spawned after the events of May 1968. See Macey, *The Lives of Michel Foucault*, p. 217.

7   See Macey, *The Lives of Michel Foucault*, pp. 257–89.

8   Macey, *The Lives of Michel Foucault*, p. 460.

9   Foucault, *Discipline and Punish*, pp. 25–6.

10 Foucault, *Discipline and Punish*, pp. 141–9.

11 Foucault, *The History of Sexuality, Vol. I*, pp. 61–2.

12 G. Rose, *Dialectic of Nihilism: Poststructuralism and Law* (Oxford, Basil Blackwell, 1984), p. 177.

13 Habermas, *Philosophical Discourse of Modernity*, p. 291.

14 Foucault, *History of Sexuality, Vol. I*, pp. 88–91.

15 Foucault, *History of Sexuality, Vol. I*, p. 89.

16 Foucault, *History of Sexuality, Vol. I*, p. 94.

17 See, for example, J. Butler and J. W. Scott (eds), *Feminists Theorize the Political* (London, Routledge, 1992); L. McNay, *Foucault and Feminism: Power, Gender and the Self* (Cambridge, Polity, 1992).

18 A. Giddens, *The Constitution of Society: Outline of the Theory of Structuration* (Cambridge, Polity, 1984), p. 256.

19 Foucault, *The History of Sexuality, Vol. I*, p. 96.

20 M. Foucault, 'On popular justice: A discussion with Maoists', in C. Gordon (ed.), *Power/Knowledge: Selected Interviews and Other Writings 1972–1977* (Brighton, Harvester, 1980), pp. 1–36.

21 For example, P. Stallybrass and A. White, *The Politics and Poetics of Transgression* (London, Methuen, 1986), p. 200.

22 For example, N. Hartsock, 'Foucault on power: A theory for women?', in L. Nicholson (ed.), *Feminism/Postmodernism* (London, Routledge, 1990), pp. 157–75.

23 Foucault, *History of Sexuality, Vol. I*, p. 100.

24 E. Laclau and C. Mouffe, *Hegemony and Socialist Strategy: Towards a Radical Democratic Politics*, tr. W. Moore and P. Cammack (London, Verso, 1985), pp. 127–34.

25 Laclau and Mouffe derive the concept of relations of equivalence from Marx's idea of (exchange) value as that which sets up relations of equivalence between materially diverse commodities.

26 Laclau and Mouffe, *Hegemony and Socialist Strategy*, pp. 105–14.

27 Laclau and Mouffe, *Hegemony and Socialist Strategy*, p. 178.

28 Laclau and Mouffe, *Hegemony and Socialist Strategy*, p. 184.

29 M. Foucault, 'The ethic of care for the self as a practice of freedom', tr. J. Gauthier, in J. Bernauer and D. Rasmussen (eds), *The Final Foucault* (Cambridge, MA, MIT Press, 1988), pp. 1–20, esp. pp. 2–4.

30 For example, C. Pateman, *The Sexual Contract* (Stanford, CA, Stanford University Press, 1988); I. Young, *Justice and the Politics of Difference* (Princeton, NJ, Princeton University Press, 1990).

31 C. Mouffe, *The Return of the Political* (London, Verso, 1993), pp. 81–8.

32 Mouffe, *The Return of the Political*, p. 67.

33 C. Lefort, *The Political Forms of Modern Society: Bureaucracy, Democracy, Totalitarianism* (Cambridge, Polity, 1986), p. 279.

34 Lefort, *The Political Forms of Modern Society*, p. 256.

35 M. Freeden, *Rights* (Oxford, Oxford University Press, 1991), p. 6.

36 Foucault, *Power/Knowledge*, p. 98.

37 See McNay, *Foucault and Feminism*, pp. 45–6. For an account of the debate between Foucault and feminists on rape see T. de Lauretis, *Technologies of Gender: Essays on Theory, Film and Fiction* (London, Macmillan, 1987), pp. 36–7.

38 Lefort, *The Political Forms of Modern Society*, pp. 256–7.

39 Lefort, *The Political Forms of Modern Society*, p. 257.

40 Lefort, *The Political Forms of Modern Society*, p. 260.
41 Lefort, *The Political Forms of Modern Society*, p. 263.
42 Lefort, *The Political Forms of Modern Society*, p. 268.
43 M. Foucault, 'Governmentality', in G. Burchell, C. Gordon and P. Miller (eds), *The Foucault Effect: Studies in Governmentality* (London, Harvester Wheatsheaf, 1991), pp. 87–104, citation on p. 103.
44 M. Foucault, 'Politics and reason', in L. Kritzman (ed.), *Politics, Philosophy, Culture: Interviews and Other Writings, 1977–1984* (London, Routledge, 1988), pp. 57–85, esp. p. 81.
45 Foucault, 'Politics and reason', p. 60.
46 M. Foucault, 'The subject and power', in H. Dreyfus and P. Rabinow (eds), *Michel Foucault: Beyond Structuralism and Hermeneutics* (Brighton, Harvester, 1982), pp. 208–26, citation on p. 212.
47 Foucault, *Power/Knowledge*, p. 186.
48 Foucault, 'The subject and power', p. 216.
49 M. Foucault, 'What is Enlightenment?', in Rabinow, *The Foucault Reader*, pp. 32–50, citation on p. 38.
50 Foucault, 'What is Enlightenment?', p. 44.
51 Foucault, 'What is Enlightenment?', p. 50.
52 For example, R. Rochlitz, 'The aesthetics of existence: post-conventional morality and the theory of power in Michel Foucault', in T. Armstrong (ed.), *Michel Foucault, Philosopher*, tr. T. Armstrong (London, Harvester Wheatsheaf, 1992), pp. 248–59; R. Wolin, 'Foucault's aesthetic decisionism', *Telos*, 67 (1986), 71–86; T. Eagleton, *The Ideology of the Aesthetic* (Oxford, Blackwell, 1990), p. 395.
53 Foucault, quoted in Macey, *The Lives of Michel Foucault*, p. 437. The speech was printed, after Foucault's death, as 'Face aux gouvernements, les droits de l'homme', *Actes: Les Cahiers d'action juridique*, 54 (Summer 1986), 22.
54 S. Wolin, 'Fugitive democracy', in S. Benhabib (ed.), *Democracy and Difference: Contesting the Boundaries of the Political* (Princeton, NJ, Princeton University Press, 1996), pp. 31–45, citation on p. 43. See, in the same volume, the essay by B. Honig, 'Difference, dilemmas, and the politics of home', pp. 257–77.
55 W. Connolly, *Identity/Difference: Democratic Negotiations of Political Paradox* (Ithaca, NY, Cornell University Press, 1991), pp. 162–3. Foucault himself was critical of Habermas's communicative solution, arguing that the notion of consensus rests on a fundamental misunderstanding of power relations as purely negative. See M. Foucault, 'The ethic of care for the self', p. 18.
56 Connolly, *Identity/Difference*, p. 13.
57 Connolly, *Identity/Difference*, p. 178.
58 A similar idea is expressed in Judith Butler's concept of performativity. See J. Butler, *Gender Trouble: Feminism and the Subversion of Identity* (London, Routledge, 1990), and *Bodies that Matter: On the Discursive Limits of 'Sex'* (London, Routledge, 1993).

59 For a critique of the liberal evasion of the political see C. Mouffe, 'Democ-racy, power and the "political"', in Benhabib, *Democracy and Difference*, pp. 245–56.

60 Foucault, 'The ethic of care for the self', p. 11.

61 M. Foucault, 'On the genealogy of ethics: an overview of work in progress', in Rabinow, *The Foucault Reader*, pp. 340–72, citation on p. 362.

62 Foucault, 'What is Enlightenment?', pp. 46–9.

63 Foucault, 'On the genealogy of ethics', pp. 350–1.

64 See L. McNay, *Foucault: A Critical Introduction* (Cambridge, Polity, 1994), pp. 154–63.

65 Connolly, *Identity/Difference*, p. 218.

66 Connolly, *Identity/Difference*, p. 138.

67 This is also a weakness in Butler's work: see L. McNay, 'Gender, habitus and the field: Pierre Bourdieu and the limits of reflexivity', *Theory, Culture and Society*, 15 (1998).

Index

Durkheim, Emile, 83, 88
Dworkin, Ronald, 139, 149, 161

Easton, David, 3
elections *see* voters; voting
elitism, 2, 39, 49–51
elitist democracy, 2–4, 27, 28, 29,
    71, 177
    see also Hayek
Elshtain, Jean Bethke, 62, 70, 72,
    208
Enlightenment rationalism, 11, 77,
    85, 103, 105, 107, 108, 112, 204,
    219, 229
essentialism/anti-essentialism, 8, 198,
    207–8, 210–11, 222, 224
ethnic rights, 12

feminism, 2, 12, 110, 113, 176
    and democracy, 180–3
    humanistic *vs* gynocentric, 198
    socialist, 197
feminist political theory, 8, 112, 166,
    188–91, 198, 208, 210, 224
    see also Pateman; Young
Foucault, Michel, 9, 11, 36
    contribution to democratic theory,
        233
    on disciplinary power, 11, 216,
        219, 220–2, 226
    on discipline and democracy,
        219–22
    Discipline and Punish, 219–20, 229
    on Enlightenment rationality, 219,
        229
    on ethics of the self, 217, 231–2
    on freedom/liberty, 216, 219, 220,
        222, 223, 224
    on government and the self, 216,
        227, 228–30, 233
    Histoire de la folie, 217
    Madness and Civilization, 219
    and 'the normalizing gaze', 198,
        201–2
    on pastoral power, 228
    and political activism, 217–18

on rights and symbolic power,
    225–7
Fraser, Nancy, 111, 188–9, 209
free market economy, 32–3
freedom, 4, 30–1, 44, 46–7, 49, 50,
    53, 61, 66, 68, 77, 161, 164,
    170
    illusory nature of, 216, 219, 220
    of the individual, 4, 23, 229
    and the rule of law, 23, 28, 29
    of speech, 25, 29, 64, 143
    see also liberty
French Revolution, 45–6, 48
Fukuyama, Francis, 17

Galston, William, 136
Gatens, Moira, 188–9
gay liberation, 12
Giddens, Anthony, 221
global citizenship, 11, 15–17
global democracy, 11
globalization, 16, 20, 33–4
group rights, 12, 224

Habermas, Jürgen, 9–10, 14–15, 16,
    62, 98, 99, 109, 146–7, 148, 197,
    205, 209, 221, 230
    approach to law, 87–9
    Between Facts and Norms, 87
    on civil rights, 87–8
    on civil society, 89–90
    commitment to democracy, 78
    on 'communicative action', 9,
        82–3, 84, 85, 88, 90, 92, 109
    on concept of 'lifeworld', 82–3,
        85–6, 87, 90
    and concept of power, 87, 89
    contribution to democratic theory,
        90–1, 93
    and deliberative democracy, 9–10,
        14, 77, 90, 91, 93
    on democracy and reason, 83–5
    and discourse ethics, 90, 91
    and discursive democracy, 91, 92
    on institutional features of
        democracy, 85–90